# OUT OF THE RUNNING

# Out of the Running

*Why Millennials Reject Political Careers
and Why It Matters*

Shauna L. Shames

NEW YORK UNIVERSITY PRESS

New York

NEW YORK UNIVERSITY PRESS
New York
www.nyupress.org

© 2017 by New York University

All rights reserved

References to Internet websites (URLs) were accurate at the time of writing. Neither the author nor New York University Press is responsible for URLs that may have expired or changed since the manuscript was prepared.

ISBN: 978-1-4798-2599-8 (hardback)
ISBN: 978-1-4798-7748-5 (paperback)

For Library of Congress Cataloging-in-Publication data, please contact the Library of Congress.

New York University Press books are printed on acid-free paper, and their binding materials are chosen for strength and durability. We strive to use environmentally responsible suppliers and materials to the greatest extent possible in publishing our books.

Manufactured in the United States of America

10 9 8 7 6 5 4 3 2 1

Also available as an ebook

*To all the women who run anyway*

*And to Jo*

# CONTENTS

# LIST OF TABLES AND FIGURES

# ACKNOWLEDGMENTS

Sincere thanks are due to the following funders, without whose support this research would not have been possible: the Center for American Political Studies at Harvard University (CAPS), the Ash Center for Democratic Governance at Harvard's Kennedy School of Government, the Institute for Quantitative Social Science at Harvard University (IQSS), the Taubman Center for State and Local Governance at Harvard's Kennedy School of Government, Marie C. Wilson and the White House Project, and Betty and Sidney Shames.

Thanks to the following institutions for permission to conduct research on their campuses: Harvard Law School, Harvard's Kennedy School of Government, and Suffolk University Law School, especially Dean Laura Ferrari.

I am indebted to the following (listed alphabetically) for their help developing the thinking and writing in this project: Marni Allen, Melanie Whitley Bowers, Hannah Riley Bowles, Kennaria Brown, Nick Carnes, Emily Clough, Caelyn Cobb, Porsha Cropper, Kelly Dittmar, Johanna Ettin, Susan Faludi, Nadia Farjood, Kristin Goss, Peter Hall, Jennifer Howk, Tracey Hyams, Sandy Maisel, Susan Marine, Matthew Platt, Beth Rabinowitz, Diane Rosenfeld, Kira Sanbonmatsu, Juliet Schor, Rachel Silbermann, Sue Thomas, Danielle Thomsen, Cameron Whitley, Vanessa Williamson, Taylor Woods-Gauthier, Miya Woolfalk, and several anonymous reviewers. Thanks also to discussant and audience comments from groups at the American Political Science Association's annual meetings in August 2013 and September 2015 and at the New England Political Science Association's annual meetings in April 2012 and May 2013, the participants of the Ash Center for Democratic Governance 2012–13 Fellows Workshop, the participants of the Gender and Sexuality Graduate Workshop, and the participants of the American Politics Research Workshop at Harvard University. Thanks as well to Ruth Mandel for her terrific book *In the Running*, which inspired both my early interest in women as candidates and the somewhat-depressing title of this book.

Special thanks to my research assistants, interview transcribers, transcription-verifiers, and data monkeys: Nadia Farjood, Johanna Ettin, Gabriel Shames, Jabari Morgan, Avery Hanger, Annalisa Klein, Kara Lessin, Chakera Hightower, Daniel Wallsten, Marion Johnson, Caroline Goldfarb, Oliver Kendall, and Kat Collins and to the research assistants of Nicholas Carnes at Duke University, who also transcribed interviews for this project.

My deepest appreciation is due to my graduate school mentors, Jennifer Hochschild, Claudine Gay, Eileen McDonagh, Jane Mansbridge, and Kay Lehman Schlozman, for their invaluable advice, assistance, and encouragement throughout this process.

Finally, and above all, thank you to all the wonderful survey respondents and interviewees who contributed their time and opinions to this project. Without you, this work could not exist.

1

## Good Reasons Not to Run

In a small conference room at Harvard Law School in 2013, Jared,[1] a twentysomething black male student, leaned over the table to emphasize to me how much he loved politics. But at the same time, he said, the "tenor" (his word) of the electoral arena bothers him:

> I think if you go back to the '60s and the '70s and further back, there were parties, so there was partisan politics, but at the end of the day, people viewed it as a joint venture. You'll hear anecdotes about people debating on the floor, but after, they'd go out to dinner and smoke some cigars and slap each other on the back. They were competitors, but there wasn't the ruthlessness that I see now, and that's very unsettling. And that just contributes to the general malaise that we find ourselves in where we can't seem to get anything accomplished, because everything comes down generally to scoring points. We could do this to get some people jobs, we could extend unemployment benefits, we could give this money to schools, but I don't want to do it because it's going to make the other party look good, so I'd just rather not do anything. It's like, why do we have this political system? Why did we elect you to represent us if nothing is going to get done?

Later in the interview, he returned to the same theme:

> [A] lack of willingness to compromise just makes the whole prospect of going into politics seem potentially unfulfilling, because I'm a very results-oriented person, and I'd just rather not bother with a headache. I love [politics], but I don't like it enough to deal with the headache of competing for the sake of scoring points. I want to get stuff done, and if I can't get stuff done, I'd rather just not bother. . . . You're looking to legislate or represent people on issues that are going to affect their day-to-day lives, and I just feel it would be tremendously frustrating . . . gridlock.

This well-reasoned frustration is fully rational—but it is also rather poignant for a political scientist like me to hear. After all, representative democracy depends on having good people willing to run for office. Here, in Jared, we have a smart, caring, and charismatic individual who could be a great political leader but who thinks it is not worth the "headache" (which word he said not once but twice).

Why not? The costs, he thinks, may outweigh the benefits. That is the essence of rational thinking, after all.[2] Jared did not explicitly provide a list, but from what he has said, we can infer. The costs he sees are primarily two: (1) partisan acrimony/lack of bonhomie (including the negative feelings of malaise and ruthlessness, springing, in his mind, from the overly competitive partisan point-scoring environment); and (2) inability to "get things done" (frustration/gridlock). These two costs are likely related (perhaps 1 leads to 2, or vice versa), but they are theoretically distinct. In other parts of the interview, Jared (and many other such interviewees) spoke of other costs, such as the feeling that one's privacy would be infringed by constant media attention or the need to raise large sums of money as a candidate.

Jared might be willing to put up with such costs as long as he felt that his work was useful, that he was getting satisfactory results. He says explicitly what he would like to come out of politics: helping people (job creation and promotion, unemployment benefits, better schools). The problem seems to be that he rationally sees some fairly high costs but not enough benefits to balance the scales. Instead, on the reward side, he sees "potential unfulfill[ment]." The real problem here for Jared's political ambition was not that he saw politics as costly but that he perceived it as lacking in rewards.

Jared was not alone. "[A]sk not what your country can do for you," President John F. Kennedy famously said, "ask what you can do for your country." Fifty-two years later, at the school of government bearing his name and at two major law schools nearby, bright and ambitious graduate students were indeed asking the question he proposed—but politics, and especially candidacy for office, tended not to be the answer.[3] Of the more than 750 law and policy school students I surveyed for this project,[4] a large majority (88.7 percent) listed "making my community a better place to live" as a major life goal. Those with whom I spoke directly, in a series of 53 one-hour interviews (diversified by race, gender, school, and year), often spoke passionately about politics, policy issues, law, and government. This is perhaps not surprising, as all of these people had already made large commitments by choosing to attend public policy or law schools, which is the reason I chose them as a sample. What was surprising was the extent to which they generally perceived electoral politics as unrewarding.

In this book I present the results from this original survey and set of interviews of elite young adults, all of whom are students at a top law or policy school that has often served as a major pipeline into either state-level or national politics.[5] Where relevant, I also bring in bits of data from the "real world," including quotations, statistics, and anecdotes from pollsters, campaign managers, candidates, and research studies. But the costs and rewards of running that this book explicates come directly from the Millennials I studied. Exploring their perspectives helps the rest of us understand what they hope for, as well as what they dislike and fear about the idea of candidacy. This knowledge, I hope, points the way to potential changes that could help bring about a different view of politics.

The evidence from my study suggests that the list of reasons why people do not run for office is long and varied and that the rationales they give are rational. They do not appear to be simple excuses based on lack of self-confidence or on selfishness but rather decisions based on common perceptions of how politics works in our democracy. In the minds of most of those I studied, running for and perhaps also holding office would likely be exhausting and unrewarding. Many see risks and barriers when they contemplate a candidacy, with few seeing high rewards. Notably, they were not convinced that, even if they won office, they could do something useful. However they define the positives and negatives of a potential run, by their calculations the good often fails to outweigh the bad.

Those for whom this is not the case, for whom the rewards appear stronger than the costs, were a narrow, unrepresentative group—and both factors should concern us from a democratic standpoint. A small pool of candidates can decrease quality and importantly hamper citizen choice, which is the key "crowdsourcing" element that is supposed to make democracy better than other forms of government. But an unrepresentative pool is a problem for a different reason. To put it simply, the United States as a country is wonderfully diverse, but its elected representatives, particularly at higher levels of government, are not. Examinations of the candidate pool find that the lack of diversity, especially by gender, race, and class, stems mostly from who chooses to run rather than from systematic voter bias.[6] The best solution would therefore be diversifying candidates—but this book and other works find that there are some very good reasons why the unrepresented often won't run.[7]

## Political Ambition

When I was working for the Obama campaign, that was probably one of the toughest jobs I've had. . . . I mean you're talking to people for ten, twelve hours a day constantly non-stop. . . . You have to have a smile on your face every single moment you're doing that, and I will say that was so darn tiring. But I really, really also enjoyed working the job where you communicate with real people every day, I loved that. And I love that about . . . the exciting thing for me about campaigns and why I can't stop working on them even though they pay you in like, you know, dog treats, the thing is that there's this . . . for me, and a lot of people in my profession, my peers, you get this adrenaline rush and they're extroverts, so they love talking to people. . . . I love talking to people. . . . But who wants to, who raises their hands and says "I want to work 80, 90 hours a week?" I mean, every single frickin' week. That's the trade-off.
—Lin, Asian American male Master of Public Policy (MPP) candidate, Harvard's Kennedy School of Government

An older model of political ambition holds that some people are just "political animals,"[8] and others aren't. Some people, like Lin, love talking to people, shaking hands, feeling that "adrenaline rush" of "communicat[ing] with real people every day." They love it enough to be worth the dog-treat level of pay and the frickin' eighty- to ninety-hour work weeks. "Politicians who live for politics are like sharks in the sea: if they do not swim, they do not breathe."[9] Some are just, in the words of Keith Gaddie, "born to run."[10] For whatever reason, they have an "intensive desire for office that transcends issues."[11]

A small handful of those I surveyed and interviewed fit the model of these "political animals," like Anne at Suffolk Law and Lin at Harvard's Kennedy School of Government. They have both been active in campaigns already, and Anne had already run once for her city council in a Boston suburb and planned to run again. These two, and a few others like them, needed little encouragement to run. They saw high rewards in running and, although like Lin they saw the costs, they were not much deterred; they figured they were more than equal to the task of overcoming whatever obstacles might arise in a campaign.

Lin and Anne and the few other "political animals," however, were in the minority; fewer than 15 percent of those I surveyed had seriously considered running for office. Far more than this proportion, however, appeared "movable" toward greater consideration of running at some point in the future if the conditions were right. This suggests that while there may indeed be political animals out there, that explanation of political ambition by itself misses a great deal.

Newer work in political science has begun to push a new version of what political ambition is. This newer model sees political ambition as malleable and contextual, which is what I also find in this study. For example, in a large recent study of state legislators, published as the book *More Women Can Run*, political scientists Sue Carroll and Kira Sanbonmatsu argue for a framework of "relationally embedded decision-making," wherein potential candidates take into account all kinds of factors about both the political system and about their own lives and the lives connected to theirs.[12] This view fits well with the data presented here; generally, the costs anticipated by those I surveyed and interviewed were not solely personal but familial, and the rewards were not just individual but communal. In line with this newer view, my findings suggest that such ambition can wax and wane according to critical perceptions in the minds of those contemplating political candidacy. And perceptions, as much good research has told us, are more important than reality in explaining people's behavior.[13]

## This Book

This is the story of a multi-year investigation into why elite, well-qualified young adults who are already on a path toward a career in policy or law are not more interested in running for office. I began this project by wondering why more women and people of color did not want to run but quickly saw that the race and sex differences in political ambition, while important, are part and parcel of larger patterns of candidate deterrence that are not just about identity factors. Race and gender, I found, operate powerfully but on the margins; the larger question for me became why more of the smart, thoughtful young people I was studying did not want to run. The reasons are not selfishness or ignorance. They are instead the result of complex, critical thinking on the part of these young people about what politics is, how it currently operates, and what it can and cannot do.

Political ambition, the desire to seek or hold political office,[14] depends on a conscious or unconscious process of cost-benefit analysis, I argue. Such ambition, I further suggest, is rationally lacking in those for whom costs outweigh rewards—and American society has made running today so costly, in so many ways, that we are turning off a whole cadre of potentially great candidates. I call this "candidate deterrence," drawing both from previous political science scholarship on the rational reasons why certain people avoid running[15] and from the idea of "nuclear deterrence" theory from international relations scholarship.[16]

This in itself is not a new idea; we know from good research that Americans, especially the young ones, mostly have negative views of politics and that young people generally do not want to run for office, for some pretty good reasons.[17] What is new in my analysis is threefold. First is the rational cost-benefit comparison (especially the focus on the perceived lack of rewards), which I argue undermines the political ambition of elite and well-positioned young adults. The idea of a "balanced scale" will serve as the central metaphor for my theoretical framework in this book: candidate deterrence occurs when perceived rewards fail to weigh significantly more than perceived costs.

Second, the law and policy school graduate students I study are very different from subjects of earlier investigations. This is an unexplored population, largely because it is very difficult to get permission to study these protected students. Because I was myself a graduate student at one of these institutions (Harvard) while conducting this research, I was able to get access that others could not. This book thus gives a glimpse into the political perceptions of a whole group of young people about whom we know relatively little. The best research thus far on the political ambition of young people, a wonderfully rich study by political scientists Jennifer Lawless and Richard Fox called *Running from Office*, studies a national sample of young people in high school and college.[18] My research uses a similar methodology but with a far more select population; and looking at law and policy school graduate students offers special insights, as this group is not only best-positioned for politics in terms of qualifications, but these individuals have already made a major life decision (attending a particular graduate school) orienting them to a career relating to law and policy. Their words from the interviews and their survey responses are invaluable tools for understanding the critical question of why they would, or mostly would not, want to run for office in the future.

Third and finally, this book takes an innovative intersectional approach, considering sex as well as race, and the two together. This kind of gender-plus-race analysis is rare in political science research. It is very difficult to get similarly situated men and women, and people of color (here, black, Hispanic, and Asian American[19]) versus whites, without socioeconomic class driving the results. While class differences are not absent in this study, they are minimized. This does not mean that all the respondents came from upper-income families; they did not. But by the time they reached relatively elite law and policy schools from which I recruited participants, the role of socioeconomic status (SES) in predicting their political behavior was minimal as compared with its role in the general population. Usually such differences are one of our strongest predictors of political activity of all sorts,[20] but in my sample, socioeconomic factors, like parents' education or family income at the time my respondents were sixteen years of age, have little predictive value for engagement in politics. And the work of the highly selective graduate school admissions committees at the schools where I recruited created an excellent sample of comparable men and women of various racial backgrounds, which is unusual and exciting if you are a social scientist.

It is also difficult to study both gender and race together, because with each identity axis you divide your sample, which can lead to problems in finding statistically important differences if you do not have enough people of color in the study. In places where they are unfortunately relatively rare, like law and policy schools, it is hard to study these small populations by both sex and race together. In this study, I worked carefully to recruit a sample that has equal numbers of men and women and that has a large oversample of people of color, to be able to address race and gender each on their own and then simultaneously.[21] This book presents, to my knowledge, the most comprehensive examination to date of how race and sex intersect in terms of political ambition.

As it turns out, in addition to being a story about costs and rewards for elite young people overall, this research also tells the story of some sizeable gaps in political ambition between women and men, and between racial subgroups of each. While most in the sample experienced some measurable level of candidate deterrence (not seeing high enough rewards to balance out perceived costs of running), it was not sex-neutral. Compared with the men, the women saw more and higher costs to running and often perceived fewer benefits.

This sex difference in perceptions stems from two processes: first, even when men and women perceived similar costs to running, the women felt the costs more keenly. At the same time, women saw additional costs that the men did not, particularly expecting to face gender discrimination in politics. Women as a group were also less likely than men to see rewards from running for/holding office. Seeing higher costs and lower benefits rationally depresses political ambition for women as compared with similarly situated men.

When I looked further by race/ethnicity, women of color stood out as those seeing the highest costs and lowest rewards. This was not a hard-and-fast rule (it was not that no black women wanted to run, for instance) but instead a description of group-based tendencies. Of those who had seriously considered running for office, two-thirds were men, even though women were half of the full sample. And women of color, although they were a quarter of the sample as a whole, were only 13 percent of those saying they had seriously considered running for office. On the whole, women were significantly more deterred from the idea of running as compared with similarly situated men, and women of color were the most deterred.

Yet the effects of minority race are far from straightforward, especially when considered in tandem with sex. Interestingly, while women of color stood out as the most-deterred subgroup, the black, Hispanic, and Asian American men in my sample were not similarly deterred as compared with white men. If anything, their political ambition was somewhat higher than that of their white male counterparts.[22] And different minority subgroups had some measurably different political perceptions and behaviors that are worthy of consideration in their own right. Later chapters of this book consider the multiple forces at work, first looking at everyone, then at men versus women, and then at women and men of color as their own subgroups.

Before delving too far into the data, however, I want to situate this project in its proper context. No work of research comes out of a vacuum. The rest of this chapter touches on themes of modern U.S. politics and key relevant concepts in political science. In particular, we live in a time of particularly acrimonious national (and sometimes lower-level) electoral politics that cannot fail to affect the perceptions of those watching and considering joining the fray.[23] This context, the lack of potential rewards as paired against what are increasingly high costs to running, is a critical and understudied piece of the puzzle of generally low political ambition among the elite young people I studied.

## Contemporary U.S. Political Context

When one is looking at the question of who does and does not run, it is essential to consider the current context of "negativity,"[24] "anti-politics,"[25] and "incivility"[26] in politics, all of which have implications for how citizens feel about government. In 2014, NBC News reported that the then-current Congress (the 113th) was the second–least productive in history.[27] It was eclipsed in do-nothingness only by its immediate predecessor Congress, the 112th. In previous Congresses, from 1947 to 2000, the average number of bills passed was about 675 per Congress; for the 112th and 113th Congresses of 2011–12 and 2013–14, the numbers of bills passed were 283 and 296, respectively. This lack of productivity seems attributable to a particularly vigorous legislative partisanship that has been increasing since the mid-1990s. Research in political science traces this increase to the combination of the institutional framework of primaries (with small and nonrepresentative sub-electorates) and changes in American political ideology, with both conservatives and liberals becoming more sharply ideological.[28]

In 1997, presidential expert Richard Neustadt asked, "What now goes on in Washington?" and then answered:

> Warfare among elites, waged since the 1960s in the name of causes, not compromises, fueled by technology, manned by consultants, rousing sup-porters by damning opponents, while serving the separate interests of particular candidates and groups at given times. President and congress-men and private organizations, and their massive staffs, all swirl around one another, seeking to manipulate public opinion and the media and one another for the sake of scoring points. They try incessantly to win a given election, to promote or to stop a given legislative provision, regulation, appointment, contract, or executive decision in diplomacy and defense. Increasingly, they all approach those givens with the same techniques consultants use, in roughly the same spirit: damn the torpedoes, full steam ahead, rouse your friends, trash the enemy, the long term's later, victory comes first.[29]

And he was writing nearly a decade ago; the trend has worsened.

The effects of this increased partisanship and polarization have not gone unnoticed by the public, whose opinion of government in general, and Congress in particular, has dropped in direct proportion to the par-tisanship.[30] Trust in government has been on a mostly steady decline for decades, with Congress in particular falling to ever-decreasing historic floors.[31] One recent study found that Congress ranks somewhere below "cockroaches, traffic jams, and Nickelback in Americans' esteem."[32] The crisis of faith has gotten so bad that President Barack Obama used his final State of the Union address in early 2016 to urge unity and an end to partisan "rancor and suspicion."[33]

In June 2015, a Gallup poll measured Americans' confidence in Con-gress at 8 percent, down five percentage points from a few years before, in 2013.[34] Scholars have noted that voters' distrust in national political institutions has increased steadily since Watergate and Vietnam,[35] but we have never seen a rating this low for Congress. Just a decade ago, the same Gallup poll measured confidence at almost 30 percent; likely, the twin trends of hyperpartisanship and gridlock since the 2008 election, along with the foundering economy, have accelerated voters' poor evaluations. Between 2009 and 2015, citizens' confidence in government fell for all three branches.[36] While in 2009, 39 percent of Americans said they placed a great deal or quite a lot of confidence in the U.S. Supreme Court, this had dropped to 32 percent by 2015. Confidence in the presidency fell from 51 percent to 33 percent, and confidence in the Congress from 17 percent to 8 percent in the same period.[37]

Where is this public negativity toward government coming from? If Richard Hofstadter is right, there is a "paranoid style in American politics" that has a "long and varied history" in this country, going back at least to 1797.[38] Certainly since Ronald Reagan's first election, politicians have run "against Washington," in a style one political scientist has called "anti-politics."[39] It is a useful campaign style when government is unpopular, with candidates on both sides of the aisle often promising to "fix" or "clean up" government.[40] The overall effects of such a strategy—while perhaps good for individual candidates[41]—likely just serve to increase voter dissatisfaction with government as a whole.[42]

Repeated portrayals of politics as embattled, acrimonious, and scandal-ridden, while perhaps useful to media outlets in drawing readers or viewers, appear to also exacerbate voter disgust.[43] Further Gallup polling suggests that "Americans' high level of disapproval is less about what Congress is doing than about what it isn't doing: putting aside partisan bickering and getting things done."[44] Joseph Nye theorizes that "[s]ome aspects of the current mood are probably cyclical, while others represent discontent with gridlock in the political process rather than deep disillusion with government."[45] Nevertheless, he concludes, there is still cause for concern as "the decline of trust may have a cost in terms of democratic values."[46] Notably for this work, political scientists Hibbing and Theiss-Morse speculate that "Public negativity . . . can affect who runs for, and who stays in, public office."[47]

## Millennials, Politics, and Political Ambition

Who are "Millennials" as a generation? Are they narcissistic and entitled "trophy kids"[48] of "helicopter parents," who expect to hear an excited cry of "Good job!" at the completion of every task? Or are they idealistic, engaged, and committed to creating a better world, as other researchers find?[49] (Note that these two possibilities are not mutually exclusive.) In sheer numbers, Millennials now equal (or, depending on how you measure it, surpass) the Baby Boomers.[50] Young people on the leading edge of the Millennial generation (born around 1982) are now in their mid-thirties, but the bulk of this generation grew up in the 1990s. They have been microscopically examined by social scientists, political pundits, and employers. The research piling up seems at times contradictory, but certain ideas come up repeatedly. Millennials tend to be skeptical about large institutions. And why not? They have watched banks, churches, and their government be rocked by scandal. Churches cover up the abuse of children, members of Congress are indicted for fraud, and bankers cause a financial meltdown and walk away while kids caught with a little marijuana go to jail.

In response, researchers tell us, Millennials turn away from the corporate cubicle and think of starting their own businesses.[51] They dream of being—and often are—entrepreneurs, not so much interested in rising through the ranks as in creating something new. According to the Pew Research Center's report on Millennials in Adulthood, "The Millennial generation is forging a distinctive path into adulthood. Now ranging in age from 18 to 33, they are relatively unattached to organized politics and religion, linked by social media, burdened by debt, distrustful of people, in no rush to marry—and optimistic about the future. They are also America's most racially diverse generation. In all of these dimensions, they are different from today's older generations."[52] The report also notes that half of them say they are not affiliated with any political party, though they tend to vote Democratic, and only 29 percent say they are affiliated with any religion.[53] Small wonder that members of this generation strongly preferred the outsider candidate, Bernie Sanders, in the 2016 primaries.

The lack of trust extends to government institutions as well. Young people who in 2002 had "appeared to be highly favorable toward government" seem to have lost some confidence in the intervening decade.[54] In 2006, Pew found a significant dip in young people's likelihood of favoring government regulation of business and a greater suspicion of government's being wasteful and inefficient.[55] Similarly, data from 2000 to 2012 from the annual Harvard Institute of Politics (IOP) poll of American youth and politics show a ten-point decrease in trust of the federal government during that period, to the point where only 14 percent said they trusted Congress to do the right thing all or most of the time.[56] As of 2012, a majority of Millennials (53 percent) said they would choose to recall *all* members of Congress, were it possible to do so.[57] In 2015, only 20 percent called themselves "politically engaged and active," a drop of five percentage points from four years before.[58]

In the 2008 and 2016 presidential elections, outsider candidates Barack Obama and Bernie Sanders, respectively, stimulated high participation among young people, both with campaigns that played on anti-Washington sentiments. On the one hand, this speaks further to the cynicism this group of young voters has about established politics. But on the other hand, the fact of such engagement suggests both hope (as the 2008 Obama campaign put it) and a willingness to work within the political system when properly inspired.[59] The evidence from these campaigns thus fits in well with the data analyses I present in this book; both suggest the possibility of change when circumstances are right.

## The Millennials in This Study

Like other studies of eligible candidates, my project studies those who could run for office but likely will not.[60] Unlike these previous works, my sample consists of graduate students in programs relating to law or policy, from schools that are proven feeders into state-level and national candidate pools. For full details on survey design, content, and methodology, please see the Methodology appendix.

No one degree leads to elective office, and most politicians have some other profession before running. However, a law degree comes closest. When I began this research, about 42 percent of the members of Congress had a JD, along with 47 percent of Massachusetts state legislators.[61] Far fewer had a policy school diploma, such as an MPP or MPA (Master of Public Administration), although these relatively new degrees seem to be gaining ground as an entrée into governmental service, with many politicians now starting out as civil servants.

The Harvard schools were a natural choice, given their reputations and the likelihood that they would attract extremely ambitious students across race and gender. Harvard Law and Harvard's Kennedy School are also well known as conduits into federal governmental positions. Harvard sends a significant number of its graduates into politics and government in the United States. More U.S. presidents have attended Harvard than any other university; seven presidents, including current President Barack Obama, attended Harvard Law School.[62] Currently, 47 Harvard affiliates hold U.S. congressional seats, constituting slightly less than 9 percent of the congressional body and more than double that of any other university.[63] Each Congress for the past two decades has had at least 34 Harvard alumni in its ranks, peaking at 48 in 1995.[64] Twelve percent of U.S. attorneys general have been Harvard graduates (more than any other single university).[65] At the state level, Harvard has the largest number of alumni in statehouses across the country (totaling 104 in number in one study).[66]

Looking specifically at graduates from Harvard's Kennedy School, we find that a substantial portion of its graduating classes each year enters the public sector. Between 2001 and 2012, of those who reported employment, the Kennedy School sent an average of 46 percent of its graduates into government jobs, with a low of 38 percent in 2011 and a high of 59 percent in 2002.[67]

I chose Suffolk Law after collecting data on current state legislators in Massachusetts and finding that Suffolk Law is the modal degree. Forty-two percent of Massachusetts state legislators with a JD came from Suffolk, a far higher proportion than the next closest competitors, New England School of Law and Boston College Law.[68] (Not all state legislators have a JD, but it was the most common form of graduate degree, held by 47 percent of Massachusetts state legislators.[69]) Suffolk Law, then, is the largest "feeder" of graduates into state-level politics in Massachusetts, just as Harvard—specifically Harvard Law and Harvard's Kennedy School—is the largest "feeder" of graduates into national-level politics. The Suffolk data also serve as a check on the Harvard data, to test which effects might be Harvard-specific and which may be more generalizable to the population of elite law students. Likewise, the Harvard Kennedy School data serve as a check on the data from the two law schools, to test for differences between highly ambitious JD students and their non-JD but still policy-minded counterparts.

Graduate school, I argue, is an ideal time to measure eligibles' perceptions of politics and a potential candidacy. The subjects are adults, old enough to have chosen a career in a field relating to politics and policy. They are usually childless, with only about a third being married. The measurements of perceptions about candidacy are more precise than we would get with undergraduates,[70] but not as colored as they would be later in life by women's disproportionate family responsibilities.[71] Because these are students who have mostly never run for office,[72] I avoid the selection bias that comes from studying people who have already chosen politics as a career.[73] This sample gives us "the dog that doesn't bark."

Yet those in my sample are not a random population of students— they have extremely elite backgrounds and have been chosen for that reason. By the time they reached the law and policy schools from which I drew the sample, these students had been extensively vetted and se- lected (by persons other than me) for many of the qualities, character- istics, and experiences that would make for good candidates. Also, by design, the schools from which I drew my sample are well known as conduits to political office. With the prestigious degrees bestowed by these schools, the background assets it took to get those in my sample into these schools in the first place, and the connections they make while in these programs, most students at any of these schools could become competitive political candidates.

Members of my survey and interview samples were all extremely am- bitious people. By the time I reached them, they were already a highly se- lective group, vetted by multiple people and committees before me (the admissions committees of their various colleges and graduate schools). Yet despite their high overall ambition, they expressed remarkably vari- able and overall low levels of political ambition. A significant portion of this group (22 percent) said categorically that they never want to run for office, and the majority (85.3 percent) said they had not thought about it seriously. On average, though, 69 percent said they would be more likely to want to be political candidates if they perceived better condi- tions for a run. Their political ambition, in other words, was generally— and rationally—low, but also quite movable.

Having spent countless hours interviewing members of this group and analyzing their responses and the statistical data from the in-depth survey, I can assure readers that most of the people in this sample would make good political candidates and/or officeholders. They are intelligent, savvy, thoughtful, and compassionate and care deeply about making the world a better place. They care about this country's politics and leadership, wishing that both were of higher quality, and they offered insightful analyses of multiple types of political issues.

Most, however, had good reasons to reject the notion of running for office themselves, at least under current conditions. As a group, they expressed deep skepticism about the ability of politics to create solutions for the problems they care about. Notably, most also saw the political world as biased in critical ways—especially by money, but also by gender and race. The extent to which respondents cared about these biases varied, but perceptions of the political world as discriminatory and nonfunctional correlated strongly with low levels of political ambition. These kinds of expectations about politics and running for office are critical fodder for our understanding of who does and doesn't run for office, and why.

Some, for example, saw strong rewards from politics, but they were a fairly small and not very representative group. In particular, those who saw more rewards than costs were far more likely to be men than women—and, if women, were more likely to be white than racial minorities. Most in my sample, however, did not think that politics was a good path toward specific policy goals or to help people or make change. Sarah, a white female law student at Harvard, said, "Sadly, I feel like I could help more and do more work not as a politician, which I feel is backwards. I feel like you would think you could do a lot more as a politician, but I think once you are, your hands are much more tied than it may appear at first."

Many interviewees echoed this assessment, saying they think they could do more good for the world through nongovernmental organizations (NGOs), social movement organizing, or even in appointed rather than elected office. For both interviewees and survey respondents considered as a whole, the life of an elected politician seemed constrained both by the amount of time one would need to spend fundraising and also by the many limitations built into the political system preventing efficient change or problem solving.

These data should give us concern about the quality, quantity, and diversity of our country's pool of political candidates. What I found suggests that we are not inspiring a diverse young cadre to think that politics is worth the costs. It also suggests that race and gender gaps in who chooses to run are unlikely to simply fade with time. And if so many people who would make wonderful representatives are deterred from running by extensive costs and low perceived rewards, then the negative perceptions of politics articulated by those in this study are likely to become a self-fulfilling prophecy.

## 2

# Political Ambition

*What It Means and Why We Should Care*

Representative democracy requires many things, among them free and fair elections, civil rights for citizens, constraints on executive power, and a free and independent media.[1] Critically, we also need people who are ready and willing to run for office (candidates)—and preferably enough of them to create good electoral competition. The better the competition, we hope, the better will be the quality of those who eventually assume office. An ideal democracy would have a bounty of high-quality, competitive candidates among whom voters could select. Even if the sovereign citizen's only real duty is to say yes or no[2] to a particular candidate, democracy can still thus afford meaningful choice among candidates, parties, and policies. This theory starts to break down, however, if we lack good candidates. A shortage of those who would be high-quality candidates, manifesting either as a shortage of candidates overall or an oversupply of low-quality candidates, constitutes a serious problem for our democracy.

Recruitment into political candidacies in the United States relies mostly on would-be candidates' stepping forward relatively independently. In stark contrast to most developed democracies, the United States has "candidate-centered politics" rather than a party-centric system.[3] Citizens rarely become candidates without some (and often a large) degree of self-recruitment. Although parties are quite important in most election and governance processes, our parties here, compared with their counterparts in other democracies, have relatively little control over who will run under their name. U.S. democracy is not simply the "competitive struggle for the people's vote"[4] but also the prior competition over who will wage that struggle. For better or for worse, candidate selection—one of the most critical functions of elite party decision makers in other countries—is "crowd-sourced" in the United States. As political scientist Joseph Schlesinger argued nearly half a century ago in his classic treatise, "Ambition lies at the heart of politics."[5]

This means that, in contrast to a system wherein it is the job of the party to convince someone to stand for office, in the United States we need people who self-identify as wanting to run. Those who run are therefore distinguished first and foremost from those who do not by their ambition to hold office. Summing up the lesson learned from a multi-year study in a book called *Political Ambition*, political scientists Linda Fowler and Robert McClure write, "Ambition for a seat in the House, more than any other factor—more than money, personality, or skill at using television, to name just a few examples—is what finally separates a visible, declared candidate for Congress from an unseen one."[6]

More specifically, this ambition means that those who run find politics meaningful or useful. Sue Thomas, an expert on women and U.S. politics, explained in her book *How Women Legislate*, "[T]he very choice of joining an organization (assuming a certain level of choice was operational) signifies that the person doing the choosing considers the organization or its goals to be generally valuable and legitimate."[7]

On the one hand, this produces a surprisingly open system, one in which ambitious, charismatic candidates can rise quickly from relative obscurity, even against the wishes of party bosses. The political career of Barack Obama makes the point nicely; in few other comparable democracies could a politician with so little electoral experience attain a country's top office. Recent Tea Party candidates similarly illustrate the system's permeability and the parties' relative lack of control; inexperienced candidates have won their parties' primaries in several high-level elections in just the past few years, going on to embarrass their parties in the general election. American history is rife with examples of such "outsider" candidates (Donald Trump in the current election springs to mind), either within the two major parties or as third-party candidates who then help to chart a new direction for one of the main parties. With enough will and work, would-be candidates in the United States, even outsiders, can often overcome the barriers to entry.

On the other hand, as open as the U.S. political system may be in some ways, the crucial individual will to run—more important here than in other democracies—is distributed neither evenly nor widely.

The barriers seem steep, even insurmountable or not worth surmounting, to many who would make good political candidates and able public servants, if only they would run. Aversion to running for and/or holding office, particularly if differentially distributed across politically relevant groups, can constitute a serious problem for a democracy. Schlesinger wrote, "A political system unable to kindle ambitions for office is as much in danger of breaking down as one unable to restrain ambitions. Representative government, above all, depends on a supply of men so driven."[8] In other words, our ability as citizens to select good leaders through an electoral process is constrained by those who choose to run. I suppose I could still vote for you as a write-in candidate, even if you did not want to run, but that is a technicality. Realistically, if you do not want to run, you meaningfully constrain my ability to vote for you. And if you would have been the best candidate, too bad for me.

A candidate-centered democracy, then, is only as good as the candidates who choose to come forward to stand for office. Reflecting in *Who Runs for Congress*, political scientist Thomas Kazee mused that his discipline has "long assumed that ambition for public office in America is widespread, that the number of people seeking elective positions is adequate to ensure both a steady supply of able public servants and a level of electoral competition sufficient to hold officeholders accountable for their actions." What if this is not the case? Candidate emergence and its lack may be, as Kazee argued, the "key to understanding American politics."[9]

The candidates we currently see run—those generally most ambitious to hold office—are a narrow and unrepresentative bunch of those who could run. Both factors (narrow and unrepresentative) are concerning. Representative government is strengthened when representatives share experiences and understandings with their constituents. An unrepresentative group of candidates vastly reduces, in important ways, the likelihood of the resulting elected officials' being like those they represent.[10] Indeed, a current crop of candidates, as measured in 2012 in a 10,000-person study of candidates at all levels of office, is unrepresentative of the American populace in multiple ways, especially in terms of race, sex, and class.[11]

So much for unrepresentative—what about narrow? That the pool of the politically ambitious is small could by itself be a problem if it meaningfully reduces competition for the seats, which could reduce the quality of those eventually chosen. And a small pool can also be a problem for democracy if it means that seats go uncontested, which turns out to be the case in a fairly large and apparently increasing proportion of elections, not so much at the national level but lower. A 2012 William and Mary College study found that only about 60 percent of state legislative elections offered voters a choice between major-party candidates.[12]

Finally, a narrow, unrepresentative pool of candidates suggests a loss of talent sorely needed to solve major national and international political crises. It could mean that people who would be excellent political leaders are choosing not to run, for reasons we have yet to fully understand. I here argue that such choices are rational, given the balance of negative to positive perceptions on the part of most potential candidates about candidacy, politics, and government. If young people—and especially young women—are averse to running, in other words, it is not because they are irrational.

## Anticipating Running for Office

Anticipation is a critical concept in political science. In an address to the 2000 American Political Science Association, renowned political scientist (and then-president of the association) Robert Keohane urged political scientists to pay greater attention to the role of what he called "rational anticipation."[13] As he put it, "Agents, seeing the expected consequences of various courses of action, plan their actions and design institutions in order to maximize the net benefits that they receive."[14] The idea is not radical; it represents the essence of rational-choice thinking. To make rational choices, individuals rely on anticipation, and therefore perceptions.

Douglas Arnold made the same point in his theory of how and why members of Congress act as they do: they are anticipating the response of constituents, even in the absence of any constituent knowledge of their actions. "The cautious legislator, therefore, must attempt to estimate three things: the probability that an opinion might be aroused, the shape of that opinion, and its potential for electoral consequences."[15]

Before both Keohane and Arnold, back in the 1950s, economist Anthony Downs had articulated a famous theory of rational action as applied to voters. Downs was careful not to equate being "rational" with being "inhuman." His "rational man" still has feelings, prejudices, and illogical thoughts—but "[moves] toward his goals in a way which, to the best of his knowledge, uses the least possible input of scarce resources per unit of valued output."[16] The benefits for a rational actor must outweigh the costs—and the rational actor's "best knowledge" (what I call "perceptions" on the part of eligible candidates) is more critical for prediction than the objective reality, although it is based upon the objective reality.

Turning his attention to why people vote, Downs offered a series of equations describing the rational actor's utility functions in voting or abstaining. His logic runs into a problem explaining the rationality of an act that has costs (voting) but few apparent benefits. The rational actor, he assumes, will correctly perceive that if no one votes, the democracy in question will collapse—but if the voter is that perceptive, she will also figure out that as long as someone else votes (and someone else always will), she won't have to. Ultimately, Downs resorts to adding a new term to his model, on the benefits side; many citizens, he explains, derive a psychological reward from the continuing existence of democracy, and this is often (but not always) large enough to counterbalance the often-small costs of voting. (Riker and Ordeshook, later interpreters of Downs, called this the "D-term," for the reward of doing one's civic duty.[17])

In my own work, faced with data suggesting high and rational perceptions of multiple, expensive costs to running, at first I had trouble explaining why logical actors *would* decide to be candidates. I discovered that the solution, for a small and unrepresentative bunch in my sample, had to do—as in Downs's model—with finding perceived rewards that offset the perceived costs. Those who want to run perceive benefits from politics and political candidacy that are not shared by those deterred from running. I elaborate more on the specific content of these costs and benefits in later chapters.

Just as with Arnold's "cautious legislator" and Downs's "rational voter," previous studies find that potential candidates are careful and thoughtful about whether and when they run. We know, for instance, that incumbents regularly collect large "war chests" of campaign funds that rationally deter challengers, including high-quality challengers.[18] We know also that minority candidates are more likely to emerge in majority–minority districts than in white districts.[19] Research also stresses the importance of eligibles' perceptions of winning. Studying strong potential challengers for House seats in the mid-1990s, Maisel and Stone write that the challengers were "most strongly influenced by what they perceived to be the chances of winning their party's nomination in their district."[20] Women may be more "rational" in this sense than men; studying state legislators who flirted with the idea of running for Congress, Fulton and colleagues find that the female legislators were more sensitive than their male counterparts to "the strategic considerations surrounding a candidacy."[21] Similarly, Lawless and Fox found in a matched sample of male and female eligibles, the women were less likely to think they would win should they run.[22]

Like the eligibles studied in this research, the young potential candidates in my study have thought ahead. About half (47.7 percent) had already been asked to run for office. A majority (63 percent) had thought about running, even if not seriously. My subsequent analysis shows that their perceptions of costs and benefits line up with their desire to run. Their political ambition strongly relates to a rational cost-benefit calculus much like that employed in a Downsian model or in other rational-actor models of political participation more generally.[23] Nearly all (92 percent of the sample on average) called themselves "ambitious," but they were not equally politically ambitious. My data analysis explores the differences and the rational reasons why some show an interest in running while most do not.

## Gaps in Who Runs: Sex, Race, and Class

I think it's very tough because I think society has kind of ingrained that it's like politics is kind of a male-dominated industry. . . . I think it's definitely become a more even playing field, but I think white males still dominate.
—John, white male JD candidate, Suffolk Law School

The United States is a country of astonishing diversity, yet public offices continue to be overwhelmingly dominated by white men. Although women constitute a majority (51 percent) of the U.S. population,[24] they make up only 25 percent of state legislators, 18 percent of big-city mayors, 19 percent of members of Congress, and 12 percent of state governors.[25] People of color are a growing third of the population, yet they hold less than 15 percent of elected political positions.[26] Across states, 9 percent of all state legislators are black, 3 percent are Hispanic, 1 percent is Asian American, and 1 percent Native American.[27] Underrepresentation by race and gender characterizes government bodies at all levels, but especially at the top; the U.S. Senate is 94 percent white and 80 percent male.[28]

One of my interviewees, Matt, a student at Suffolk Law School, proposed a useful test for visualizing such gaps. When asked about the current ratios of men to women or whites to nonwhites in Congress, he said he did not know exactly, but that "they're not where they should be." When queried further, he elaborated: "I think that my . . . ideal situation would be if I walked into a room full of politicians [and] the first thing that goes through my head shouldn't be, oh my God, there's a lot of white men here." By his proposed test, we're currently failing.

Time alone is not solving this problem of disproportionality; in the past two decades, gains for both women and racial/ethnic minorities have been at best incremental and have sometimes reversed course.[29] Figures 2.1 and 2.2 depict the levels of women and minorities in Congress and state legislatures, and minorities in Congress and state legislatures, respectively. In nearly twenty years, blacks have increased their proportion in the U.S. House by about two percentage points, from 7 to 9 percent.[30] Black, Asian American, and Hispanic members of Congress come almost exclusively from majority–minority districts, where racial minorities make up a majority of the population. However, these districts may decrease in number in the future as a result of the recent Supreme Court ruling in connection with the Voting Rights Act (*Shelby County v. Holder*).

In the same twenty-year period, women have increased their share of state legislative seats by only four points (from 21 percent in 1994 to nearly 25 percent now).[31] In 2010, for the first time since women began running for public office in their own right in significant numbers, women lost rather than gained ground in Congress, and that year also saw the largest drop of women in state legislatures.[32]

State legislative term limits—which feminists, political reformers, and scholars of politics used to think would increase the diversity of legisla-

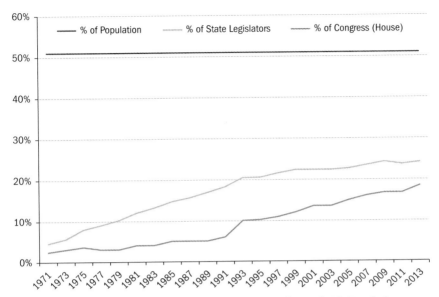

Figure 2.1. Women as a Proportion of U.S. Legislative Bodies and U.S. Population, 1971–2013. Source: Compiled from data given in CAWP 2016, U.S. Census 2014, Congressional Research Service 2014a.

tive bodies—seem to have had the opposite effect, at least for women.[33] As elected women are term-limited out of office, other qualified women are not coming forward to take their place, causing a decrease rather than an increase in elected women overall.[34] This led political scientists Jennifer Lawless and Richard Fox in 2005 to conclude that the problem of under-representation of women is one of willingness or ability to run.[35] I too find that the political ambition of women is lower than that of similarly situated men but emphasize the rationality of women's lower ambition, in contrast to some less-rational explanations.[36]

Few studies have investigated race and political ambition until recently. Works by Marschall, Ruhil, and Shah suggest that black candidates are more likely to run in places where blacks have previously held political power.[37] Similarly, another study of minority groups beyond blacks found that minority candidates were more likely to run when their racial/ethnic group held a larger share of the population in that area.[38] Relatedly, other studies suggest that that a lack of "political

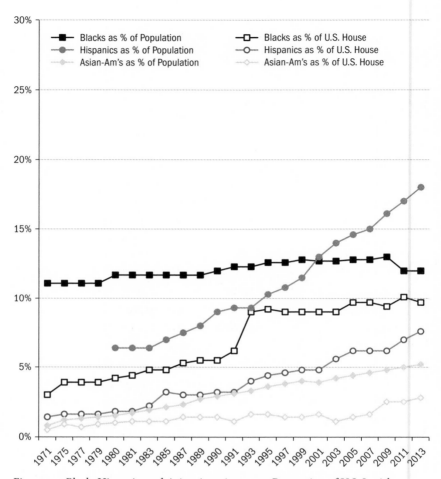

Figure 2.2. Black, Hispanic, and Asian Americans as a Proportion of U.S. Legislative Bodies and U.S. Population, 1971–2013. Sources: Compiled from data given in: *Biographical Directory of the United States Congress 2014*; Congressional Research Service 2014a, 2013, 2012; U.S. Census Bureau 2010, 2002, and 2001; and NCSL 2009. Note: "Hispanic" was not a U.S. Census designation until late in the planning for the 1970 census, and the question was asked only on the long form, sent to 5 percent of households. Also, the 1970 questions asked were confusing, and the resulting data inconsistent (see Haub 2012). Reliable statistics on this category are not available until the 1980 datasets.

empowerment," usually defined as blacks' holding positions of power like a mayoralty, may be at least partially responsible for lowered political ambition among black citizens in those areas.[39] Putting the two perspectives together might suggest that such a lack of empowerment could be a negative feedback cycle, leading to fewer candidates of color. People of color, in other words, are quite understandably more likely to run where they think they have a chance of winning. Their perceptions of their chances appear to depend on both the history of elected leadership at that level or in that area and on the concentration of their racial/ethnic group in the population. In this case, gender and race are not alike, because of geographical residential segregation by race but not by gender.[40]

In the general population, socioeconomic status is likely the most important predictor of who will be deterred by structural barriers, particularly given the necessity of campaign fundraising. In an era of what Nick Carnes calls "white-collar government," the most severe underrepresentation in our representative government may be by class rather than by race or gender.[41] Even those I spoke with in interviews, who were generally quite privileged in many ways, still seemed to think politics was for richer, more powerful people; we can only imagine how removed from politics the truly poor must feel. Future research could usefully examine what kind of candidate-deterrence effects might exist for different socioeconomic strata.

In this work, however, my goal was to minimize class differences. We already know that socioeconomic status is one of the most critical factors affecting any form of political participation.[42] This project therefore attempted to study the differences in political ambition between men and women, and between whites, blacks, Hispanics, and Asian Americas, separated (as much as possible) from class. This is easier said than done, though the pre-screening by admissions committees to which I previously referred was especially helpful. Even if a student at Harvard Law grew up in a Los Angeles ghetto (as did one of my interviewees), the very fact of the Harvard Law degree will go a long way toward leveling the playing field when he or she leaves school.

We would expect at least some of the race and gender differences that show up among the larger U.S. population, and which are tied to income and education, to be minimized among these students of elite law and policy schools. Yet the research presented here tells us that gender—and some race—differences persist among even those with relatively high levels of income and education.[43] In particular, my survey and interview data suggest that women, and especially women of color, are far more likely than their male counterparts to perceive the barriers to electoral office as insurmountable or as not worth surmounting, even when socioeconomic differences are minimized. For female potential candidates, the costs just seem higher, and sometimes the rewards lower.

## Unrepresentative Democracy: Why We Should Care

Leadership is by nature unequal; it is an elite pursuit. In many ways, we should expect people in leadership positions to resemble one another more closely than they resemble ordinary members of the community. Why should we be concerned that a group of leaders is homogeneous in a gendered and raced way, if we are not concerned that leaders are also homogeneous in terms of personal characteristics (intelligence, ambition, aggression, charm, organizational skills, and dedication to a group or cause)?

The answer takes us beyond the personal characteristics of leadership into the function of a leader.[44] Having leaders who are disproportionately dedicated, charismatic, and ambitious is not particularly concerning philosophically, as this is the purpose of a leader—to show dedication to his or her group or cause, to attract and keep members, to organize the group's actions and affairs, to act as a public icon of the group, to ensure the care and well-being of group members. That leaders are disproportionately male and white should pose a concern, as these features do not seem necessarily related to the function of a leader but instead appear tied to historical and cultural prejudices and constraints about who is allowed to demonstrate ambition, intelligence, public responsibility, and aggression. As political theorist Will Kymlicka notes with regard to gender, which we should also apply to race, "almost all important roles and positions have been structured in gender-biased ways."[45]

Following several works by political theorist Jane Mansbridge, underrepresentation is appropriate in a democracy only when the perspectives and interests of the under-represented group are well represented by others in situations where diverse perspectives are needed and interests conflict.[46] Severe and continuing under-representation is thus just only if the axes of unequal representation are irrelevant to the interests of members of the under-represented group. This is the case with neither race nor gender.[47] Lawless and Fox explain, "A central criterion in evaluating the health of a democracy is the degree to which all citizens—men and women—are encouraged and willing to engage the political system and run for public office."[48]

To be clear, justice within the context of representative democracy does not demand full, unchanging equality among all groups. That inequalities exist between groups is not in itself a problem; that these inequalities affect the representation of the groups' perspectives and interests, that the inequalities persist rather than rotate, and that the inequalities derive from a history of state action—as is the case with both race and gender inequalities—makes these significant and a matter of justice for the democratic state to address.[49]

Beyond the question of the intrinsic justice of more equal distributions of offices, there are also instrumental questions of policy output and governance process to consider. Both theory and empirical evidence suggest a link between substantive representation of issues and descriptive representation of people. There are good reasons why "blacks should represent blacks and women represent women," in Mansbridge's words. She explains that in certain contexts, and often for some good reasons, "[D]isadvantaged groups may want to be represented by 'descriptive representatives,' that is, individuals who in their own backgrounds mirror some of the more frequent experiences and outward manifestations of belonging to the group."[50]

On the policy side, many studies support the conclusion that policy results change when legislatures become more representative by race and gender, although party and ideology complicate the effects.[51] On the process side, several studies find that the inclusion of women and people of color changes the style as well as the substance of legislative decision making.[52] In addition to the concerns about justice and political equality as ends in themselves, then, lack of gender and racial diversity among the elected leaders in a representative democracy seems to carry implications for interests and self-understandings of its citizens and the process and results of the political system as a whole. It is therefore

alarming, from a democratic standpoint, that there seem to be some serious gaps in individuals' willingness to run for office by key and politically relevant identity categories, including race and gender.[53]

## What We Know about Why Gaps Persist

Considerable scholarly attention has given us important, insightful hy-
potheses about the motivations prompting certain people to run for
office. Until the mid-1990s, however, this "political ambition" or "candidate emergence/recruitment" research studied only people who had
already run (such as elected officials or candidates who ran but lost) or
those who were actively deciding.[54] A recent wave of research examines
the political ambition of people who would make good candidates but
most likely won't run. In particular, several projects examine how such
political ambition varies along identity lines.[55]

Why are white women and people of color less likely to run for office
than white men? Existing literature has addressed this question better
for gender than for race, pinpointing several important mechanisms that
contribute to the continuation of male dominance of U.S. politics. Some
studies, however, also provide insight into the racial issues at play, sometimes tying race to socioeconomic status and sometimes examining it
from a social-psychological perspective for its symbolic motivating or
de-motivating power. For both race and gender, existing explanations
address structural, institutional, and individual-level factors.

First and foremost, on the structural side of the gender question,
many have noted the primacy of women's disproportionate work–family
conflict as compared with men, which keeps far more women than men
away from time-intensive jobs, including politics.[56] At the same time,
because of a persistent wage gap and the concentration of women
in lower-prestige and lower-paying jobs, women tend to have lower
incomes than men. They therefore collect fewer of the resources that
stimulate political interest and participation.[57] Women of color, who
are disproportionately lower-income compared with their white female
counterparts, are particularly vulnerable to the effects of both of these
structural factors, which may in large part account for their paucity as
candidates. A third structural barrier is incumbency, because incumbents overwhelmingly win reelection and the vast majority are male.[58]

(As Laura Liswood, founder and secretary general of the Council of Women World Leaders, frequently says, "I don't believe there is a glass ceiling; I think it is just a thick layer of men.") Finally, the structure and functioning of U.S. political parties may limit entry for political outsiders of various stripes, including women.[59]

Some of these structural factors, however, may be changing. Researchers used to attribute the relative dearth of women as candidates to the fact that women did not acquire as much education, as measured by college degrees. Also, men used to greatly outnumber women among graduates from law school. Both of these factors have changed in the past few decades. Women now are more likely than men to graduate from college, and law school cohorts are increasingly gender-balanced or close to it.[60] Although there is no one degree for becoming a politician, a JD comes closest; lawyers make up a larger proportion of Congress and state legislatures than any other profession.[61] The gender gaps in salary[62] and wealth[63] persist but are attenuated for elite women, who are more like elite men than they are like their lower-income female counterparts. The same could be argued of well-educated, wealthier minorities when compared with their lower-income counterparts.

Moving to more specific institutional factors, scholars have pointed to several that seem to affect the political behavior of both legislators and citizens in ways connected to race and gender.[64] For example, when women (non–race-specific) hold greater power within a political institution or are seen as prominent in that institution or are visible as high-level candidates, this power and visibility may stimulate greater interest, participation, and/or efficacy on the part of other women.[65] Some research also suggests the same pattern among blacks (non–gender-specific), where black citizens are "empowered" to participate politically by seeing black leaders.[66]

We can imagine several possible mechanisms connecting the presence or absence of members of one's group in positions of power to one's own likelihood of participation, feelings of efficacy, or political interest. Seeing members of one's group may have a role-modeling effect ("I could be like her/him"). Alternately, or in addition, it could act as a powerful signal of acceptance by the institution ("Look, s/he made it"); this may have been part of the dynamic in the nomination and subsequent election of Barack Obama as president. Relatedly, but not identically, the presence of women or people of color in an institution may lead outsiders to see the institution itself differently ("Perhaps it isn't as sexist/racist an environment as I thought").[67]

With some notable exceptions, most of the key writings on how institutions affect eligibles' political ambition are in the comparative field of political science rather than American politics research. Those who study women's political participation and ambition in countries like those in Europe and Latin America have focused on institutional constraints and opportunities.[68] Much of the recent comparative literature about women's ascent in politics concerns gender quotas, which occur in some form (mostly as reserved legislative seats or as party-based quotas) in more than one hundred countries worldwide.[69] Another major strand of research in the comparative literature investigates party-based recruitment into candidacies.[70] Studies in both veins assume strong and relatively centralized political parties that have a good deal of control over choosing their candidates. These studies are thus able to fairly effectively assign blame for women's continuing under-representation.[71]

In U.S. politics, where individual eligibles generally shoulder the burden of self-recruitment, the political science literature dealing with parliamentary systems—mostly institutionalist in style—is not as relevant to help us understand political ambition. Prominent recent studies about why more eligible women do not run for office in the United States have disagreed about whether to emphasize individual initiative or institutional factors.[72] Here, I follow the lead of the emerging "contextual" model of political ambition, drawing from both the institutionalist and individualist literature.[73] Individualized political ambition, I suggest, in line with this emerging model, depends deeply on eligibles' perceptions of the institutional costs and rewards involved. In a U.S. context where individual political ambition is vital, we must be aware of the components of individual decision making about what politics is and whether to participate in it—but we must also acknowledge that such individual decisions are deeply informed by perceptions of the institutional barriers and opportunities one will face.

Moving from the research on structures and institutions to individual-level factors and political ambition, recent studies have identified a major gender-based confidence gap, with women generally being much less likely than men to think of themselves as qualified to hold public office.[74] There is also powerful evidence of gender-role socialization effects. In contrast to men, women are socialized from infancy to believe they should prefer the private to the public sphere—or at least be able to participate fully in both, which in practice tends to reduce the time available to women for public leadership, relative to men.[75] Women see few women in office and therefore may believe, consciously or not, that politics is not for them.[76] Other studies have found that, as a group, women are more risk-averse than men, and in political campaigns women attach greater importance than men do to winning the race.[77] Finally, a group of studies finds that women continue to be treated differently from men as candidates, particularly in media coverage but also in recruitment and treatment by party leaders, biases that eligible female candidates anticipate with distaste.[78]

Eligible candidates who feel different from the political "norm" may expect that their qualifications will not be seen as enough for them to win an election or do the job. They may also feel that they will have to work harder than a white male to get elected or once in office. Indeed, studies find that women candidates and legislators *do* work harder than their male counterparts to raise the same amount of money[79] and that, as legislators, they bring home more pork to their districts.[80] Last, expectations about the usefulness of politics to solve problems or create positive change may be crucially related to the reasons women and people of color do not seek elective office. We know from research that women's primary motivation in running for office is to affect policy and "create change."[81] Yet this factor has not been examined or tested enough as a crucial component of individual political ambition among eligible candidates[82]—and an explanation for how and why women's desire for office may differ from men's.

Overall, differential expectations (about bias, barriers, disproportionate work, and the usefulness of politics) between women and men, and/or between whites and people of color, could help us explain why white men continue to be the most likely to seek political office. Understanding such expectations is critical to solving the problem of underrepresentation for two reasons. First, removing structural barriers alone may not be enough to create greater equality in elective offices if political-psychological challenges persist. And second, large structural factors are unlikely to change overnight.[83] Even if structural barriers persist, it may be that changing the expectations held by women and people of color could convince more of them to run. In a costs-rewards framework, it is crucial to know what costs good potential candidates anticipate—but beyond this, as costs may be difficult to change, we also need to know what rewards they do or do not see.

3

# The Costs of Running

I cannot envy any elected official. They have a hard job. Having worked for elected officials, I think it's a difficult position to be in. . . . You're just constantly fundraising. It costs a lot of money. You have to raise a lot of money to be viable . . . and that's a really big impediment. I hate the fact that money plays such a large role. . . . [And] you have to be on the job day in and day out, you can't stop. . . . I mean, any elected official, whether you think they're a great legislator or not, just the stamina that is required to be in these positions is absolutely amazing. If you want to be in elected office, you really have to bust your butt.
—Lin, Asian American MPP candidate, Harvard's Kennedy School of Government

We tend to assume in political science that political behavior is for the most part rational, even though this assumption sometimes flies in the face of evidence of daily human unpredictability. But we do not mean that people act like robots; we simply mean that the rewards of a behavior generally outweigh the costs. If not, an individual is unlikely to engage in that behavior. Or, across a large group of people, most people would not, so that the assumption holds generally even if some people fail to act rationally some or even all of the time.

Rational voters weigh the costs and benefits, both to themselves and to society more generally, of voting or not voting.[1] So too do rational citizens make decisions about other forms of political participation such as donating money or time to a campaign, putting a sign in their yard, talking with others about politics, or writing letters to the editor or to their representatives.[2] We would expect potential candidates, for whom far more time and resources are at stake, to be even more circumspect in their calculations.

What, then, are the potential costs and benefits of running for political office? This chapter looks at the costs by themselves first. When we begin to look carefully, we see myriad costly elements involved in candidacy, many of which are unusual compared with those of other advanced post-industrial democracies. The largest costs are financial; our unique U.S. system of campaign funding is particularly burdensome to the individual candidate, who generally raises personally the large bulk of the money need to run. But the costs of the U.S. system of candidacy and holding office go far beyond the obvious financial ones. As a headline from *The Onion* put it humorously following Barack Obama's first election in 2008, "Black Man Given Nation's Worst Job." The satiric article read, in part:

> WASHINGTON—African-American man Barack Obama, 47, was given the least-desirable job in the entire country Tuesday when he was elected president of the United States of America. In his new high-stress, low-reward position, Obama will be charged with . . . having to please more than 300 million Americans and cater to their every whim on a daily basis . . . The job comes with such intense scrutiny and so certain a guarantee of failure that only one other person even bothered applying for it.[3]

## Huge Financial Inputs

The costs of time, effort, and money for even a low-level campaign in the United States are high, even before the major costs of high-level campaigns—paid media and consultants—kick in. Running for a state legislative seat averages about $88,000, with large differences across states.[4] The most expensive state legislative races (for the lower chambers) were in California and Texas ($354,455 and $274,734 on average, respectively), while the least expensive averages were in Maine ($4,916), Vermont ($2,434), and New Hampshire ($677).[5] Running for Congress is yet more expensive; winning U.S. House candidates raise about $1.5 million on average, and the number continues to increase with each election cycle.[6] A winning Senate campaign in 2012 cost on average $11.5 million, again with large differences by state. And running for president is immensely

TABLE 3.1. Average Costs of Winning Key Political Offices

| Cost of Winning an Election in 2014, in U.S. Dollars (Thousands) | |
| --- | --- |
| U.S. President | $784,000 |
| U.S. Senator (Average) | 9,700 |
| U.S. House of Representatives (Average) | 1,500 |
| Mayor of Major U.S. City (At least) | 1,000+ |
| U.S. State Leg (Average) | 88 |
| Canadian Member of Parliament Spending Limit* | 97 |
| UK Member of Parliament (Average) | 53 |

* Based on a thirty-seven-day election period; the spending limit can increase if the election period turns out to be longer (Elections Canada 2015).
Sources: Campaign Finance Institute 2016 (for House and Senate); Metcalfe/City Lab 2012; Elections Canada 2015; Hardman/Spectator (UK) 2014, with British pounds converted to U.S. dollars based on 2014 exchange rate of 1.55 dollars per pound.

expensive and growing more so with each race. In 2012, each presidential campaign spent around $1 billion.

Even running for local office is no walk in the park; CityLab, a project of Atlantic Media, reported in 2012 that increasingly, candidates for city- or county-level political office are seeking funding from outside their localities.[7] Races for mayor in some cities can become "extravagant carnival[s] of cash,"[8] requiring multimillion-dollar budgets for serious candidates. Compare this with headlines in the Toronto *National Post*, which reported in a headline, "It costs a *grotesque* amount of money to become Mayor of Toronto" (emphasis added) when it was revealed that then-candidate Rob Ford spent about $40,000, in violation of several campaign finance rules there.[9] Yet this level of campaign fundraising in any major U.S. city would seem more "minor" than "grotesque." Among comparable countries, the United States is a major outlier on campaign spending at all levels.

In 2014, *Time* magazine reported that, as an industry, spending on campaigns has greatly outpaced the increases in health care, income, and GDP in the past decade. Since 1998, federal campaign costs, as reported by the Federal Election Commission (FEC), have increased by more than 200 percent.[10] If measured since the mid-1980s, the figure is more than 500 percent.[11] Overall, more than $2.6 billion was spent in the 2012 elections.[12]

## A Highly Irregular "Candidate-Centered" System

Running for office anywhere requires resources, both material and non-material. However, the extent to which parties shield candidates from the brunt of campaigning costs varies widely across countries, with the United States near the bottom of the heap. Ours is a "candidate-centered system."[13] Many democracies nationalize some or most campaign expenses, seeing them as part of "the costs of their democracy."[14] We can see this with a simple comparison between the countries that are part of the OECD, the Organisation for Economic Cooperation and Development, which includes the economically developed democracies most comparable to the United States. Every other OECD country except two (the United Kingdom and Switzerland) provides public funding to political parties, while the United States does not.[15] Unlike the United States, however, the United Kingdom and Switzerland both provide candidates free or subsidized media access.[16]

Meanwhile, in this country, and especially for higher-level candidacies, television advertising can consume the largest portion of a campaign's budget, and most candidates get little to no help from government[17] and often not much from parties, particularly in primaries. With oft-questioned logic,[18] the U.S. Supreme Court has pronounced money to be speech and corporations to be people, thereby striking down hard-won limits on political donating and major pieces of public financing systems.[19] The result has been that the majority of money for most campaigns in the United States comes from large individual contributions and large contributions from PACs (political action committees), which candidates themselves solicit.[20]

Although outsider PACs have had a striking influence on U.S. campaigns for some time, especially since the "Swift Boat" ads against John Kerry in 2004, the *Citizens United* Supreme Court decision in 2010 fueled further intensification of the negative campaigning environment, with so-called "super PACs" engaging in pro- and anti-candidate messaging campaigns independently of actual candidates. Compared with the usual practices in other democracies, this is, to put it mildly, odd and confusing.

Table 3.2 compares the United States with the rest of the OECD countries in terms of campaign financing structures and other aid for

TABLE 3.2. Comparing United States with Other OECD Countries on Campaign Assistance for Candidates

| | Public Funding to Political Parties? | Free/ Subsidized Media Access? | Tax Relief for Candidates/ Parties? | Expenditure Limits? |
|---|---|---|---|---|
| Australia | Yes | | Yes | |
| Austria | Yes | | | Yes |
| Belgium | Yes | Yes | Yes | Yes |
| Canada | Yes | Yes | Yes | Yes |
| Chile | Yes | Yes | Yes | Yes |
| Czech Republic | Yes | Yes | Yes | |
| Denmark | Yes | Yes | Yes | |
| Finland | Yes | | Yes | |
| France | Yes | Yes | Yes | Yes |
| Germany | Yes | Yes | | |
| Greece | Yes | Yes | Some | Yes |
| Hungary | Yes | Yes | Yes | Yes |
| Iceland | Yes | Yes | Yes | Some |
| Ireland | Yes | Yes | Some | Yes |
| Israel | Yes | Yes | Some | Yes |
| Italy | Yes | Yes | Yes | Yes |
| Japan | Yes | Yes | Yes | Yes |
| Korea | Yes | Yes | Yes | Yes |
| Luxembourg | Yes | | Some | |
| Mexico | Yes | Yes | Yes | Yes |
| Netherlands | Yes | Yes | Yes | |
| New Zealand | Yes | Yes | | Yes |
| Norway | Yes | | Yes | |
| Poland | Yes | Yes | | Yes |
| Portugal | Yes | Yes | Yes | Yes |
| Slovak Republic | Yes | Yes | Yes | Yes |
| Slovenia | Yes | Yes | Some | Yes |
| Spain | Yes | Yes | Some | Yes |
| Sweden | Yes | | Some | |
| Switzerland | | Yes | Some | |

TABLE 3.2. (*cont.*)

| | Public Funding to Political Parties? | Free/ Subsidized Media Access? | Tax Relief for Candidates/ Parties? | Expenditure Limits? |
|---|---|---|---|---|
| Turkey | Yes | Yes | Yes | |
| United Kingdom | | Yes | Some | Yes |
| United States | | | | Some |

Source: International IDEA 2014

candidates and parties. Most of the other countries provide political parties and/or candidates with free or subsidized access to media (especially television), and with tax exemptions for the costs of conducting campaigns (and often to those who donate to them). Those countries that do not provide tax relief for the waging of campaigns mostly offer other forms of indirect support, such as providing free postage and/or meeting facilities/space. And most require campaigns to hold their expenses to pre-set limits (which occasionally happens in certain U.S. presidential elections, if both parties agree, and in some U.S. states and localities, but not as a general rule and not widely). As can be seen in table 3.2, the United States provides the lowest levels of government support for and intervention in campaigns of comparable countries.

Table 3.2 could reasonably lead to more than one conclusion. Perhaps what is needed is not greater government support for candidates but more self-funders like former Mayor Michael R. Bloomberg of New York, 2010 California gubernatorial candidate Meg Whitman, or presidential candidates Mitt Romney and Donald Trump. Should parties and interest groups just try harder to recruit millionaire candidates? This would certainly help alleviate the problem of candidate deterrence by fundraising, but it would do little to increase diversity of the candidate pool. Millionaires and billionaires are disproportionately white and male, as a result of persisting income gaps and wealth gaps by both race and gender.[21] Recruiting the wealthy to run (which tactic has certainly been tried by many recruiters already) also exacerbates the large class differences between representatives and those they represent, which distorts policy outcomes in favor of policies preferred by the rich.[22] If the goal is more representative government, by identity and life-experience factors like gender, race, and class, more government intervention in campaign financing (public funding, matching funds, spending limits, free but limited media time for candidate ads, real ceilings on political donations to PACs as well as to candidates) would appear to be a better solution than recruiting more Romneys or Trumps.

## Time, Effort, and Double the "Butt-Busting"

In addition to direct financial resources, individual candidates at all levels in the United States are responsible for creating and managing new entities (campaign operations) for each new election, which require sometimes-large startup costs and a large input of time and energy that then cannot go to actual campaigning.[23] The costs rise with the level of office but are not insignificant even for lower-level campaigns. One campaign handbook tells potential candidates, "[Y]ou will be running an operation the size of a small business for several months. . . . [E]ven if you do not . . . advertise or hire staff, the cost of materials can be steep. Too often, candidates underestimate the costs of campaigning, attempt to raise money when it is too late, and incur major debt. . . ."[24] Campaign guidebooks also strongly recommend hiring professional staff: "[Y]ou will need to build an organization that will manage the bulk of the operational and administrative tasks of the campaign for you. . . . [R]unning a successful political campaign requires expertise."[25] Suggested paid positions in a campaign include campaign manager, treasurer, fundraising director, volunteer coordinator, scheduler, webmaster, office manager, field/outreach director, and, if possible, yard-sign coordinator, to say nothing of office rent, supplies, transportation, and pizza for the volunteers. In other democracies, most of this would be handled by the party rather than by the individual candidate.[26]

In addition to the financial costs, there are enormous time, start-up, and other resource costs involved in the most basic activities of a campaign at any level of office. Factors that might usually be handled by parties in other democracies here mostly fall to individual candidates, including: deciding to run in a primary, submitting papers to officially become a candidate, building a campaign operation, recruiting volunteers, planning public campaign events and talks, buying and distributing bumper stickers and yard signs, vying for party support, building coalitions with local/state/national organizations, soliciting individual- and group-level donations, holding campaign fundraising events, choosing a platform and key issues, communicating the campaign's message, buying and earning media attention, obtaining crucial endorsements, convincing voters to support you, registering voters, and convincing people to vote at all.

All of this goes on for quite a while; campaigns here last longer than almost anywhere else. In an interview with a campaign manager who recently managed a losing gubernatorial campaign, I was told that the candidate's greatest fault was starting too late. "We only had eight months," he lamented. "Realistically, we needed eighteen."[27] This length (540 days), which sounds familiar to anyone who follows presidential elections, contrasts starkly with the average for "unscheduled" campaigns in European democracies (about 60 days) as well as with the "scheduled" campaigns (180 days).[28] Justin Trudeau's successful campaign to become prime minister of Canada in 2015, for example, lasted 78 days according to CBC News.[29] Here in the United States, by contrast, the 2016 presidential hopefuls were well into campaign assembly by the start of 2015, about 660 days (nearly two years) before the election.[30] Campaigns here are more marathons than sprints, but the candidates and their staffs generally have to sprint the whole way anyway.

The U.S. system is further differentiated from almost all others in its use of a primary system to pre-select candidates who then run again in the general elections. Whatever the merits of such a system in terms of democratic openness—and such merits are hotly debated, still, relative to the disadvantages of this system[31]—it is irrefutable that it creates more work for the individual candidates. She who would hold office must generally mount two separate campaigns, with separate audiences, strategies, opponents, and electorates. Whatever input of time, energy, money, and other resources are required, in other words, must generally be doubled if one is lucky or good enough to win the first round. In the words of Lin, the public policy graduate student quoted at the start of this chapter, that is a whole lot of "busting your butt."

## Anticipating the Headaches

The upshot is that campaigns can be costly, in both financial and non-monetary terms. They can also be rewarding in various ways, which the following chapter will enumerate and explore. And some of the costs or rewards might matter differently to different people.

All of this is useful information for political science. It helps us figure out how people behave politically and what kinds of personal or institutional incentives they respond to. The Millennial students I interviewed were happy to discuss their perceptions of candidacy, especially regarding potential challenges. Nearly all brought up campaign financing and the need for candidates to raise often-large sums to be competitive. Most also spoke about costs relating to privacy and scrutiny—either of themselves or of families and friends. Some brought up the risk of having one's income depend on electoral outcomes. Others spoke of their dislike of conflict and confrontation, some level of which is essential to American democracy, but which seem particularly salient in the past few years. Some simply disliked the idea of so much public speaking, while others perceived this as a reward.

Not all interviewees perceived the same costs, but there was enough overlap to form a suggestive list. Table 3.3 presents this list of perceived barriers to electoral candidacy, in order of salience in the minds of interviewees. The table summarizes what those in my interview sample thought were the major barriers to running for, or holding, office and gives an indication of how prevalent this perception of cost was among them. Generally, as the table suggests, the young people I talked to not only were very aware of the potential challenges in store should they choose to run, but they found many of those challenges particularly distasteful.

The same is true of those in the survey sample, although the proportions differ. Likely this has to do both with sample size—the survey sample was far larger—and with methodology. In the interviews, I asked open-ended questions and let interviewees bring up costs and rewards on their own. On the survey, I asked a long series of questions about various aspects of politics and campaigning, most of which were answered by most respondents.[32] The interview format encouraged deep feedback on a few key issues while the survey format solicited fairly shallow data

TABLE 3.3. Costs Mentioned in Interviews (in Order from Most- to Least-Mentioned)

| Perceived Cost | % of Interviewees Mentioning |
|---|---|
| Fundraising/asking for money | 69 |
| Sex or race bias/double standards | 49 |
| Corruption/politics as lobbyist-driven | 47 |
| Lack of privacy, scrutiny/judgment | 42 |
| Dealing with party officials | 36 |
| Politics feels inauthentic to R ("gripping and grinning") | 33 |
| Long hours/exhausting/time away from family | 31 |
| Having to fit well into major party | 27 |
| R does not enjoy networking/"schmoozing" | 27 |
| Not meritocratic | 27 |
| Attacks/negativity/need thicker skin than R has | 26 |
| R does not enjoy "playing politics," horse-trading | 26 |
| Bureaucratic/inefficiency | 22 |
| Hyper-partisanship/gridlock/lack of thoughtful deliberation | 22 |
| High stress | 16 |
| Having to deal with unreasonable/short-sighted people | 15 |
| Geography | 13 |
| R does not enjoy public speaking | 9 |
| Low pay/financial sacrifice | 9 |
| Heavy weight of responsibility, decision making | 9 |
| R prefers to avoid conflict | 9 |
| R is more of an introvert | 9 |
| Incumbency as barrier to R's running/winning | 9 |
| Risky | 7 |
| Dealing with the media | 6 |
| R has one or more skeletons in closet | 6 |
| R thinks he or she would need to be more physically attractive or look different | 4 |
| R can't remember names/faces well | 2 |

Source: LPS-PAS, Interview Sample (N = 53); R = Respondent

on a broad set of questions. On the whole, there is much agreement. Table 3.4 gives data from the survey sample, on many of the same cost factors as the interview data in table 3.3, and some new factors.

The quantitative nature of the survey data allows for some useful data visualization. Figure 3.1 arranges, in order of importance, the factors that survey respondents said might make them more likely to want to run for office.

One common set of items are things that would make running easier (public financing, having a lot of support already, feeling sure you would win). These factors reduce the costs of running. Public financing, for instance, reduces the enormous cost of having to laboriously raise money through individual contributions. Feeling sure you would win reduces the cost of riskiness, which worries some potential candidates.

Another set of seemingly important items in the figure, however, seems more tied to the rewards of running than to the costs; factors like feeling you could "make a difference" if you ran or if you won, and knowing you could "help your community" are the kinds of things interviewees mentioned as key benefits of running—and it seems, from the analysis of the survey data presented in this chapter, that they do indeed matter for the survey sample as a whole, not just to the subset of interviewees. Using the words of interviewees to illuminate the survey data, the rest of this chapter further develops the reasoning behind the most critical of these perceived costs and quantitatively measures how much they seem to matter.

This chapter will deal only with the costs side of the equation, but soon we will look closer at these rewards and whether they matter enough to offset the perceived costs. Generally, the data from the interviews, coupled with quantitative data from the survey which will be presented in this chapter, lend credence to the theory that negative perceptions on the part of Millennial eligibles about the various costs involved in running can be severely offputting.

## Hating Having to Solicit Money (and to Be Indebted)

Anticipating having to ask for money may be the single most deterring factor I studied. Several interviewees said it would be hard for them to ask (and perhaps also accept) donations, which are essential parts of a

TABLE 3.4. Costs Data from Survey, with Question Wording and Means (in Order from Highest to Lowest Mean)

| Perceived Cost | % Agreeing (Mean)* | N |
|---|---|---|
| It is important to me that I can "[Be] sure of always having a relatively well-paying job" | 88.6 | 761 |
| I would be more likely to run if "It would not interfere with [my] family's privacy" | 78.2 | 760 |
| I would be more likely to run if "Campaigns were fully publicly financed, so [I] would not have to raise money for [my] campaign" | 77.7 | 760 |
| I would feel negative about "Calling people to ask for donations" | 73.7 | 760 |
| I "Hate to lose at anything" | 63.8 | 761 |
| I "Avoid conflict whenever possible" | 50.7 | 761 |
| The consideration of being expected to contribute financially to my family of origin is "very or somewhat important to [my] choice of future job(s)" | 46.5 | 550 |
| I "will be expected to contribute financially to [my] parents, siblings, or other relatives in the future" to a large or moderate extent | 46.0 | 546 |
| I would feel negative about "Dealing with the media" | 38.7 | 760 |
| I would feel negative about "Facing hostile questions" | 37.2 | 760 |
| I am not "Thick-skinned" and I believe "It takes a thick skin to survive in politics" | 37.1 | 660 |
| "In today's media environment, you'd have to be crazy to run for office" | 36.8 | 760 |
| I would feel negative about "Dealing with party officials" | 33.5 | 760 |
| I am not "Willing to take risks" | 32.8 | 761 |
| I believe that politicians often "lie" | 29.0 | 760 |
| I do not fit into either major political party | 28.1 | 760 |
| I would feel negative about "Going door-to-door to meet constituents" | 28.1 | 760 |
| I would feel negative about "Making public speeches" | 18.4 | 760 |
| The term "Ethical/moral" describes me well or very well, and I think politicians often "Act immorally" | 14.8 | 736 |
| I would be more likely to run if "[I] had fewer skeletons in [my] closet" | 11.2 | 761 |

Source: LPS-PAS, Survey Sample

* Note: Because each variable is collapsed to a binary variable (0 or 1), the mean (weighted) gives the percentage of the sample scoring "1," or saying that the statement is true for the respondent.

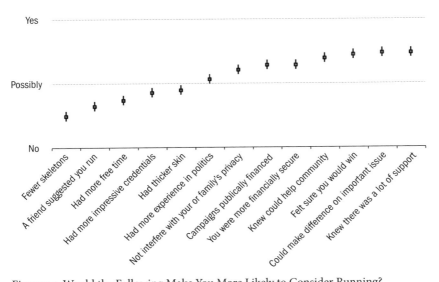

Figure 3.1. Would the Following Make You More Likely to Consider Running?
(Weighted means with 95 Percent Confidence Intervals). Source: LPS-PAS, Survey
Sample. N = At least 716 for all questions, and 763 for certain questions ("help commu-
nity," "make difference," and "support") that were in the final round of data collection.

campaign. Esther, a policy student, explained, "I hate asking people for
money. That would be incredibly hard for me. I have tremendous guilt
doing that. It's hard to ask. It doesn't feel like it's something I should
be asking people for. I don't like to borrow money from friends or my
parents. Even when I go home to Connecticut and my parents want to
send me off with $40 they slip into my pocket, it's really hard for me to
accept that." If Esther found it hard to accept the occasional monetary
kindness from family members, she might have a very hard time asking
strangers for the amounts needed to wage a successful campaign, as she
seemed to understand.

The task of having to solicit money for a campaign (and having to
do it every day for a long period of time) loomed large in the minds
of the interviewees. When asked about how they might feel as a candidate about "calling people to ask for donations," survey respondents
expressed negativity (the weighted[33] mean was 73.6 percent).[34] Of these
who felt negatively, a third chose the option "so negative it would deter
me from running." In interviews, respondents explained this aversion,

some with evident disgust. Sofia explained, "The idea of asking people for money really skeeves me out." Omar, a law student, referenced the growing costs of campaigns, saying, ". . . it certainly can't be fair for people who don't have personal money to draw upon. [T]hey don't want to make calls for 5, 6, 7 hours a day. They want to legislate, they want to talk about the issues, they would rather, you know, knock on a thousand doors as opposed to making a thousand calls asking for money."

Many of the interviewees referenced the *Citizens United* decision by name. These were, after all, law and policy school students, and that decision seemed to have had a large effect on many of them. Lin, the MPP student quoted earlier, was ambivalent about the idea of public financing of campaigns but expressed overall unhappiness with the current system:

> [W]ith *Citizens United* . . . it's just going to be so interesting to see in these upcoming cycles the impact of essentially, you know, unlimited donations from corporate entities. I think it's just going to be so interesting what that impact will be on the electoral process. And if that court decision holds for an extended period of time, that's going to spur further campaign finance reform moving away from spending limits writ large. I think that would be really interesting, but . . . at the end of the day, I hate the fact that money plays such a large role. . . . I think that the system would be a lot better if we tried to minimize the impact of money.

In the survey data, more than half (52.4 percent) of the sample stated that they would definitely be more likely to consider running "if campaigns were fully publicly financed, so you would not have to raise money for your campaign."[35] Another quarter (25.3 percent) said that such public financing would "possibly" make them more likely to consider a run for office. Together, then, nearly 80 percent of those surveyed were somewhat or very bothered by the current process of campaign financing.

Data from an additional question, asked only in the final wave of the survey, suggest also that the absolute amounts of money involved matter. Perhaps deterrence effects would not be so strong if candidates had to raise some money but not so much. A question in the final wave (targeting students of color in the newest first-year class at Harvard Law) asked respondents, "Would you be more likely to consider running for public office if the amounts of money involved were not so high?" Although this question was unfortunately asked of only forty-seven respondents, the responses showed a clear sample preference; thirty-nine of the forty-seven said this would make them more likely to consider running.[36]

## The "Ick" Factor

Beyond not wanting to ask, however, there is a second and perhaps more damaging psychological effect on potential candidates of the way we finance campaigns in this country. Simple distaste at having to do the asking is one thing—but what if eligibles are so disgusted by the system that it leads them to see politics in general as corrupt? The interview data suggest that the U.S. system of campaign finance may have this result, if not for everyone then for a good proportion of the sample. Many of the interviewees struggled to maintain idealism while also confronting the realities of the political system.

Take, for instance, a black female law student, Tonya, who said, "I think by and large politicians want to do good. I do, I do believe that. That they really have an issue they care about [and] they think the best way to effect change is by doing something in politics. And I think somewhere, within that system it gets—that desire changes into something else. I don't know if I would use the word *corrupted* but I think that the focuses shift from helping to staying in your position."

Sarah, a white female law student, also used the word *corrupt*, although modified by *almost*. She then added,

And that's a strong word. I don't necessarily think all of the politicians do this consciously . . . I think it's just easy to fall into that. It doesn't matter what you personally think, it's what your job is, and I think [corruption is] easy to fall into, and that can lead to problems because that's not what we want. . . . A lot of politicians are influenced by interest groups and who has the money, and what's going to get them re-elected, rather than what's the best thing for the country as a whole.

George, a Suffolk law student, was more blunt: "I think [politicians] start going into the system as, you know, very idealistic, but as they go along through time they become, I would say, pawns for corporations or other, you know, interest groups." When I suggested that *pawn* was a strong word, he laughed and explained, "I don't think there's any bribery or fraud going on, but I think that you know they lose their independence . . . because they're always trying to appease somebody. . . . I think they've been influenced by the stronger people with more money or whoever can keep them elected."

Data from the survey suggest that a lot of people felt as George did. It is not that these young folks thought that politicians were outright corrupt, on the whole; only 14.8 percent said that politicians "often" acted immorally.[37] But 67.5 percent said that politicians "sometimes" acted immorally. It is not clear that these mentions of immorality refer to money, as nonfinancial scandals about politicians (particularly those related to their sex lives) are often in the news. But the interview data suggested that at least some of this perception of generally high levels of occasional immorality relates to the way campaigns are financed through donations, and the need for the individual politician to raise them. Some may relate to compromising one's values, either for money or for popularity (which also appeared to be linked, in the minds of interviewees). In response to a different question, only about 3.4 percent of the survey sample said that they thought politicians would often "Do what they think is right even if it's not popular."[38] On that question, the majority (58.6 percent) of the sample thought that politicians would "never" or "rarely" choose what was right over what was popular.

This kind of skepticism about politicians may help explain comments by Omar, a black male student at Harvard Law, who said that he wouldn't rule out running, but added,

> I think that in terms of what it actually means to be an elected representative at the national level on a day-to-day basis is much less glamorous than people understand. I think that especially in the House of Representatives it's just fundraising, you know, you get here and OK, over the next three months, you have this sort of fundraising quota. . . . [E]ven when they are elected, they can give less and less of their time to the things that were really important to them in order to raise money. I think that because of those constraints you attract people who are kind of empty suits.

Although he did not say he would never run, the idea of joining the ranks of the "empty suits" did not seem appealing to Omar or to others in his elite law/policy graduate student cohort. In fact, one of the most popular terms of self-description in the survey was "authentic/sincere," which 95 percent of survey respondents said described them well or very well (with 61.3 percent choosing "very well").[39] The prospect of compromising one's morals or beliefs to be elected or reelected, which seemed linked in these students' minds, at least partially, to the need to raise large sums of money to run, was downright off-putting.

Tamika, a black female law student at Harvard, spoke in more direct terms about what she called "the negative implications that come with that idea of being a politician." When I asked what she meant, she elaborated: "Just in terms of corruption or not necessarily being completely truthful when you're making these promises. . . . I feel like some people really get caught up in the politics and totally forget where they may have come from or what their ideas were before they got power. So I guess it's the effect that politics can have on the politicians themselves."

Mario, a Hispanic male student at Harvard Law, called this, with a half-smile, "selling your soul," adding quickly, "for lack of a better word." Many in the survey seemed to agree (although the survey avoided asking about souls). When asked how much they agreed with the statement "Politics corrupts even good people into doing bad things," 39.3 percent chose "agree" or "agree strongly."[40] Another 31.8 percent chose "neither agree nor disagree," suggesting ambivalence; less than a third of the sample disagreed outright, with only 4.0 percent disagreeing strongly. The whiff of corruption (a word used twenty-five times by interviewees, and never by me unless in a follow-up question) seemed, in the minds of many potential candidates, to pervade politics.

When I asked Tamika if she would ever run, she was adamantly opposed to the idea. She explained: "I don't know if I'm necessarily willing to. . . . I want to keep my idealism. It's nice. I think it's nice. So having to . . . the idea of me making a promise to a large group of good people and then completely going back on that, I can't. It doesn't sit well with me at all. I can't see myself doing that." I asked if she thought politicians could ever keep a promise. She replied that perhaps they could, but she did not think it happened most times. She added, "I think that people sometimes do what they have to, to win, which also doesn't sit well with me."

One particularly verbose interviewee, Dave, put the matter starkly, while putting his Harvard education to good use. He laughed out loud when I asked why he wouldn't run for office, explaining his views thus:

> I [would] risk capture by going into a political process as corrupted, and sclerotic, and generally putrescent as the American one, so full of money, really, that it ends up attracting people who understand that and don't care, or the few silly idealistic ones who think they can change the system from within. I mean, say what you will about Obama, it's quite possible that he never intended to be anything but a shill, but that's what he's become. And anyone who thought that he could do otherwise, assuming of course he wanted to, is kidding themselves, given the kind of machines he was fighting against.

No matter if you agree with him or not, Dave's comments are indicative of the kinds of negative feelings my interviewees have about the process. On the whole, the young people I interviewed expressed strong negative emotions (revulsion, disappointment, disgust, anger) when contemplating raising money for campaigns, particularly from lobbyists, corporations, and rich individuals. Regardless of the objective legal status of financing campaigns through large individual contributions and the Supreme Court's equating of such donations with speech, most of the potential candidates I talked to perceived the system as tainted, if not outright corrupted, by money. The flow of money into campaigns, they thought, distorted the representational process, swayed representatives' priorities, made representatives callous to the needs of "real people" (and therefore "inauthentic," which my respondents did not want to be), and forced representatives and candidates to spend a good portion of their time raising money. The eligibles in my sample not only did not want to do the work of raising all the money; they disliked and questioned the system of having to raise it in the first place. A large part of the job of being a candidate was, to a sizeable majority of them, distasteful.

## Perceptions of Privacy Invasion as a Further Deterrent

Besides money, another important deterrent to a rational eligible candidate might be the fairly reasonable and widespread dislike of being under constant media surveillance. Yet as media outlets and technologies have proliferated, competition for a "scoop" has increased drastically in the past few decades. At the same time, post-Watergate cynicism has given rise to a subspecialty of scandal journalism.[41] With network news viewership and newspaper readership in decline and a plethora of other potential sources available, media outlets from cable news stations to HD radio stations to blogs to e-mail news services to comedy-news shows[42] fight one another to "break a story."

At the same time, current information technology helps us get news almost instantaneously, even while specialized cable channels, radio stations, and blogs have an unprecedented amount of time/space to fill with news. CNN runs twenty-four hours a day, seven days a week, while Internet sources do not have the same word limits as traditional newspaper stories, and even newspapers now regularly refer readers to their online sites for extended stories. The need for political news, in other words, is insatiable. Increasingly, everything a candidate says and does is reportable and reported.

Filling the need for ever more conduits of potential stories to various forms of media outlets, campaigns have become increasingly reliant on "opposition researchers" to dig up dirt on the opposing candidate(s) and then strategically feed it to the press. Many of the potential candidates in my samples were extremely aware of and sensitive to the thought of always being under such a microscope. It is perhaps too easy to romanticize the past, but these eligibles might have been more willing to run in a far earlier era of American politics when even a president could have an off-camera life. For example, Omar, the black male student at Harvard Law quoted earlier, said he disliked the "gotcha" media flurries around moments like when President George H.W. Bush underestimated the price of a gallon of milk in a debate with his election opponents. Omar explained, "I don't want to give up that amount of privacy."

"The media," when referred to by interviewees, was generally seen as intrusive—and not in a helpful way. Jen, a white female Suffolk Law student, referred to media focus on appearance, personal lives, and scandals as "static around what the real issues [are]." Such "static," as Kim, an Asian American female law student at Suffolk, pointed out, can "distort your image." She added, "I would hate that [and] hate [for] my family to have to go through that."

Juan, an MPP candidate at Harvard's Kennedy School, explained that the "reputational costs" would be too large both for him to bear and for his family. He recounted his anger at what he saw as media invasion into the family of Sarah Palin when she was a vice presidential nominee and related this to his own lack of political ambition:

> Years ago you would have had the three or four major news outlets and we've gone from that to today [when] you just have so many megaphones and so many people sitting on their soap boxes. . . . So I think more than any other objection I recoil from that prospect at least in the near term just because of the reputational costs that it might have on my family and myself. . . . If there [were] some magical situation where all the Bristol Palins of the world would just be protected from the spotlight . . . that's just great. Then I have to say that I absolutely would [be more interested in running], yes.

In the survey data, anticipated privacy invasion concerned many such Millennial eligibles in a way that appeared related to their contemplation of candidacy. Almost half of the survey sample (45.5 percent) said they would be more likely to consider running if they knew that doing so would not interfere with their families' privacy.[43] Another 32.6 percent said this would "possibly" make them more likely to consider running, for a total of nearly 80 percent of the sample suggesting that this factor has some importance in retarding their political ambition.

Relatedly, some survey respondents feared they already had some "skeleton" in their closet that would surely be dug up and displayed in public, likely in a way embarrassing for the potential candidate and possibly damaging or even fatal to their candidacy. Of the survey sample, 11.2 percent said they definitely would be more likely to consider running if they had "fewer skeletons in [their] closet," and another 23.4 percent indicated that the absence of skeletons in their closets would "possibly" increase the likelihood of their considering a run.[44]

A final media/privacy–related item on the survey put the matter starkly. In a pre-test of the interview protocol, before the collection of either survey or interview data, one beta-tester responded to a question on political ambition by telling me, "In today's media environment, you would have to be crazy to run for office." I found the statement intriguing and wondered how many in the eventual survey sample would agree with it, and how strongly. I added it to the "agree/disagree" section of the survey, allowing respondents five possible responses to gauge their agreement or lack of such, ranging from "disagree strongly" to "agree strongly."[45] Responses clustered in the middle of the range, rather than in the extreme ends; 9.5 percent agreed strongly while 7.4 percent disagreed strongly. With regard to simple agreement versus not, about a third agreed and nearly a third (30.4 percent) chose "neither agree nor disagree." Again, this is more suggestive of ambivalence than strong negative feelings, but two-thirds of those surveyed (67.2 percent) did not disagree with the statement. And for the third who agreed outright, the word *crazy* suggests a strong perception of the media environment as a costly part of running.

Survey responses and further interview data support the idea that privacy concerns matter to eligibles. In a free-response answer in the survey, a white female law student wrote, regarding running, that she would be "[i]nterested, but likely wouldn't want to put myself or family through the media scrutiny." A white male law student echoed this response, noting that "[l]ack of consideration for my family" would turn him away from electoral politics.

In response to a free-response question on the survey asking what would make the respondent feel more likely to run, one white female policy school student wrote, "I think the media would probably [tear] me apart if I ran being fairly openly bisexual so will probably never run for office. Would love to work as a non-elected advisor in politics someday." Another public policy student stated simply what would make him more likely to run: "Perhaps not having to deal with the media environment of today." A Latina law student wrote she'd be more likely to run "If the media didn't dig up people's past indiscretions." One respondent chimed in that s/he would feel more qualified to run if s/he had "more of a filter on the things that I say." And perhaps in reference to undoing such a past indiscretion, another anonymous survey respondent wrote, "Invent a time machine."

Lately in several European nations there has been debate and court cases about the "right to be forgotten"—for example, the ability to force search engines like Google to destroy old data about you. In time, this may become a human rights norm, although I anticipate a fierce debate in this country, where free speech often gets prioritized over other rights. Until we get a time machine, then, the likely trend is that privacy concerns will only increase. Considering the data from the various survey questions together, and in tandem with the qualitative data, it appears that privacy seemed a key element weighing on the mind of eligibles, at least those with malleable political ambition.

## Not Fitting into Either Major Party

Few in the sample (less than 5 percent) thought that politicians often worked across party lines. Instead, the mean answer for that question hovered between "sometimes" and "rarely." The partisan polarization we have seen reach new heights lately, and its attendant gridlock, may leave out those who feel closer to the middle ideologically.[46] In the survey sample, most respondents (like those of their age and education level across the country) identified more with the Democratic than the Republican Party, but the majority did not seem themselves as strong partisans of either. And, like Americans at large, there were in the middle a fair number who think of themselves as independent (or, when pressed, perhaps only very weakly partisan). On the standard political science party summary scale, where 1 is a strong Democrat and 7 means strong Republican, 28.5 percent of the sample scored between 3 and 5—so, in the middle rather than at the partisan ends of the scale.

For those falling more in the middle, the enhanced role of partisanship involved in governing, even if not in campaigning, can be frustrating. One interviewee, a white male student at Suffolk Law, used the word *hate* twice to get across his sentiment: "I hate political parties, and I wish everything [were] nonpartisan and everyone [were] independent and we can have a large amount of candidates where . . . the two parties weren't running everything . . . only giving the country two options. . . . I hate that."

Months later, a white female Suffolk classmate of his said something similar to me: "I think the partisanship is really hurting people a lot. That's sort of the main thing I see. I think there's really a lot of diversity in both of the parties, and they're agreeing on things that, if you look at them logically, they shouldn't even be agreeing on. But because they're in the same party, they feel they have to. So I think that's really the biggest issue [for me]." When she said this, I asked directly, "Do you think it would help if we had more than two parties, or is it just parties in general that are a problem?" Her response was that the number of parties (in our case, just two) is a critical problem in her mind, and she did not see much cause for optimism about change in the future:

> I think the more parties you have, the less control [each party has]. . . . Both in the Democratic and the Republican [parties], if politicians don't vote on party lines, they're not going to be promoted by their party or org [*sic*], they're not going to get the funding for the next campaign, they're not going to get the support, they're not going to get high-ranking members coming on the campaign with them. And if there were more parties, maybe you could really get substantial [change]. With three, I think it's harder to gang up, in a way, because two parties are fighting for that third party to stay on their side, whatever the triangle formation is. So, three would probably be . . . potentially it could be a more reasonable solution. But at the same time, if the parties are still just stuck in their ways, then it will be back to the same.

Some interviewees thought their personal views basically disqualified them from candidacy, so they did not expect to run for office in the future, unless it were perhaps nonpartisan (as with some local offices). Jim, a white male law student at Suffolk, said he "disputed" the two-party system, as he did not think that any one political party could encompass his beliefs. When I asked if he would ever run, he said, "I'm very socially liberal and at this moment in time, being socially liberal is not congruent with being conservative, so . . . ." He trailed off after the *so*, as if to imply, "oh well!"

A white male student at Harvard Law, Jack, said something similar in terms of frustration about partisanship and the lack of options for those who might be financially conservative but socially liberal, or vice versa. Then, as he talked, his comments became more far-reaching, circling back to campaign funding (which is of course implicated in the partisanship that frustrated so many of the interviewees) and to a "pathetic" lack of really representative government (including, important to him because of his engineering training, the lack of scientists elected to high office):

But I think more than that is another thing that's always bothered me about politics today . . . I consider myself financially conservative but when very socially conservative people, the people who I feel basically take ideas from their religion or the ethics of their upbringing, try to apply it across the general population. . . . I think that a logical and rational basis for decision-making is largely very lost nowadays where things are so partisan and it, if you do what the Republicans are supposed to do, and if you do what the Democrats are supposed to do in nature and nobody compromises with anybody, it's not based [on] what's the best way to go about solving this problem. Or what makes some sort of metrics to do something, which is the way I'm comfortable with problem solving because I'm an engineer.

I think it's sort of a sad and scary position that we're in with basically just a bunch of extremely partisan talking heads who don't seem very interested in advancing the country more than they do their own political career.

Dave, at Harvard's Kennedy School, spoke of feeling closest to the Green Party, noting that the two major parties often had strong geographical ties or bases of support. He made the excellent point that young people are increasingly free from geographical constraints, often moving about among large cities. ". . . [M]any of us are deterritorialized elites. We don't have territorial communities in which we can follow politics," he explained. For Millennials, who often like to think of themselves as "citizens of the world" rather than geographically bound, the traditional geographic nature of partisan politics may itself be a stumbling block. Low political ambition for these "deterritorialized elites" could be a rational response to not feeling "rooted" in a geographical community in and from which politicians are elected.

## Relatively Low Pay and High Job Uncertainty

Most political jobs do not pay big bucks. Local offices like school board, city council, county commissioner, and the like, which can be the stepping stones to higher office, are often unpaid or paid at extremely low rates. Even the salaries of the highest offices are not comparable to the pay these graduates could expect in the private sector—the salary as of

2014 for U.S. senators and U.S. House members is $174,000[47]—but most hold lower office for several years (or decades) before even being able to run for these higher-level positions. State legislators earn, on average, $35,000 annually, not counting expense reimbursements and with wide variation across states.[48] In many states, serving as a state legislator is a part-time job supplemented by one or more other paid positions. By contrast, the average starting salary for students with a law degree from Harvard the year I started this project (2012) was $143,000; by midcareer, such individuals were earning $234,000 on average.[49] Overall, it is safe to assume that a career in politics can mean the opportunity cost of a higher private-sector salary for those in my sample.

Even putting aside the salary differential, there is a related factor at work here: working in electoral politics is more of a risk than working one's way up through a law firm or even having a salaried position as an elected politician's aide. As one of my interviewees (a white female student at Harvard Law) explained, she would be worried about voter irrationality and inconsistency—not unreasonable concerns if your job depends on them. With a law career, there is an established career ladder and a clear set of steps to reach the top; with politics, nothing is ever certain.

The survey sample appeared to agree. "Earning a great deal of money" was considered a "very important" life goal by only 9 percent of respondents in my survey data[50]—but 31.8 percent said it was "very important" in their lives that they could be "sure of always having a relatively well-paid job."[51] Another half of the sample (52.3 percent) indicated that this would be "important," leaving only 11.4 percent who said that "being sure of always having a relatively well-paid job" was not important in their lives. And lest those who wanted to be certain of a relatively well-paid job appear selfish, consider that nearly half of the sample, 46.0 percent, said they would be expected to contribute financially to their family of origin (parents, siblings, etc.) in the future.[52]

## Personality Clashes

Finally, several interviewees brought up an important set of potential costs that found support in the survey data as well, relating to personality. Personalities vary widely, and certain types of people might be better suited than others to be political candidates. In particular, extroverts would likely find it easier (less costly) to run than introverts. Those who can speak off-the-cuff to a large crowd may not see as many costs to running and a political career as those who loathe and want to prepare in depth for each public speech. Those who like a good fight may see the constant conflict of political dealings as a fun challenge, while those who try to avoid conflict might see that kind of life as their own personal hell.

Even among a group of elite, intelligent, ambitious young people, personality still matters. And for some, the way we set up campaigning, campaign financing, media scrutiny of candidates and politicians, and other aspects of running clashes deeply with their personalities. One interview quote (from Liz, a white female MPP student at Harvard's Kennedy School of Government) nicely encapsulates the point: "I'm a natural introvert. I'm also naturally sarcastic and overly honest. The moment of the tenth day of, say Fourth of July celebrations, or the moment that I said something that was entirely true while strongly wrong, would be the day I'd be entirely willing to throw everything else out. To leave the system. It's one of those things where the smaller flaws will just wear on you. And I just . . . I wouldn't have the patience. Those are the moments that would just break me." "Entirely true while strongly wrong," in her words, meant, as far as I gathered, something that would be true but not popular, such as something politically incorrect or that people would not want to hear. She seemed to fear most having to keep up a front, to pretend to be someone she was not.

Another personality aspect that could make for a large difference in political ambition is what researchers refer to as having a "thick skin,"[53] as in not minding what others think of you and/or being able to brush off criticism. Following the lead of these other researchers, I asked in my survey if respondents felt they had a thick skin and whether they would need one to run for office. A large majority of my survey sample, 89.8 percent, agreed that "It takes a thick skin to survive in politics."[54] However, in rating the thickness of their own skin, more than a third (37.5 percent) said the term *thick-skinned* did not describe their personality at all or described them only "a little."[55] When asked if having "thicker skin" would make them more likely to consider running for office, 26.7 percent said "yes" outright, with another 36.5 percent saying "possibly."[56]

Other personality facets relate to this idea but are worth discussing in their own right, too, such as comfort with confrontation. We can imagine someone's being personally thin-skinned, as in sensitive to personal criticism, but still willing to engage in political dialogue and put forward opposing opinions or challenging another's argument. In the survey data, it is readily apparent that there is a range of willingness to engage in confrontation. One question asked, "How likely are you, if at all, to challenge a professor in class if s/he were to present an argument that you strongly disagreed with?"[57] The answer choices ranged from "Not at all likely" to "Very likely." Some people strongly disliked the idea, while others felt no compunction about jumping into the fray, even with someone in a position of authority. Overall 66.4 percent of the sample said they would be likely to challenge the professor, but only 20.6 percent called themselves "very likely" to do so.

Culture, particularly of one's family and where one grew up, likely plays a large role in one's willingness to challenge. Geographic and ethnic heritages differ widely in the social value they place on confrontation; those who grow up in the Midwest or Deep South are often far less likely to engage in direct confrontation than those who grow up in New York City. Ethnic subgroups have different practices, too; Amartya Sen once wrote an engaging book, *The Argumentative Indian*, on the role of argument, especially verbal confrontation, in Asian Indian culture and identity. Being derived from argumentative New York City Jews myself, I found that this made sense to me; I learned early that to ever get a word in at family dinners, I needed to interrupt and speak loudly, which I still do. After this training at home, challenging professors in class was second nature.[58] A third of the survey sample, though, said they would be unlikely to challenge the professor. For many, the idea of confrontation, which is hard to avoid in politics, could be a real turnoff.

## Building a Model of Deterrence

The costs as enumerated thus far include having to ask for money (and the accompanying "ick" factor), privacy intrusion, gridlock and partisan polarization, job uncertainty and relatively low pay, and the rough-and-tumble, often-confrontational nature of politics. For many, this combination of costs could be particularly unappetizing, but none by itself tells a full story. To get a better overall picture of how individuals respond to potential deterrence factors, we need to find a way to aggregate costs, which we will tackle a bit later in chapter 5. For now, the qualitative and quantitative evidence together, as shown in this chapter, paint a picture of some fairly high potential costs. But whether or not they are perceived as costly, and how much they matter, may vary greatly from one person to the next. This is something we can measure, and test against perceptions of rewards, as chapter 5 will also do. Deterrence, then, would be the result of seeing high costs but not seeing enough rewards to make running seem worthwhile.

## Do Costs Matter to Political Ambition?

Before beginning to stack up perceptions of costs, and before comparing these with perceptions of rewards, we should know if costs seem at all related to the idea of wanting to run for or hold political office (political ambition). If these things are not related, the idea of candidate deterrence holds no water. The quantitative data from the survey offer an ideal way to test this question, and the answer is an unequivocal yes. Table 3.5 gives correlation coefficients, measuring the direction and degree of correlation (how much the variables "move together") for each of these with a scale variable measuring whether (and how seriously) each respondent has thought of running for office.[59] Most of the individual measures of potential costs, discussed earlier, correlate—many strongly—with their having thought about running for office.

Individually, these correlations suggest that certain factors (privacy, public funding for campaigns, asking for money, job uncertainty, fear of corruption, and feeling like one's skin is not thick enough) relate in some way to considering a run for public office, although correlations by themselves do not tell us what form this relation may take, or how it might be affected by other factors. For now, the correlations provide at least a basis for continuing the investigation into candidate deterrence as relating to costs and benefits.

Another way to test the relationship between costs-perceptions and political ambition is with regression modeling. This form of analysis

TABLE 3.5. Correlation Coefficients with Having Thought of Running (Seriously, Somewhat, or Not at All)

| Survey Question | Corr. Coef. (Pearson's R) | N |
| --- | --- | --- |
| Would be more likely to consider running if campaigns publicly financed | 0.222*** | 753 |
| Would not mind calling people to ask for money | 0.085** | 753 |
| Thinks politicians do what is right instead of merely what is popular | −0.023 | 753 |
| Thinks politics corrupts | −0.103*** | 753 |
| Would be more likely to run if privacy ensured | 0.264*** | 753 |
| Thinks you would have to be crazy to run in today's media environment | −0.223*** | 753 |
| Would be more likely to consider running if fewer skeletons in closet | 0.115*** | 716 |
| Would be more likely to consider running if less gridlock (note: asked only in final wave, so sample size is small) | 0.175 | 47 |
| Thinks politicians work across party lines | −0.07* | 753 |
| Thinks politicians talk a lot but do not get much done | −0.091** | 716 |
| Not a strong partisan of either party | −0.063* | 753 |
| Would want to always have a relatively well-paying job | −0.129*** | 553 |
| Would be more likely to consider running if had thicker skin | 0.113*** | 716 |

Source: LPS-PAS, Survey Sample
* $p<.1$, ** $p<.05$, *** $p<.01$

is an improvement over correlation testing, as regression allows us to separate and control for other factors that may be driving the observed correlations in table 3.5. Women may be more sensitive to privacy concerns, for example,[60] so we could control for respondent gender or other demographics and see if those mattered to the overall role of costs in predicting political ambition. And we know from research that certain experiential factors (such as having been asked to run for office in the past) can strongly predict one's wanting to run, so we want to control for those.[61] The size of the regression coefficients also gives us information about how much of the variation in one variable can be explained by variation in another.

Table 3.6 gives coefficients for a series of regression models. It is useful to do more than one model to see what changes when we do things differently, and to make sure that the tentative conclusions we might draw are not based on only one formulation of a model. The dependent variable (that which is being explained) in all models is some measurement of

TABLE 3.6. Regression Models of Political Ambition, with and without Costs

| | Model 1 (Logistic) | Model 2 (Logistic) | Model 3 (Ordered Logistic) |
|---|---|---|---|
| | Dependent Variable: Had thought seriously of running for office (binary) | Had thought seriously of running for office (binary) | Three levels: had not thought of running, had thought but not seriously, had thought seriously |
| **Independent Variables/Controls** | | | |
| Female | −.773*** | −.798*** | −.741*** |
| Nonwhite | .195 | .199 | −.151 |
| In law school (versus public policy program) | .045 | −.017 | −.129 |
| At either Harvard School (versus Suffolk) | .155 | .154 | .262 |
| Family income at about age 16 | −.039 | −.081 | −.089* |
| Mom's level of ed. | .285* | .344** | .119 |
| Dad's level of ed. | −.080 | −.128 | −.022 |
| Has been asked to run | 2.515*** | 2.414*** | 2.126*** |
| Would prefer public financing of campaigns | — | .005 | .602*** |
| Would not like asking for money for campaign | — | −.157 | −.084 |
| Thinks politics corrupts | — | −.704*** | −394** |
| Thinks you would be "crazy" to seek office | — | −.200 | −.466*** |
| Is concerned about family's privacy if run | — | .201 | .267 |
| Would be more likely to run if had "thicker skin" | — | .216 | .328* |
| Constant | −3.891*** | −3.420*** | 3.347*** |
| N | 728 | 685 | 685 |
| R-Sq | 0.186 | 0.201 | .191 |

Source: LPS-PAS, Survey Sample
* p<.1, ** p<.05, *** p<.01

political ambition, but we can try different forms of the dependent variable. So in the first column in the table, the dependent variable is a binary variable testing for whether that respondent had thought of running for office seriously (1) or whether he or she had not done so (0). The second column shows the same form of model, with the same dependent variable, but adding in a series of "costs" variables as independent (explanatory) variables. The third column uses the same explanatory variables as the second but uses a different form of the dependent variable (now a 3-point scale testing for not only whether the respondent had thought of running for office or not, but then if he or she had thought about it seriously versus just in passing).

Overall, the three columns in table 3.6 point to some tentative conclusions. First, being male and having been asked to run for office are two of the strongest predictors of having thought (seriously or not) of running for office, so we will explore these factors in more depth in chapter 6. The other demographics, such as family income, parents' education, type of school or program, and being nonwhite versus white do not by themselves explain very much at all about the political ambition of someone in this sample. Although class (one's and one's family's education and income levels) may explain a great deal about political participation in the general population, here in this elite sample and for this specific form of participation—considering running for office— class does not help us predict how someone will behave. Neither does race, so it is not true that, separate from class, being white or nonwhite is by itself activating or depressing the sample respondents' consideration of running from office.

The costs factors, however, seem to show some promise of helping us explain political ambition; several are both statistically and substantively significant. Preferring public financing is very significant in one model but not in the other, as is thinking one would be "crazy" to seek election in today's media environment, while fearing that politics corrupts is significant in both. The issue of perhaps needing "thicker skin" is slightly significant, but only in one model. Together, though, the data suggest that costs perceptions are indeed worth pursuing as an explanation, in more depth. Chapter 5 takes up the question of how better to quantify these perceptions and combine and compare them with perceptions of rewards from politics.

## Other Factors Implicated in Political Ambition

As shown in table 3.3, interviewees for this project raised a host of concerns about running. Many of these are not included in the "costs" scale and calculations as there were not matching survey items. It is worth taking a moment to consider these "other" costs, which I had not anticipated in designing the survey. Some of these were felt narrowly (as in, by few people) but strongly enough to deter those people from thinking they would ever seek office. Two good examples are religion/denomination and geography. One's religion/denomination and religiosity, it turned out, could be either a motivator or a de-motivator for pursuing a life in politics. One Mormon interviewee mentioned that her church strongly pushed members toward public service and government. Several Jewish interviewees said the same, referencing the Jewish mandate to "heal the world" (in classic rabbinical texts, *tikkun olam*).

However, different religious beliefs could lead to the opposite effect. One interviewee who was a Jehovah's Witness explained that his church taught that "all earthly government is false, and the only true government is the Kingdom of Heaven." Such a belief could logically turn someone away from the idea of running for office. There also may be a slight deterrence effect for those who are not religious, either because American politics is steeped in religious language or (and) atheist interviewees expected voters to be on the whole religious and thought their atheism could be a source of bias against their candidacy. In general, in the survey data those who were most politically ambitious were more religious than the non–politically ambitious, although there is no way of testing the direction of causality. I therefore do not include this factor in future analyses, even though I find it theoretically fascinating and well worthy of future study.

Geography is another complicated factor in an attempt to understand political ambition. While the Suffolk students in the sample were mostly from Massachusetts, or at least New England, those from Harvard's Kennedy School and Harvard Law School were from all over the country (and in some cases, the world, although all were American citizens). Many had traveled extensively, and most had moved from somewhere else to attend graduate school in the Boston area and did not plan to remain in that geographical area. Recall how Dave described himself and his fellow students as "deterritorialized elites."

This probably would mostly have the effect of deterring political ambition, as one usually needs roots in some sort of geographical community to run. Some interviewees had a clear sense of where they wanted to live, but most did not and seemed ready to go where a job took them in the future, and perhaps to move many times if the job required it or they changed jobs. Many said emphatically that they would not want to live where they grew up, so they wouldn't know where they would run. Such rootlessness conflicted with their sense of what it would mean to run for office. On the flip side, those who had a very clear idea of where they wanted to live (Jasmine, who owned a house in Atlanta to which she knew she would return after law school, for example, or Anne, who lived and planned to stay in the Boston area) were much more interested in the idea of running for local office (and Anne already had done so). So although I do not have a good way to measure it and therefore exclude it from future quantitative analysis, this is a key factor in the political ambition of young people that future research should consider.

Another potentially de-motivating aspect of geography in respondents' minds related to partisan residential clustering.[62] Several interviewees mentioned that they didn't think they could get elected in the places they wanted to live, comparing their partisan and/or ideological beliefs with the majority beliefs in those areas. Research tells us that eligibles are far more likely to express political ambition if they think they have a good chance of winning a race.[63] Interviewees who were conservatives, for example, seemed resigned to the idea that they couldn't win office in the big cities in which they planned to live, like Boston, New York, or Washington. And for some this turned into a more general discussion of not feeling as if they fit into one of the major parties (e.g., interviewees who were fiscally conservative but socially liberal), who wondered aloud what kind of geographic constituency might fit their particular set of beliefs.

There is another hugely important factor that we have not yet discussed, as it is difficult to tell whether it is a cause or a consequence (or both) of political engagement. We know from research on political ambition that being *recruited* (in the sense of being told by others that you should run for office) is a major predictor of one's having thought seriously of running.[64] In my survey data, too, there is an extremely strong correlation between one's having been asked to run at some point in the past and one's having seriously considered running.[65] This might make it look as if being asked to run leads to greater political ambition.

However, it is far from clear that the causal arrow goes that way; what if one is asked to run because one already is in political places (campaign headquarters, political party gatherings, city council meetings) and around the people (elected officials, party leaders, other candidates) who are likely to ask? Regression models (using the same control variables) show extremely strong results the other way too. Just as one's having been asked to run predicts strong political ambition (in the sense of one's having seriously considered running or wanting to run for higher versus lower or no office), so too does one's having strong political ambition predict being asked to run.

Also, previous candidacy may predict future candidacy—but where did the previous political ambition come from? School office candidacy (as in having run for student council in high school or college) correlates strongly with both one's being asked or told to run for nonschool public office[66] and with one's having thought seriously about running for nonschool public office in the future.[67] Of those who had volunteered on a political campaign in the past two years before the survey, 73.3 percent had been asked or told to run for office.[68] Only 40.1 percent of those who had not volunteered were similarly asked. Clearly there is a connection; already being interested in politics and campaigns, wanting to run, and being asked or told to run all "move" together as variables—but it is far from clear what comes first. Thus far being asked to run has not been included in cost-benefit analyses because of its uncertain causality—is it a reward? Being asked could perhaps make you think there is or will be support for your candidacy, and it's nice to feel that people believe in you. But it also might act to lower costs in your mind; if I'm being recruited, maybe it won't be a total uphill climb. Or perhaps having been asked should simply be considered a kind of flashing red light signaling to us those respondents who already have a strong interest in electoral politics and political campaigns.

## Summary

Thus far the data suggest several facts about candidate deterrence for young eligibles in the United States: running as a candidate in the United

States, particularly for higher office but even for local office, can be difficult, risky, energy-consuming, and costly in terms of time, money, and other resources. The constant media surveillance accompanying politics, while perhaps important in holding elected officials accountable once they are in office, may also deter good potential candidates from tossing a hat into the ring. Other costs like personality features that clash with the way we "do" politics in this country correlate, at least for some people, with political ambition.

The respondents' political ambition thus seemed fairly malleable and tied to what they perceived as better conditions for a run. This gives us a good basis for thinking that political ambition is not simply innate; if it can wax and wane according to conditions, then it could be activated in a whole lot of people at different times and under different circumstances.[69] The graduate students in this study not only perceived these costs clearly, but many also appeared to find these costs overwhelming. In other words, costs matter, and rationally, to most of those I studied. Only a few (perhaps the "political animals" in the group) were insensitive to costs.

4

## The Rewards of Running

[P]olitics is . . . community leadership by passionate individuals, and there's a good and a bad to all of that. They could be passionate about themselves, they could be passionate about the community, they could be passionate about certain issues that they really want to push forward. . . . I think that in many cases politics is very good because a group of people can get together and push forward an agenda to make a serious change, and people may agree or disagree as to whether that's a good change, but I think the political process is a good thing and the ability to effect change is a very good thing.
—Anne, white female Suffolk Law student

At the same time as they reflected on the various costs of running for or serving in elective office, many of the young people I interviewed also brought up positive features of politics, policy, and/or government. All of them had already made big life decisions orienting them toward law, politics, policy, and/or government as a career—they were enrolled in top law or policy schools, and they had each chosen one of the three institutions most likely to send graduates into national or state-level politics. Of those in their age group, those in my survey and interview samples should be among the most likely to have an interest in politics and possibly in running. (Indeed, a small number of those I spoke with and surveyed were already running—or had already run—for elective office.[1]) Their impressions of the costs of running for and holding political office, while thorough, sometimes cynical, and often strongly worded, were not one-sided. Many also saw great potential in politics, government, and governance and cared deeply about politics and policy.

This chapter therefore articulates and explores the possible rewards that could help balance out the negative costs described in the previous chapter. In interviews, subjects spoke about many potential rewards of

TABLE 4.1. Rewards Mentioned in Interviews (in Order from Most- to Least-Mentioned)

| Perceived Reward | % of Interviewees Mentioning |
|---|---|
| Policy goals | 49 |
| Solving big problems, making positive change | 47 |
| Likes idea of community leadership (esp. local) | 33 |
| Helping individuals solve their problems | 31 |
| R likes problem-solving/strategy | 29 |
| Having power/influence | 26 |
| R enjoys networking/people | 24 |
| R likes system of democracy, representative government, would enjoy being part of structure of collective decision making | 22 |
| R enjoys challenge | 16 |
| Sees running as exciting | 11 |
| R enjoys public speaking | 11 |
| R thinks would lose weight door-knocking | 2 |

Source: LPS-PAS, Interview Sample

holding office, including helping people, changing policies they cared about, feeling powerful, and other perceived benefits. Table 4.1 presents interviewees' perceived rewards of running for or holding political office and gives the proportion of interviews where students brought up that particular form of reward, in order from most- to least-mentioned. The most-mentioned rewards were policy goals, solving big problems, community leadership, helping individuals solve specific problems, the challenge of problem solving, enjoying people and networking, and generally appreciating democracy and collective decision making.

As we might expect in a sample of law and policy school students, this group had a marked interest in public policy; half of the interviewees mentioned policy goals as a possible reward of a political career path. Nearly half talked about solving big problems and making positive change as a potential reward. A third liked the idea of community leadership, particularly at the local level, and nearly a third cared about the idea of helping people with specific problems. Nearly a third mentioned that they enjoyed, or would enjoy, the challenge of problem solving and strategic decision making involved in a political campaign.

Writing in a foreword to a 2004 book about young people running for office (*Born to Run*, by Keith Gaddie), David Boren, then president of the University of Oklahoma, praised the desire he saw on the part of students to "get involved and give something back to their communities." Far from seeing Millennials as the stereotype of a selfish, self-involved, selfie-taking group of kids, Boren wrote, "This generation is a very caring generation. These young people contribute a great deal of their time volunteering for community service. They organize and participate in blood drives, renovate homeless shelters, serve food to those in need, pick up trash along the roads, tutor younger students, and help in many ways. They are continuing and enhancing the great American tradition of volunteer service which has been one of our greatest national strengths. . . . These students are eager to make the world around them a better place."[2]

I too found this spirit in my interviews and in the survey data I collected. By the end of more than fifty hour-long interviews, I was impressed with the dedication of these students and with their deep desire to do something meaningful with their lives. Some made the connection between that need and politics, seeing public administration, public law, public policy, and/or government as the way to make the kind of change they wanted to see in the world. For these people, the perceived rewards of politics measured high. Others, however, saw little connection with making the changes they cared about. For them, either the rewards of politics were low or the costs they saw overpowered the rewards. Quite rationally, these people had little interest in running for or holding office.

As with chapter 3, on the costs of running, this chapter delves into various potential rewards as gleaned from the data provided by the Millennials in my study. As the previous chapter did for the set of variables relating to the costs of running, this chapter explores and quantifies, as much as possible, variables relating to the benefits side of the equation. The words and numbers both say that rewards matter too. As political scientists Jennifer Lawless and Richard Fox wrote in *Running from Office* in 2015, "How can we get more young people to aspire to run for office? The simple solution is for government to function more effectively, politicians to act more responsibly, and the news media to cover politics more substantively. If young people saw politics as a vibrant, effective way to engage with and improve their communities and society, then more of them would not be turned off by the thought of entering the fray."[3] Indeed. In my sample, for certain individuals the rewards mattered quite a lot, and collectively rewards as a whole related strongly to political ambition overall. The initial suggestion from the data, in fact, is that rewards may matter more than costs, an intriguing finding that should be tested more directly in future research.

## Power and Leadership

As we might expect in a highly ambitious group—and more than 90 percent of all those in the survey sample identified themselves as ambitious or very ambitious—some of the rewards people brought up had to do with fame, prestige, and the excitement of leadership and power. One interviewee, Kelly, a white female student at Suffolk Law, mulled over what political position she might want to hold, explaining that she would like to be close enough to "see the problems, but [also] be in a position of power enough to actually get something done." She concluded that she liked the idea of serving in state-level government rather than local or national, saying that she would be "high enough that I could actually change something . . . but low enough that I could still see the people I'm trying to help."

For Kelly, seeking power was for that more altruistic reason of being able to help others, but a number of interviewees also speculated that people who run "want power," in the words of a different white female Suffolk Law student whose tone suggested this was negative, or at least not definitely positive. A third white female Suffolk student, in a separate interview, speculated that some would-be politicians are "earnest, honest, want to change the world" types of people, while others "get into it for the money or for the power or for the ego."

The quantitative data suggest that many of those in this study like being in charge or at least think themselves good at it. The vast majority (nearly 90 percent) of those surveyed said that "good at being in charge" described them well or very well.[4] (About half said "well" with another nearly 40 percent saying "very well.") Far fewer people, but a not insignificant number (12.5 percent, or one in eight), said in response to a different question that being famous was "important" or "very important" to them.

But as others noted, power may just mean the capacity to get something done on a large scale. Jim, a white male Suffolk student, mused:

> I think one of the allures of politics is that regardless of how wealthy you become in your life, whether or not—wealth is determined person to person, whether you achieve your goals in that way, there's a sense of . . . power sounds like a bad word. It's somewhat of a dirty word, I guess. There's that feeling of influence that politicians have that you can't buy. You can be a billionaire and not have necessarily the political influence of being [a] Senator. Being involved with something . . . makes you think you are part of something greater. So it's something it would be interesting at least to be involved with.

Matt, another white male student at Suffolk, echoed this idea of leadership as power, saying he would like to start in local politics and "see what I can do for my community" and through that "learn the ropes and learn the reality of politics. And kind of learn that and move forward." He continued:

> I think regardless of whether you're the president or whatever the lowest form of political offices, when you see a direct result of your efforts and you see things that are good happening in society or benefits that occur in society I think that's a great feeling. . . . Learning from that, do all things from that so that hopefully when you do get to other positions and you have more power, and you have more responsibility, you can effectively hold that position and then you'd do a good job.

The survey data on political, civic, and volunteer activity suggest that this was a fairly participatory group. The mean number of political/civic activities in which these students had engaged in the previous two years (voting, writing letters to the editor or to a member of Congress, volunteering) was 3.12 acts. The most common political act was voting, which 80.9 percent of respondents indicated they had done in the previous two years. But significant chunks of the sample had also written letters to the editor (15.8 percent), volunteered in their communities (46.1 percent) or on a political campaign (22.8 percent), contributed money to a political candidate (33.3 percent), contacted an elected official (38.0 percent), served on a nonprofit organization's board (11.5 percent), or attended a city council or school board meeting (13.0 percent). Overall, 79.1 percent of the sample reported engaging in some form of political or civic behavior beyond voting in the previous two-year period. In the general population, far fewer people vote or go beyond, making this group unusually politically engaged.

In looking to their beliefs about politicians, however, we find a rather sharp divide. Some (but a minority of the sample as a whole) held positive beliefs. For instance, 23.7 percent believed that politicians often worked for the public good, while 17.6 percent believed that politicians often helped people with problems. Both of these could be counted as important rewards if one were in office, and some people saw these as factual statements. Many, though, did not. These data point toward a split between the few who saw politics as rewarding and the many who did not.

Cory, a black male student at Harvard Law, was one of those who believed in the rewards. He spoke of how he had always had "a real passion for politics" while growing up. He explained:

> [When I was] growing up, people around me in my neighborhoods, they used to always blame Ronald Reagan or George W. Bush for why things were so terrible in their communities. So at that time I was under the impression that presidents had so much power, and made the concrete decisions. When I got older, though, I realized it doesn't really work that way. I still think that politics . . . could have profound effects on marginalized groups in society. So it's something that I continue to follow.

Power in this sense could be a good thing, the capacity to do good. Yet perhaps not surprisingly, given that so many saw power (or the wanting of it) as having potentially negative implications, almost no one I interviewed came out and told me directly that they wanted power because they liked to be in charge. No one, that is, except Esther, whom we met in the previous chapter—an outspoken and very politically active white/Jewish MPP student at Harvard's Kennedy School of Government. Esther had had a great deal of campaign and activist experience, and, when I asked what she might like about holding office, she came out and said what no one else dared to:

Well, and this is one of those dirty, inside secrets—I like having power. I like being able to have some influence on what I think would be better for others. I think . . . having the ability to at least—even if I'm the lone progressive vote in the Kansas House, at least I could be loud and vocal and make some waves and maybe it drives some additional attention to Kansas, and maybe it provokes some other people to get involved whose voices might not otherwise be heard.

Others, while not as blunt as Esther, spoke freely about their desire to be leaders—and most had some form of leadership experience, from clubs or such in high school or college years. Their public-minded goals and desire to make a difference in the world fit in well with an idea of leadership, especially at the local levels, where they thought it was less likely that they would lose touch with those they would represent. Seeking prestige, fame, or power for its own sake was generally seen as negative (and you'll notice that even Esther's quote about wanting power was not just for her own sake, but for doing something, like changing policy or empowering marginalized people)—but the idea of having power/ influence to do something good was a popular point.

## Seeing Politics as a Good Way to Effect Change

Indeed, one of the most powerful potential rewards of politics, as described by my interviewees and seconded by the survey responses, was the opportunity to do something meaningful. Like the character Tracy in *The Phila-delphia Story*, those I talked to hungered "to be of real use to the world!"

One terrific example of this mindset comes from sitting Congressman Juan Vargas (D-CA), who, in a 2014 interview with LatinasRepresent,[5] said that he saw politics as "a life worth living." He explained:

I'm frankly a very religious person, and I do believe in social justice and I do believe that you fight for other people and that at the end of the day, you know, your life matters, and it matters that you did something good. If you accumulate all these things that don't matter, at the end of your life, you're going to have a life that was worthless. So for me, the fight's always worth it. Fighting for undocumented people, fighting for people [who] are poor, fighting for people [who] are struggling to get by . . . it's worth it.[6]

The idea of "making a difference" has several testable components, as table 4.1 suggests. People might have specific policy goals, some issue(s) about which they feel strongly and would like to see resolved in a particular way (this was true for fully half of the interviewees). We could therefore imagine that having strong opinions on policy issues might make the idea of working in politics more rewarding to an individual.

But also interviewees spoke of the idea of solving big problems in a way that was not necessarily related to specific issues. The idea here might be that they liked the idea of working together with other people on issues important to a political community, be it local, county, state-level, or national, and coming up with collective solutions, more in the way in which Congressman Vargas spoke about his work in politics. Because interviewees used a wide variety of different words, phrases, and sometimes hand gestures to explain their thoughts and feelings, it is sometimes difficult to parse their meaning into discrete categories. But generally nearly half of those interviewed spoke in broad terms about wanting to solve big problems or make positive change, with a fair proportion (about a quarter) making specific reference to the idea of collective decision making, democracy, and/or representative government in connection with the idea of working together with others to solve problems or make things better.

There is a third component to "making a difference," a more person-centered idea of helping a particular individual or group with their problems. About a third of the interview sample noted that this was important to them. Helping make life better for someone else does not have to be tied to a particular issue or policy stance but may just impart positive feelings (altruism, joy, pride, meaningfulness) to the helper, and many of those I studied thought this achievable through political office.

As in the previous chapter, we can also draw on survey data to examine rewards systematically. Table 4.2 lays out the survey questions relating to possible rewards, and the sample mean scores for each. In the survey data, one of the most critical rewards of running for or holding office seemed to be the belief that politics can solve important problems. A question asking this directly (measuring respondents' agreement or disagreement with the statement "The problems I most care about can be solved through politics") found an interesting discrepancy. While 40

TABLE 4.2. Rewards Data from Survey, with Question Wording and Means (in Order from Highest to Lowest Mean)

| Perceived Reward | % Agreeing or True of (Mean)* | N |
|---|---|---|
| Considers self "Good at being in charge" | 87.5 | 713 |
| Would feel positively about "Being a part of history" as a candidate | 84.6 | 47 |
| Considers "Feeling useful, doing something good in the world" an important life goal | 83.7 | 48 |
| Considers self "A good public speaker" | 75.2 | 713 |
| Would be more likely to run if "Cared about an issue and knew [I] could make a difference if [I were] in office" | 59.0 | 760 |
| Would feel positively about "Going door-to-door to meet constituents" | 54.4 | 760 |
| Would be more likely to run if thought, "Could help [my] community" | 52.7 | 760 |
| Would be more likely to run if thought, "It would help [me] get a better job later" | 45.1 | 47 |
| Thinks, "The problems I most care about can be solved through politics" | 39.7 | 760 |
| Considers self "Very competitive" | 38.0 | 48 |
| Would feel positively about "Attending fundraising functions" | 31.0 | 760 |
| Has strong opinions on policy issues | 25.5 | 760 |
| Believes one person can "make a difference in politics" | 23.8 | 760 |
| Thinks politicians often "work for the public good" | 23.7 | 760 |
| Would be "very likely" to interrupt professor in a class | 20.6 | 760 |
| Thinks politicians often "help people with their problems" | 17.6 | 760 |
| Considers becoming "famous" an important life goal | 12.5 | 761 |

Source: LPS-PAS, Survey Sample
* Note: Because each variable is collapsed to a binary variable (0 or 1), the mean (weighted) gives the percentage of the sample scoring "1," or saying that the statement is true for them.

percent of the survey sample said they agreed this was true, only 7 percent said they "strongly agreed." This probably should be read in the context of the contemporary U.S. politics of negativity, partisanship, and gridlock, discussed earlier. Generally a plurality of the sample agreed that politics can solve problems, but few agreed strongly that this was happening at the moment.

More generally, the opportunity to make a specific policy difference—as in raising awareness of or writing legislation about a specific policy issue—is a key possible reward of running for or holding office. Those in the survey sample who had strong policy views (in any direction) were significantly more likely than those who did not to find politics useful in solving the problems they saw as important.[7] Having strong policy opinions, in other words, correlated with the belief that politics could solve problems. It is impossible from these data to know what causes what here (believing that politics matters to solving problems could lead to the holding of strong views, or vice versa), but the correlation tells us at least that they move together.

The individual words used by those I studied show some strong belief in the use of politics to solve problems. In interviews, respondents expressed a great desire to "help people" or "make the world a better place," and some saw politics as the way to do this. Anne, the white female Suffolk Law student who was quoted at the start of this chapter and who had run for her city's school board the year before the interview, said she had ambitions to run again and for higher office someday. She said, "The idea . . . really appeals to me because I think I may be able to [affect] policy and make a difference."

Kim, an Asian American female student at Suffolk Law, used an unusual word. She said, "It's actually a phenomenal thing to do. I think it's something that could really help me make an impact on the country." She was not sure if she ever would run, but the sense I got from talking with her was of a deep admiration for those who would dedicate themselves to helping others in this way. (She was, for the record, the only interviewee to use that interesting word *phenomenal*.)

Similarly, Cory, a black Harvard Law student, said he had thought before about running and felt he would like to do so. "I feel like there are a lot of important issues that I care about that can be solved through the political process. Particularly as I get older, and if these issues remain, that may encourage me to say, you know what? It's time for me to be a voice for the people. The people that I feel have been ignored for too long." In his mind, then, running for office could be a great way to help a particular set of people, those who he feels are currently left out of the political system.

These findings from the young eligibles fit in well with data from the "real world." Those who have already chosen a life in politics cite the opportunity to make a difference and help people as some of the most important rewards they derive from their work. In a study of why sitting state legislators would or would not run for Congress, Fulton and her co-authors found such ambition for higher office to be strongly linked to the state legislators' perceptions of how much of a difference they could make were they to win a congressional seat.[8] Similarly, in a recent survey of female state legislators, Lake Research Partners found that three-quarters (74 percent) were most motivated to run for office by the potential to make what they perceived as positive change.[9]

On the flip side of the "making a difference" reward is the fear that something (gridlock, say) might block this as a reward. The low productivity of Congress did not pass unremarked by the law and public policy graduate students I interviewed. Indeed, what would be the point of all that butt-busting, many wondered, if you couldn't get much done once elected? Like Jared, from chapter 1, Jack (a white male Harvard Law student) thought he just wouldn't be able to "change things" as an elected official: "I think being a U.S. senator or a U.S. representative would be really cool and [a] really great position to sort of be able to get your ideas . . . out to a broader base of people. But if I really wanted to be able to change things [I'd work in one of the] independent agencies like the FBI and EPA or the DOE or DOD. . . . Like they can really do whatever the hell they want to a degree." Bureaucrats might disagree with this assessment of their flexibility, but the point is that Jack, like Jared and many others, perceived elected officials in particular to be constrained in a negative way. Apart from whatever negatives these young folks perceived about the process of campaigning, then, they also saw steep barriers to efficiency and effectiveness facing those who make it to office.

One way to measure this is to ask an agree/disagree statement: A survey question asked respondents how much they agreed or disagreed with the statement "Politicians talk a lot but don't really get much done." A majority (59.4 percent) agreed (choosing "agree" or "agree strongly"), and nearly another quarter of the sample chose "neither agree nor disagree." Only about one-seventh of the sample (14.2 percent) disagreed with the statement outright. If "getting a lot done" was important to respondents, as it was to Jared, the survey suggests that few saw politics as the clear avenue to doing that.

Last, we could measure feelings about gridlock by simply asking directly. This has the potential disadvantage of suggesting an answer in the phrasing of the question but the advantage of getting much closer to what we might really want to know. So it is worth trying, even while taking the answer with a grain of salt. One question from that final wave of the Harvard Law students asked: "Would you be more likely to consider running for public office if there were not so much gridlock once you got into office?" Having seen the results from the first several rounds of the survey, and speculating that gridlock was a cost in the minds of many eligibles, I wanted to test the proposition directly in the last chance to do so with this population, even with a small sample. Again, there were only forty-seven respondents, but the pattern was clear; forty-four said less gridlock would make them more likely to consider running (weighted, this is 92.4 percent). Even if the question wording had an effect, and it probably did to some extent, it is interesting to see the strong response these students had to the idea of less gridlock.

## Different People Interested in Different Levels

So far, I have discussed running for office as just a monolithic idea, but we can begin to break it down by different types and levels of office. Some people may see rewards at more local levels of office, for instance, while others might really care about politics only on a national level. When asked what kind of office they could ever imagine running for, 39.8 percent indicated interest in national office; 52.4 percent said they could imagine someday running for state legislator, governor, or other statewide office (such as attorney general); and 58.7 percent expressed interest in possibly running for local or state-level offices like school board, city council, or mayor. Overall there was a nice distribution of interest in offices across levels, although more than a full quarter of the sample (28.0 percent) said they never wanted to run at all, at any level. The overall picture painted in figure 4.1 is one of at least mild interest in multiple types and levels of office. As we might expect, the office that holds the least interest for this sample was president, but perhaps we would not have guessed that city council was the most appealing across the sample. Local office, several of my interviewees told me, would be better because you could really see the people you were trying to help.

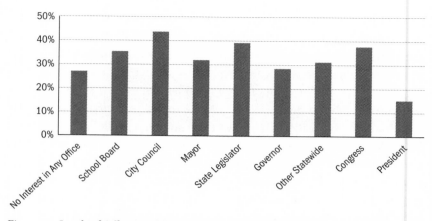

Figure 4.1. Levels of Office: Could You Ever Imagine Yourself Running for the Following? (% Saying Yes) Source: LPS-PAS, Survey Sample. N = At least 716 for all questions, up to 763 for some.

## Enjoying Challenge, Strategy

Finally, a good many interviewees mentioned that political campaigning, and perhaps also serving in elective office, would involve the kind of strategy and problem solving they enjoyed. These were, after all, people who had already chosen career paths in law or policy, by virtue of being in these particular schools, so it makes sense that many of them would enjoy certain features of candidacy, like the challenges of arguing over policy, getting votes, picking the right issues to discuss, and building political alliances and coalitions.

For instance, Kelly, a white female law student at Suffolk, said she enjoyed solving problems. Many others echoed this idea, like Ahmed, an Arab American Suffolk Law student, who said, "I would enjoy sitting down and let's get this discussion on the table. What do we like? What do we dislike? Why is it good? Why's it bad? Who's against and who's with us? You can make a decision and come up with a plan, a strategy and implement it. I like that."

Similarly, Juan, the MPP student quoted earlier in the costs chapter, after a very long pause, told me that he supposed there were parts of being a candidate that he could get excited about: "I guess the aspect that I would enjoy would be crafting the strategy, whether it's the marketing and the message construction or assessing what areas of the state or district or region or municipality or township . . . or country that I could focus on and why. What are the areas [where] I could shore up support, that sort of thing?" He ended by saying he would find these parts of a campaign "enjoyable" and "satisfying," even while he resisted the idea, as quoted earlier, of his family's privacy's being invaded by the media.

Nick, a white male student at Harvard Law, said that he would particularly enjoy debating. After all, he had always enjoyed arguing. He remembers that right after September 11, 2001, when he was in seventh or eighth grade, he argued with a teacher that the attacks had been planned by Osama bin Laden and not Saddam Hussein. "So I've always been interested in politics and world events, things like that," he explained. He linked that willingness to argue to his reasons for being in law school. "I'm a pretty argumentative person," he explained.

The survey, unfortunately, lacks a good measure for this kind of "argumentation" reward. In a series of questions on personality variables, however, I asked a few questions that might bear on the topic. None of them measure exactly the right thing, but together they give us at least some information. In the series on personality, respondents were asked how well a set of terms described them, ranging from "not at all well" to "very well." One such term was "good at being in charge" (mentioned earlier), which 87.5 percent of the sample said described them "moderately well" or "very well." Another term, "willing to take risks," showed more variation; about a third of the sample (32.8 percent) said this term did not fit them that well (choosing "not at all well" or "a little"). The other two-thirds, however, who said this described them "moderately well" or "very well" could conceivably derive rewards from the risk taking.

Some of these quantitative data are more directly related to the question of enjoying the challenge or strategy of a campaign than others, and those that are only somewhat related are hard to read as clear "rewards." In developing an overall index of the benefits of running, I do not include all of these personality features, because of the difficulty of theoretically connecting them to clear rewards. For that purpose, I include only the most relevant and defensible "rewards" bits of information. But the observed means do give us a hint that, as we might expect, personalities vary and could easily lead to some people's deriving more rewards than others from the same set of actions or processes. As in the previous chapter, where some people's more introverted personalities led them to see more costs to candidacy, those with extroverted personalities might get great satisfaction from being in charge and taking risks. (As a real-life example, Bill Clinton springs to mind.)

## How Much (If at All) Do Rewards Matter to Political Ambition?

As earlier, with the costs, it is reasonable to ask whether perceptions of these rewards of politics/candidacy correlate in a meaningful way with wanting to run for office or not. Indeed, they do. As we would expect if the rational candidate deterrence theory holds water, those who saw higher rewards were far more likely than those who did not to have thought about running.

Table 4.3 gives correlation coefficients and $p$-value levels for several key rewards variables. (Note that the sample sizes vary, because not all of these questions were asked of all respondents.)

Overall the table shows some strong and statistically significant correlations. Some of these variables seem very related to having thought of running for office, especially believing that politics solves important problems, wanting to be famous, thinking politics could help one's community, liking the idea of going door-to-door to talk to potential constituents, liking the idea of making public speeches, enjoying the prospect of being a part of history, and describing oneself as "competitive." Some of the other possible rewards discussed earlier, like having strong policy opinions, do not show a strong correlation with respondents' having thought of running for office, even when there is plenty of data to test. And others do not show a significant correlation, but that may be because of a low sample size on those particular questions (several were asked only in the final version of the survey, which yielded forty-eight respondents, one of whom skipped several of the questions, so this does not give us a large sample for certain questions). On the whole, though, it appears that these perceived rewards do indeed show strong correlations with political ambition. Whether—and if so how—these perceptions of rewards relate to perceptions of costs both within and across individuals is the subject of the next chapter.

TABLE 4.3. Correlation Coefficients between Key Rewards Variables and Political Ambition, as Having Thought of Running

| Survey Question | Corr. Coef. (Pearson's R) | N |
|---|---|---|
| The problems I most care about can be solved through politics | .260*** | 753 |
| Holds strong policy opinions in either direction on both of two policy issues (the legality of abortion in the first trimester and government's role in reducing income differences between rich and poor) | .049 | 753 |
| Politicians often work for the public good | .111*** | 753 |
| Politicians often help people with their problems | .164*** | 753 |
| The term "good at being in charge" describes me moderately or very well | .191*** | 716 |
| Becoming famous is an important or very important goal in my life | .301*** | 753 |
| I would be more interested in running if I cared about an issue and knew I could make a difference if I were in office | .234*** | 753 |
| I would be more interested in running if I knew I could help my community | .307*** | 753 |
| I would feel positive or very positive about going door-to-door to meet constituents as a candidate | .267*** | 753 |
| I would feel positive or very positive about making public speeches as a candidate | .356*** | 753 |
| I would feel positive or very positive about improving the lives of my fellow citizens as a candidate | .139 | 47 |
| Feeling useful/doing something good in the world is an important or very important goal in my life | .221 | 48 |
| I would feel positive or very positive about being a part of history as a candidate | .322** | 47 |
| I would be more interested in running if it would help me get a better job later | .032 | 47 |
| The term "competitive" describes me moderately or very well | .348** | 48 |

Source: LPS-PAS, Survey Sample
* p<.1, ** p<.05, *** p<.01

## Summary

I think I would most like seeing the changes happening, even if it's really slowly; just seeing that would be really fulfilling.
—Mariana, Hispanic/white Suffolk Law School Student

It is perhaps a basic human desire to feel that, as Congressman Vargas put it, "[Y]our life matters, and it matters that you did something good." While the costs of running for and being in office may be high, for some people the rewards could be a powerful motivation to run anyway. Although some survey and interview respondents simply wanted to be famous or to have power for its own sake, the far larger proportion related the rewards of politics to the idea of helping people or making the world a better place. Perhaps the many failings of the political system could be overlooked, or minimized in the mind of a potential candidate, if she truly felt that politics was useful to solve the kinds of problems she cared about. The interviewees or survey respondents who saw politics as useful were in fact the least likely to say they would be deterred by having to raise money or an intrusive media or other features of the campaign environment. High perceptions of rewards, in other words, could balance out even high perceptions of costs. But as the following chapter will show, not many in this study saw enough rewards to make the idea of running seem worth their while.

# 5

## Weighing the Costs and Rewards of Political Careers

As much as you might want to help everybody, you can't
please everybody. And not everything you're going to do is
going to help everybody, because I think it's a hard balance,
and it seems a lot of times like you're trying to pick the least
bad situation. I think that's kind of a little bit of a . . . I can't
think of another word besides *depressing*.
—Katie, white female Suffolk Law student

The combination of seeing relatively high costs and ambivalence about
possible rewards is not a good recipe for political ambition. Instead, I
argue, the rational result of that combination is candidate deterrence.
In my study, even those well positioned for future candidacy, coming
from the institutions most likely to produce political candidates, were
for the most part rationally deterred from throwing hats into rings anytime soon. Low or even moderate rewards are simply not enough to
balance out the generally high costs these eligibles saw in the prospect
of running.

And they are not alone. One old friend who has long served as a city
councilor in his small town in Maryland perhaps expressed best the sentiment of rewards' not exceeding costs. When he said he was stepping
down, I asked why, and he shook his head. "There's just nothing enjoyable about it anymore," he said sadly.

His comments echoed the frustration expressed by long-serving and
recently retired U.S. Senator Olympia Snowe, who began her farewell
speech by pointing out that she and her husband (a former U.S. Representative and Maine governor) had a combined history of fifty-six years
in office. She said, "We've had a passion for public service . . . and we've
never regretted a single moment." She said, "Throughout my tenure, I've
borne witness to government's incredible potential as an instrument
for the common good. I have also experienced its capacity for serial

dysfunction." However, she implied that the latter was winning out, citing as a main reason for her exit the "excessive political polarization" that was endangering Congress's ability to "tackl[e] our problems at a time of monumental consequence for our nation."[1]

If those who have been there feel this way, should we be surprised that so many bright young people are saying thanks but no thanks? Not all young people are deterred; some great Millennial candidates are certainly out there running. One organization, Run for America Action, has been working to recruit and support twelve Millennial congressional candidates for the 2016 elections.[2] For these highly politicized "political animals"—the ones Gaddie called "born to run"[3]—the perceived rewards seem to outweigh the costs.

But for the rest of us, and for the majority of those I studied for this project, the perceived rewards were rarely enough to balance out some pretty high-seeming costs. The idea of candidacy for many starts to feel a lot like a public good subject to the classic collective action problem; we would like to have good people in office, we would like a steady and high-quality stream of qualified, competitive, and interesting candidates, but we just do not want to do it ourselves. And, perhaps more dangerous than the widespread nature of candidate deterrence is its uneven effects—it does not affect everyone equally. Those least likely to be deterred look a whole lot like our current crop of elected officials; they are disproportionately partisan, higher-income, white, male, and already very politically engaged. Why does this cycle seem to be repeating itself? Answering this question requires a close look at how costs and rewards compare, both on a per-person basis and across different groups of people.

## Stacking up Costs versus Rewards

Most of the individual potential costs and benefits enumerated in interviews and the survey data, as reported in previous chapters, show a direct relationship with political ambition. But it is probably the rare person who cares about a single cost enough to say that only because of that she or he would never run for office. It is far more likely that costs kind of "stack up"—and that they are then measured against stacked-up rewards. The next step then is to simulate that kind of mental (conscious or unconscious) thought process, using the survey data.

The ideal process in describing scientifically how costs and rewards measure up against each other would be to be able to quantify and aggregate each, and then compare them. This process runs the risk of making assumptions about how much each element matters and counting it in a nonrealistic way for that individual. Someone may care deeply about the idea that he or she would be under constant media scrutiny, for example, and only mildly dislike the idea of having to ask for money. To account for the possibility of varying sensitivities to costs, then, we need data not just on the direction of a person's feelings about each potential cost (positive or negative), but also its magnitude (strong or weak). The same is true for each potential reward; for each, we should know if that is something which motivates this person positively or not, and if so, how much. Fortunately, the survey responses are thorough enough to provide data on magnitude as well as direction for each of the major potential costs and benefits described in the earlier chapters. The next several sections describe the measurement and quantitative process of constructing indices for both costs and rewards.

As a caveat before I delve too deep into the data, I want to express clearly the many limitations of this process, and the study on which it is based. This was not a nationally representative sample; it was instead a highly selective sample of a small elite population whose members would be well-positioned to run for office, should they choose to do so. In some ways, this is good; it presents what we might call a "hard test." If even these well-positioned, elite eligibles have good reasons not to run, it is likely that those less well-positioned might have the same or better reasons for avoiding candidacy. But we do not know just from these data whether the results are generalizable to larger/broader populations (a task I happily leave to future researchers).

In terms of the measurement and quantification of costs and rewards, this is at best an approximation, based on a survey taken at a single point in time. To my reasoning, it was the best point in time I could think of; the sample is people who have made a significant life-direction decision by attending a law or policy graduate school, but it captures their feelings about politics and candidacy before a lot of the "real life" factors (especially children and other careers) that keep people from running get in the way. That said, if political ambition is truly malleable and situational, those very factors could be what makes someone want to run for office, whereas that person did not as a graduate student. Again, we will need further and better studies than mine to more fully understand the factors that over time affect the kind of rational cost-benefit analysis preceding candidacy. The evidence I have, however, points in the direction of such a rational calculation existing in the first place, which itself gives us useful information. Even if the quantitative analysis here gives only an approximation, it suggests to us a useful way of understanding what political ambition is and how to study it. I suggest here that we can empirically investigate both the costs and the benefits that potential candidates perceive, measure them, and then compare them to each other on a per-person basis.

## The Costs Index

In constructing a per-person "costs index," I stick very closely to the empirical data and try not to assume much. Instead of starting with assumptions about how people think, beyond the assumption that they will in some way add up costs versus benefits, I start with just what the data say about what they told me on their surveys. The index as a whole, then, will tell us how many, of all the possible costs tested in the survey, did that person respond to negatively? For each individual respondent, we can make a little scale out of all the survey variables relating to the costs of running.

Each question from the survey gives us one (or sometimes two) piece(s) of information about that respondent in terms of his or her sensitivity to the costs of running, and what counts for that individual as a "cost." Take, for example, the question about whether the person would not want to have to ask for campaign donations. Each survey respondent chose one answer on a 1–5 scale (ranging from not at all to very well) to tell me about his or her feelings about that prospect, with 1 meaning that the person felt very positively about it, 2 meaning positively, 3 meaning neither positive nor negative, 4 meaning negative, and 5 meaning "So negative it would deter me from running."[4] Those who said that they felt negatively about the idea of calling up potential donors to ask for campaign contributions (a 4 on this scale), would get a 1 in the costs index, while those who marked themselves as a 5 on this question would get a 2 in the index. This single survey question, then, gives us two pieces of information about people's level of negativity about donation-based fundraising—are they negative about the idea or not, and, if so, whether it is strong negativity (to the point of deterrence) or not.

If this were the only item in our index, we would thus have people who scored 0, people who scored 1, and people who scored 2. Those with a 0 on the index would be those to whom this prospect was not problematic, and those scoring 1 would mind but not as much as much as those scoring 2. Using the same method, to this index I then added lots of other variables relating to "costs," capturing in the same way both the direction and the magnitude of their answers on key questions. Table 5.1 gives information about each cost variable included in the index and how each was scored and why, if it was not obvious. The original question wording can be found in table 3.4. The costs index overall thus aggregates many factors that may have made a difference to the individual respondents, or may not have, and gives each person a single "costs" score. It tells us overall how much that set of costs factors I measured with the survey matter to that person. While there may indeed have been cost-related factors I did not measure, this costs-score gives us a pretty good sense of whether someone saw running as a costly enterprise or not, in a variety of ways.

Finally, I divided each respondent's score by the total number of potential "costs" points possible. The resulting numerical value this creates is a ratio, which standardizes all scores on a scale between 0 and 1. Because not all of my survey waves asked exactly the same questions, some respondents did not have a chance to answer certain questions, while they may have been asked others that were not asked in a different wave. The overall score thus tells us how many points a respondent scored out of the total points possible.

For respondents in the non–first waves, for instance, the top-scoring respondent on the "costs" scale received 27 points. The lowest-scoring respondent on that same scale received 3 points, so this respondent saw very few costs to running. Meanwhile, the person with a 27 saw a huge number of costs and felt them all keenly. Most people were somewhere in the middle (the mean for respondents not in the first wave was 12.77). If we divide each respondents' score by the total possible points (37), the person scoring 3 still gets a very low score (0.03), but the person who got a 27 now gets a 0.73. And those around the mean, with 13 or so points on the

## TABLE 5.1. Costs Index Variables

| Potential Cost Variable | How Scored in Index? | Asked in Which Survey Wave? |
|---|---|---|
| It is important to me that I can "[Be] sure of always having a relatively well-paying job" | 1 point if "important," 2 points if "very important" | Not asked of first wave |
| I would be more likely to run if "It would not interfere with [my] family's privacy" | 1 point if "possibly," 2 points if "yes" | All waves |
| I would be more likely to run if "Campaigns were fully publicly financed, so [I] would not have to raise money for [my] campaign" | 1 point if "yes" | All waves |
| I would feel negative about "Calling people to ask for donations" | 1 point if "negative," 2 points if strongly negative | All waves |
| I "Hate to lose at anything" | 1 point if describes person well, 2 points if very well | All waves |
| I "Avoid conflict whenever possible" | 1 point if describes person well, 2 points if very well | All waves |
| The consideration of being expected to contribute financially to my family of origin is "very or somewhat important to [my] choice of future job(s)" | 1 point if "important," 2 points if "very important" | Not asked of first wave |
| I "will be expected to contribute financially to [my] parents, siblings, or other relatives in the future" to a large or moderate extent | 1 point if agree, 2 points if strongly agree | Not asked of first wave |
| I would feel negative about "Dealing with the media" | 1 point if "negative," 2 points if strongly negative | All waves |
| I would feel negative about "Facing hostile questions" | 1 point if "negative," 2 points if strongly negative | All waves |
| I am not "Thick-skinned" and I believe "It takes a thick skin to survive in politics" | 1 point if both are true | All waves |
| "In today's media environment, you'd have to be crazy to run for office" | 1 point if agree, 2 points if strongly agree | All waves |
| I would feel negatively about the time that politics takes | 1 point if agree, 2 points if strongly agree | |
| I would feel negative about "Dealing with party officials" | 1 point if "negative," 2 points if strongly negative | All waves |
| I am not "Willing to take risks" | 1 point if describes person well, 2 points if very well | All waves |
| I believe that politicians sometimes or often "lie" and the term "ethical/moral" describes me well or very well | 1 point if both are true | All waves |
| I do not fit into either major political party | 1 point if weakly true, 2 points if strongly true | All waves |
| I would feel negative about "Making public speeches" | 1 point if "negative," 2 points if strongly negative | All waves |

TABLE 5.1. (*cont.*)

| Potential Cost Variable | How Scored in Index? | Asked in Which Survey Wave? |
|---|---|---|
| I would feel negative about "Going door-to-door to meet constituents" | 1 point if "negative," 2 points if strongly negative | All waves |
| The term "Ethical/moral" describes me well or very well, and I think politicians sometimes or often "Act immorally" | 1 point if both are true | All waves |
| I would be more likely to run if "[I] had fewer skeletons in [my] closet" | 1 point if "possibly," 2 points if "yes" | All waves |
| **Total points possible if in first survey wave:** | **31 points** | |
| **Total points possible if in later survey waves:** | **37 points** | |
| **Index mean once the per-person scores were calculated (points scored out of points possible in that wave):** | **0.339** | |
| **Index standard deviation once the per-person scores were calculated:** | **0.117** | |

Source: LPS-PAS, Survey Sample

costs scale, would get 0.34 (the new mean of the standardized ratio scale of costs).

Meanwhile, in the first wave I did not ask as many questions about costs, so the highest someone in that wave could get was a 31. For those respondents, I divided the overall score by 31, so theoretically a person could still get a 1 (if he or she had seen all possible costs and felt each one very strongly). Those scoring very highly on the standardized ratio scale were those who saw as many costs as they possibly could, given the questions I asked on their version of the survey, and were bothered by each, while those scoring low saw relatively few of those costs about which I asked or, if they saw them, were not as bothered by them. Those scoring in the middle saw some but not all costs compared with those scoring very high or very low.[5] Figure 5.1 shows the distribution of scores across the survey sample.

The curve of costs-index scores has a nice bell-shape, suggesting a pretty normal distribution of perceptions of the costs of running for office. Some people see few costs, some see a large number, but most fall somewhere in the middle. The mean falls around .34, with a standard deviation of .12. The curve skews a bit away from normal by having a

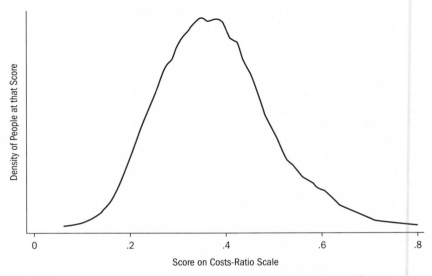

Figure 5.1. Distribution Curve of Standardized Costs-Ratio Scale (Kernel density estimate). Source: LPS-PAS, Survey Sample. N = 763.

longer tail on the right—this means that some group of people see very high costs, way above the average, but they are not the majority. Who sees these high costs, and how their perceptions of rewards compare, are critical questions I will address in the following chapters. For now, though, I will focus just on this costs-perceptions index.

By itself, this per-person score of costs can serve as an explanatory variable; even without knowing what rewards people see, we would expect those people who see fewer costs to show more interest in running. This is indeed what we see in both correlational and regression analyses using the costs index as an independent variable, with the dependent variable being political ambition. The costs index correlates extremely highly (and negatively, as we would expect) with both whether the respondent has thought of running at all[6] and what level of office the respondent might ever want to pursue.[7]

In regression-testing, using as the dependent variable the question about having thought of running and using the costs index as the only independent variable, we find that the coefficient on the costs index is relatively high compared with the constant, and the p-value is extremely significant.[8]

This suggests that the costs index is strongly related to political ambition, and in a negative direction, because the coefficients are negative (in both the correlation and regression tests). However, the R-squared value of the regression model, which measures how much of the variation in the dependent variable is explained by variation in the independent variable, is low.[9] This means that there are probably many other factors which make a difference above and beyond the costs index, even though it seems to be an important explanatory variable in part.

Running the same regression but this time including a series of demographic controls (sex, race, family income, degree program, and school) does not decrease the strong significance of the costs index as an explanatory factor, and it is still clearly a negative effect.[10] Some of the demographic controls also show significance, particularly sex: women show far less interest in running. Interestingly, the strength of the association between being female and having lower political ambition has decreased once we have taken into account costs (more on this to come later in this chapter and in chapter 6). Degree program and school also mattered; Harvard's Kennedy School students were more politically ambitious, compared with students from either law school, while Harvard students overall showed more interest in running than Suffolk Law students. But the costs index was still strongly statistically significant and showed the largest coefficient, as table 5.2 shows, giving both regression models. The R-squared value has increased some, but not much, suggesting that while the second model (including demographics as well as costs) better explains the variation in the dependent variable, a lot is still left unexplained by this model. Overall, the numbers suggest that costs matter deeply, but that they are far from the only factor that matter.

Also, as a note: the way I set up this analysis is based on the assumption that political ambition is a dependent variable (it is the thing being caused) and the costs and the demographics are the independent variables (what is doing the causing). However, the causal logic here could go in the other direction; perhaps those already interested in running are minimizing in their minds the costs of something they already want to do. Political psychology tells us that our human thought processes, while internally rational in our minds, may involve a whole lot of post-hoc justification.[11] It is hard therefore to assert simply that perceptions of costs drive political ambition with a one-way causal arrow. Regressions

TABLE 5.2. Regressions with Costs Index Predicting Political Ambition

| Independent Variables/Controls | Model 1 (Ordered Logistic) | Model 2 (Ordered Logistic) |
|---|---|---|
| | Dependent Variable, for both models: Had thought of running for office (not at all, in passing, or seriously considered) | |
| Costs Index | −3.762*** | −.3.371*** |
| Female | — | −.832*** |
| Nonwhite | — | .009 |
| In law school (versus public policy program) | — | .296* |
| At either Harvard School (versus Suffolk) | — | .509** |
| Family income at about age 16 | — | −.051 |
| Constant | −2.002 | −1.882 |
| N | 753 | 748 |
| R-Sq | 0.026 | 0.059 |

Source: LPS-PAS, Survey Sample
* $p<.1$, ** $p<.05$, *** $p<.01$

run either way are strongly significant; political ambition (in the sense of thinking about running for office in the future) strongly predicts perceptions of costs, even controlling for other variables, but so too do perceptions of costs strongly predict political ambition.

For now, it is enough to know that the two are strongly linked. Perceptions of costs relate in an important way to political ambition. The next section explores whether the same is true for perceptions of the rewards of running, and, if so, how we can begin to combine costs and rewards into a unified framework of analysis.

## The Rewards Index

Having examined the individual rewards-related variables from the survey data in chapter 4 and noting their connections with political ambition, we are ready to build a rewards index in the same way we did earlier for costs. The variables used for constructing this new index of rewards/benefits are listed in table 5.3, along with information on how

## TABLE 5.3. Rewards Index Variables

| Potential Reward Variable | How Scored in Index? | Asked in Which Survey Wave? |
|---|---|---|
| Considers self "Good at being in charge" | 1 to 2 points | All but final wave |
| Would feel positively about "Being a part of history" as a candidate | 1 to 2 points | Only in final wave |
| Considers "Feeling useful, doing something good in the world" an important life goal and believes politics "solves" important problems | 1 point if both are true | Only in final wave |
| Considers self "A good public speaker" | 1 to 2 points | All waves |
| Would be more likely to run if "Cared about an issue and knew [I] could make a difference if [I were] in office." and believes politics "solves" problems | 1 point if both true | All waves |
| Would feel positively about "dealing with the media" | 1 to 2 points | All waves |
| Would feel positively about "Going door-to-door to meet constituents" | 1 to 2 points | All waves |
| Would be more likely to run if thought "Could help [my] community" and believes politics "solves" problems | 1 point if both are true | All waves |
| Would be more likely to run if thought "It would help [me] get a better job later" | 1 to 2 points | Only in final wave |
| Thinks "The problems I most care about can be solved through politics" | 1 to 2 points | All waves |
| Considers self "Very competitive" | 1 to 2 points | Only in final wave |
| Would feel positively about "Attending fundraising functions" | 1 to 2 points | All waves |
| Has strong opinions on policy issues | 1 to 2 points | All waves |
| Believes one person can "make a difference in politics" | 1 to 2 points | All waves |
| Thinks politicians often "work for the public good" | 1 to 2 points | All waves |
| Would be "very likely" to interrupt professor in a class | 1 to 2 points | All waves |
| Thinks politicians often "help people with their problems" | 1 to 2 points | All waves |
| Considers becoming "famous" an important life goal | 1 to 2 points | All waves |
| Would feel positive or very positive about "improving lives" as a candidate | 1 to 2 points | Only in final wave |
| Would feel positively about the time that politics takes | 1 to 2 points | All waves |
| Would feel positively about "Dealing with party officials" as a candidate | 1 to 2 points | All waves |
| Would feel positively about "Making public speeches" as a candidate | 1 to 2 points | All waves |
| Would feel positive or very positive about "improving the lives of fellow citizens" if elected | 1 point if true | Only in final wave |
| **Total points possible if in final survey wave:** | **37 points** | |
| **Total points possible if in earlier survey waves:** | **32 points** | |

TABLE 5.3. (*cont.*)

| Potential Reward Variable | How Scored in Index? | Asked in Which Survey Wave? |
|---|---|---|
| **Index mean once the per-person scores were calculated (points scored out of points possible in that wave):** | 0.34 | |
| **Index standard deviation once the per-person scores were calculated:** | 0.14 | |

Source: LPS-PAS, Survey Sample

many points each could receive in the index. Again, with several of these rewards variables, I take advantage of the difference between "agree" and "strongly agree" or other questions where the answer choices fall on a scale that captures both direction and magnitude.

Also as before, I had to construct the ratio differently depending on which wave of the survey each respondent was in, as certain questions were not asked in all waves. The denominator of the ratio is thus 32 points if R was in any survey wave but the last one, and 37 if R was in the final wave of the survey (where some additional questions were asked). The resulting standardized scale gives us a measure of how many rewards each R saw out of all the possible questions he or she was asked about rewards. This makes the rewards index comparable to the previously built costs index, as both give a ratio of points-scored to points-possible for each individual, and both are on the same 0-to-1 scale.[12]

The maximum score one could theoretically get on the standardized rewards-index ratio is thus 1 (if R saw every single possible reward, and at the highest level), and the minimum is 0. I can again plot the distribution of scores for all respondents, as shown in figure 5.2. The chart shows good variation across the scale, but also a strong skew, suggesting that on the whole, perceptions of rewards were closer to 0 than to 1. The mean is .34, with a standard deviation of .14. This curve looks somewhat similar to that shown in figure 5.1, showing the distribution of perceived costs, but with a longer right-hand tail.

Again, as with the standardized costs ratio above, the standardized rewards ratio correlates strongly with political ambition, however we measure it, in both correlation and regression testing (not shown, but with extremely small p-values for each). In an ordered logit regression (not shown), with one's having thought of running as the dependent

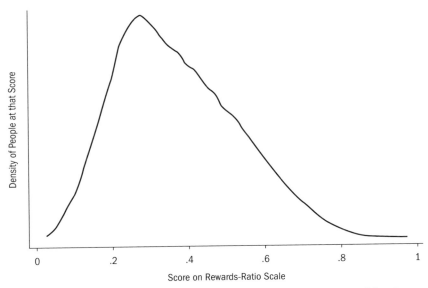

Figure 5.2. Distribution Curve of Standardized Rewards-Ratio Scale (Kernel density estimate). Source: LPS-PAS, Survey Sample. N = 763.

variable, the p-value of the standardized rewards scale as an explanatory variable was less than p = .001 even when controlling for school, program, sex, nonwhite race, and R's family income at about age sixteen (as in table 5.2).

Generally, the costs and rewards scales described here do what we would want them to do: they seem to capture reasonably well the sentiments of my sample toward politics, candidacy, and government. There is reasonably good variation on most of the items composing the scales, which we can exploit quantitatively. The overall scales give us nice distributions, wherein some people see high rewards and others see low rewards, and the same goes for costs. Statistically, both scales correlate strongly and in the expected directions with measures of political ambition, as they should if we expect potential candidates to act rationally. Each scale has been standardized as a ratio rather than as an absolute number. The next step is to begin to compare perceived costs with perceived rewards on a per-person basis. For this, we need to aggregate the costs and the rewards within each person, so that each respondent gets a kind of "total score" of rewards versus costs.

## Evaluating the Costs-Rewards Scales and Constructing Combined Measure

Ultimately our goal is to compare the costs and rewards ratios and numerically combine them to get an overall score of costs versus rewards. Before we can combine the costs and rewards indices into one unified scale, however, it is important to be sure that these indices are not simply measuring the same thing. Are perceptions of costs theoretically (and, in the survey data, practically) a different thing from perceptions of rewards, or are they just reverse images of each other? Theoretically they are different things, because each scale uses different survey questions (about totally different things) to build its own index. And practically, they seem to be doing something different. One neat way to test these indices is through that old social science standby tool, the 2x2 table. If the costs and rewards scales are simply measuring the same concept, we should not see anyone who sees high costs but also high rewards, or low costs but also low rewards. But as figure 5.3 shows, splitting both indices at their means, we do see this. In fact, each of the four cells in the 2x2 matrix contains at least one-seventh of the sample population.

Some people see high costs but also high rewards, others see high costs and low rewards, some see high rewards but low costs, and others see low costs and also low rewards. Costs and rewards, in other words, are operating relatively independently, even if they show correlation.[13]

Overall, then, we have a scale of perceived rewards that appears to measure something different from our scale of perceived costs. We can now begin to aggregate the indices into the same scale in an attempt to simulate quantitatively the kind of rational cost-benefit calculus we would expect to go on in the mind of a rational potential candidate.

If we consider rewards as positive and costs as detractions, the logical way to combine the scales would be to subtract costs from benefits. If someone saw all of the possible rewards (1 on the rewards scale) and also all of the possible costs of running (1 on the costs scale), for instance, that person's overall ratio comparison score would be 0. Meanwhile, if the individual saw half of the costs but only a quarter of the rewards, his or her score would be 0.25 minus 0.5, for a total of -.25 overall. The additive measure can thus range from -1 (if someone sees all costs and no rewards) to 1 (all rewards and no costs). In real life, it is probably not true

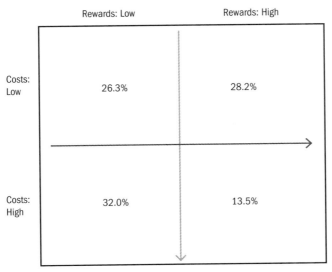

Figure 5.3. 2x2 Matrix: Costs Dummy versus Rewards Dummy. Source: LPS-PAS, Survey Sample. N = 763. Notes: "Low" here means below the sample mean for that index. "High" means above the sample mean. Chart gives percentage of overall sample falling in each cell.

that each of these factors would be weighted equally in someone's mind, but we do not have enough information about individuals to know how they would weight each factor in their own cost-benefit calculus. Our additive scale is very approximate, but it is a useful exercise that can give us hints about this group overall, and how costs and rewards stack up in the aggregate.

Figure 5.4 shows the distribution of the resulting scores when the costs index is subtracted from the rewards index. This quantitative comparison suggests that for most of the survey respondents, the potential costs and rewards more or less balance out; the mean for the overall sample hovers right around 0.

This does not bode well for a whole slew of future candidacies' resulting from this group, at least not anytime soon. Unless one expects to get something out of the experience of running, it would be irrational to be politically ambitious. We cannot be certain at what point along the combined costs-rewards scale each individual might judge a run to be "worth it" to him or her—but we can infer that any negative number

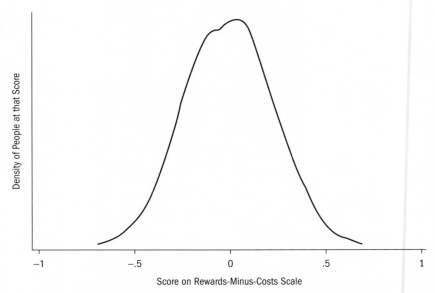

Figure 5.4. Distribution Curve of Rewards-Minus-Costs Ratio. Source: LPS-PAS, Survey Sample. N = 764.

or anything too close to 0 likely means rational candidate deterrence rather than political ambition. And the mean of the "rewards-minus-costs" variable for the sample as a whole is pretty close to 0 (0.004 to be exact). But interestingly, there is a relatively high standard deviation (.22), suggesting wide variation across this sample on the question of whether rewards balance out costs.

This is not to say that those scoring around 0 or even below it will never run. Under the emerging model of malleable political ambition, it is likely that the costs-benefits calculus will change as these individuals have new experiences, glean new information, and are recruited into or repelled from candidacies by future events. Research has found that women in particular often come to candidacy later in life and for policy-oriented reasons,[14] such as having kids and then getting interested in the politics surrounding local schools. Life happens.

For now, however, in that moment of time frozen and encapsulated in these survey and interview data, for most of these folks the perceived rewards do not appear to be enough to outweigh the perceived costs. For only 14.2 percent[15] (or to put it in absolute terms, 110 people out of

763 surveyed) did the rewards score minus the costs score equal at least .25, to give just a rough estimate of how few people saw low costs but high rewards. For the rest of the people, the other 653, the average of rewards minus costs was negative (−.05). In other words, some people see rewards that more than balance out the costs—but generally, running looks to the large bulk of people like effort, time, energy, and money expended for not much reward.

## How "Movable" Are They?

As noted earlier, democracy requires a large, fairly competitive, and steady pool of candidates for all the 500,000[16] offices across U.S. federal, state, and local governments that need to be filled through election, most of them coming open again every two to four years. It is in the public interest to have a good supply of candidates that is constantly replenished by a strong pipeline to ensure the kind of competition that increases the chance of our getting good and accountable officeholders. In recruitment-centered countries this means that parties must constantly be finding and persuading new people to run. In a candidate-centered system as in the United States, this means that far more young people must self-identify as eligible candidates and be willing to put up with the unusually high costs in our system.

Logically, if we would like to see more of these young people show interest in running for office at some point, and if we consider their decision to be at least mostly rationally based on perceived costs and rewards (and if their perceptions of those costs and rewards are more or less correct), then we have two options for increasing their political ambition. We can lower the costs or increase the rewards. Ideally, we would do both. If the costs did not seem so costly, would these graduate students be more likely to think about running? What if the rewards looked more rewarding?

The survey data allow us to put into effect some thought experiments along these lines. The survey asked about various contextual factors that could perhaps affect political ambition, such as whether or not people were recruited or asked to run and whether they might feel more willing to run if certain things were true (their spouses would support them, they knew they would have community support, they had more experience

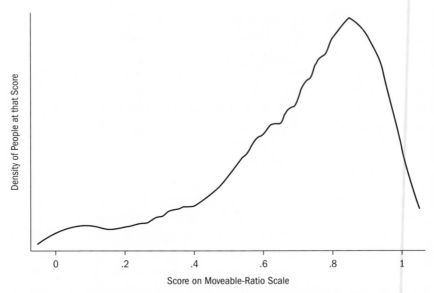

Figure 5.5. Distribution Curve of "Movable" Ratio Scores. Source: LPS-PAS, Survey Sample. N = 764.

in politics, they knew they could make a difference on an issue, etc.). Overall, across the various survey waves, more than twenty survey items had to do with changing conditions under which the eligible candidates might run. If we put these all together, as we did for costs and rewards, we can create a scale of how "movable" someone is given the conditions of a potential run.

Figure 5.5 tells this story graphically, offering a kernel-density plot showing the distribution of the "movable" ratio scores (which have been standardized to fall between 0 and 1). The relatively high mean of this variable (0.69)[17] suggests that generally these respondents were quite "movable" in their political ambition depending on the conditions they expected to encounter. There is a long left tail in the distribution, suggesting that there are some people who just would not budge; they did not want to run, and different conditions did not much appear inclined to change their minds. Indeed, we can find and count these people; of the 763 usable returned surveys, 123 of the respondents scored 0.45 or less on the "movable" scale.[18] We could consider these people total "candidacy refusers." But that is not where the bulk of the data lies; such refusers were only about 16.6 percent of the sample as a whole. Everyone else, the other 83.4 percent, appeared sensitive to the conditions of a possible run.

The quantitative data tell an extremely clear story along this vein: context matters. On the whole, people could be pretty movable if they thought the conditions were better for a run. "Better" may not mean the same thing for everyone, and there was a fair amount of variety in what mattered to individuals, but the bulk of those in the survey sample were "movable," providing yet more suggestive evidence of malleable political ambition.[19]

One way to further test this idea of being "movable" is by using regression tools to create "predicted probabilities." This procedure uses the available data from my survey sample to predict how much one variable would change another, holding everything else constant. In figure 5.6, the dependent variable is one's having thought seriously of running for office, as a binary (yes or no). The predicted probabilities tell us how likely it is, at different points on the rewards-minus-costs index scale, that someone will have thought seriously of running.

Someone who sees very low rewards but high costs, at the far low end of the rewards-minus-costs scale, has a 0.4 percent (rounded to 0 in chart) probability of having thought seriously about running. Someone at the mean on the rewards-minus-costs scale, scoring around 0 (such that costs and rewards were about even in their minds), has an 11 percent probability of having thought seriously of running for office—still low. But someone at the top of the rewards-minus-costs scale, who sees high rewards and few costs, has a 77 percent probability (quite high!) of having thought seriously of running for office. Perceived rewards and their relationship to perceived costs thus seem to matter a great deal for political ambition among those in this sample.

## Summary

The first few chapters of this book explored the concept of political ambition and what we know about it from research, and then delved deeply into what might be the costs and the rewards in the minds of potential Millennial candidates. Both chapters 3 and 4 on costs and rewards, respectively, developed tools for understanding and measuring these

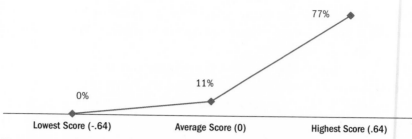

Figure 5.6. Predicted Probabilities of Having Thought Seriously of Running for Office, by Level of Score on Rewards-Minus-Costs Index. Source: LPS-PAS, Survey Sample. N = 764.

perceptions in people's minds. In this chapter I have worked to simulate how these costs and rewards might "stack up" against each other. Going back to that image of a balanced set of scales, the answer is: pretty evenly. Generally across this sample, the rewards do not outweigh the costs, resulting in candidate deterrence rather than a whole lot of political ambition.

I argue that it is not because these young people are dumb or selfish; while a few wanted to be famous or make a lot of money, these were a small minority of the group as a whole. Mostly, it appeared that these graduate students wanted to do good things for the world (help their communities, solve problems, improve lives) but were highly ambivalent about their ability to do good through electoral politics. The indication from the data so far is also that rewards may matter more than costs; seeing low costs and low rewards does not seem to stimulate political ambition, but high rewards—even if coupled against high costs—can. What is most damning for the political ambition of these young people was that most just did not see high rewards from running.

According to this analysis so far, some "political animals" in the sample did indeed want to become candidates, but they were a small, non-representative group. In particular, they tended to be far more male than female, a topic to which I turn in the next chapter.

# 6

## Inefficient and Unappealing Politics

### *Women and Candidate Deterrence*

You do begin to at least understand why more women [than men] would look at [running] with clear eyes and say "No, thank you."
—Liz, MPP candidate, Harvard's Kennedy School

Liz was a white female Kennedy School student who had experience working with government and had been working with some friends on a startup project to create a smartphone app to help people vote. It is fair to say that she was a political creature. But she was also deeply introverted and said she couldn't stand the idea of being scrutinized and judged the way she thought she would be as a political candidate. And, she said, it would be worse for women. They wouldn't get a fair shot at the game.

Liz's idea of looking at the decision to run or not with "clear eyes" fits in well with this book's overall theme of rational decision making. Rational, in the sense of comparing costs with benefits, can still take into account the "relationally embedded" kind of decision making about which Carroll and Sanbonmatsu write. Their work finds, as I do, that both costs and rewards matter greatly as someone considers running for office. For women especially, they argue, a simple lack of costs is not enough; increased political representation "is produced by both the *absence* of impediments and the *presence* of encouragement and support."[1] Costs matter, but so too do rewards.

Interestingly, as this chapter will show, the costs-benefits comparison looks different for women on the whole from the way it does for men. In particular, women—even in this sample of well-matched elite, ambitious young people—were more likely to see high costs and low rewards. The bulk of the sample had good reasons to be deterred from running, in other words, but women on the whole ended up having more good reasons not to do so. And when we look more closely at those factors enumerated in earlier chapters, and especially campaign finance and privacy, we see that women seem to feel the costs more keenly. This can show up in the quantitative data even if everyone perceives a cost, if women were more likely than men to say that they "strongly agree" with a question rather than simply "agree." They are also significantly less likely than men to see holding political office as useful, in the sense of solving problems they think important, a key predictor of political ambition, as we saw previously.[2] As Taylor Woods-Gauthier, at the time an executive director of a state-level women's candidate-training program, explained to me in 2013, "Women just have a harder time seeing politics as an efficient means to their ends."

Women are also strongly likely to see additional costs relating to their gender, in the form of expectations of gender biases on the part of various political actors (voters, media, party leaders, and funders). This seems related to the gender gap in feeling qualified to run, which turned up both in my sample and in earlier research.[3] Given the expectations about double standards and other gender biases, however, I interpret the gender gap in "feeling qualified" somewhat differently from the way other researchers do; it is perfectly logical for women to discount their qualifications if they think they will be subjected to a double standard (as in, judged more harshly because they are female). Finally, as in prior studies, women in my sample are far less likely than men to have been asked to run, another factor strongly predicting political ambition.[4] This, though, could be correlation rather than causation; if one is not already active in politics, one will be less often recruited to run. Likely, all of these processes are at least partially connected, if not strongly interlinked.

Multiple expectations and experiences on the part of women result in differing perceptions of the costs and benefits of running compared with those of similarly situated men. We end up with measurably different levels of political ambition across gender even when all in the sample are ambitious, well-educated, and studying in the schools that send people into politics. This chapter suggests that, while most in the sample are rationally deterred from running, women are more deterred than men.

## Equal Ambition but Unequal Political Ambition

Respondents did not differ by sex in their level of ambition overall. As we would expect in this elite sample, nearly all respondents described themselves as "ambitious." There are no significant differences in describing oneself as ambitious across sex, nonwhite race,[5] or graduate school/program. As figure 6.1 shows, ninety-one percent of women in the survey sample, and the exact same percentage of men, agreed that the term *ambitious* described them well or very well. There was no sex difference, either, in the proportions of men versus women calling themselves "very ambitious" instead of merely "ambitious"; 49.3 percent of the men[6] and 50.0 percent of the women chose the "very" category.

However, not all respondents were equally *politically* ambitious. When asked if they had ever thought about running for public office (not including student government), significantly more men than women answered in the affirmative. Men were much more likely than women to say both that they had "seriously considered" running and that the thought had "crossed their mind."[7]

Only about half of all women had thought about running in either way (fleetingly or seriously), while nearly three-quarters of the men had done so. Looking at who had thought seriously about it, we see that

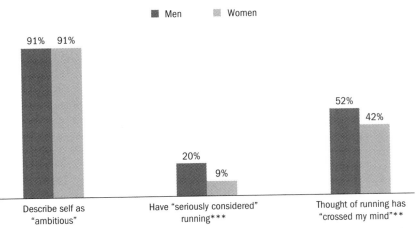

Figure 6.1. Ambition and Political Ambition, by Sex. Source: LPS-PAS, Survey Sample. * $p < .1$, ** $p < .05$, *** $p < .01$ (for difference between sexes). N = 716 (ambitious Q). N = 753 (thought of running Qs).

20.3 percent of men but 9.2 percent of women had done so. To look at it another way, of those who had seriously considered running for office, fewer than a third were women.[8]

The figure sets up an intriguing and important question. Why, in a sample of highly ambitious women and men, are the women significantly less *politically* ambitious than the men? The men and women in this elite sample should be, and in many ways are, more alike than they are different. The work of the highly selective admissions committees at these schools served to ensure a sample matched on all kinds of characteristics that tend to have a gender skew in the general population, such as ambition, family income, and education. In my survey sample, there is no gender skew to these characteristics among respondents. Also, one of the biggest differences between adult men and women—time spent engaged in child care—is mostly absent among my sample, as few of my respondents had children.

Yet even after we control for family responsibilities, general ambition, education, and income, there is still a large difference in the political ambition levels of the men and women in my sample, as shown in the illustrations earlier. One interpretation is that these differences could be tied in some way to biology (perhaps women are just genetically averse to politics?). However, the data that respondents gave about their previous political activities contradict such an interpretation. More female than male respondents said they had been active in student government in high school (although there is debate about whether this bears any relation to running for office later in life).[9] And there is no difference by sex in reports of participating in politics outside of school while in high school. If anything, the women report having been more active in politics in high school and report about the same level of activity relating to politics in college. Some research has found that girls in general are differently socialized in families as far as politics is concerned.[10] But among the ambitious and elite group of my sample, men were not more likely to have been politically socialized than women (in the sense of discussing politics with their families while growing up),[11] and the women were just as likely to have run for school office in high school or college.[12]

Significant sex differences do not begin to emerge until respondents' recent reports of political activity, in the past two years (in college or immediate postcollege). Something seems to happen to young women that changes their perceptions of the relative costs and rewards of politics, and the change, as far as I can tell from these data, comes between high school and college or in college. As I did not expect to find this, I do not have sufficient measures on this point in my study, either in the interviews or the survey data—future research is needed to evaluate this seemingly critical political development phase in a gender-conscious way. For now, I will stick to my data and tell you what I know for sure: the young men and women I surveyed and interviewed, by the time I got to them, saw the political world differently from each other.

In terms of women's lower political ambition when compared with those of men, research has suggested various answers, including that women lack confidence,[13] that women see bias in politics,[14] that women are more strategic about how and where they spend their time,[15] that women are less likely to be asked to run (recruited),[16] that the prospect of electoral competition itself is more offputting to women than to men,[17] and that women are more risk-averse.[18] I find support in my data for all of these explanations and can also add a new consideration: in addition to seeing more and higher costs (to put into my cost-benefits framework what research has found), I also find that women see fewer *rewards* in the idea of candidacy. Not only do the costs seem higher when compared with those of similarly situated men, in other words, but the benefits seem lower.[19] That, I argue, is a crucial and missing piece of our explanation of women's political ambition. In this chapter, I walk through the data on both the costs and the rewards sides, now looking at women and men separately.

## Women's Greater Sensitivity to the Costs of Running

Previous chapters suggested that young and elite prospective candidates perceive multiple costs to running for office, such as the need to raise large sums of money and the perception of privacy invasion by media or opposition research. These costs were perceived by large proportions of the sample and seemed to deter those who did not see corresponding rewards to balance out these costs. Men as well as women perceived and were deterred by these barriers—but as the data in this section will show, women were more deterred than men.

If we return to table 3.4, giving survey data on the costs of running, we can now look at whether women and men perceive and react to these costs similarly or differently. Table 6.1 replicates that first table, but now for each cost I give the means for women and men separately, as well as an indication of whether the difference is statistically significant. For many variables, there is no significant difference between men and women. But a few do show differences; for example, men in general perceived invasion of family's privacy, losing at anything, and having skeletons in their closet to be more costly. On the other hand, women were more likely to perceive as costly things like dealing with the media, facing hostile questions, needing a thick skin, and taking risks.

The final row in table 6.1 gives the average scores of men versus women on the overall costs index developed in the previous chapter. This gives us a sense of how the costs stack up for women versus men as groups and tells us that on the whole, even before we add in any new costs, women overall perceive running as more costly than men do. The difference in means is not huge, but it is strongly statistically significant.[20]

When I run regression analyses looking at the factors that affect political ambition, as shown in table 6.2, the coefficient on the costs index is strongly significant, despite the inclusion of multiple controls, including respondent sex. And when I use the costs index itself as a dependent variable, as shown in the second column, the coefficient on being female rather than male, while not large, is strongly statistically significant. In other words, costs matter collectively for political ambition, and women see more of them in general than men do.[21]

## Women See Lower Rewards

Separately from the analysis of costs, we can look at whether perceptions of the potential benefits of running for or holding political office differ by sex. As one might expect, there is indeed a difference; women see fewer of the possible rewards and are sometimes less enthused about those they do see. If we look again at the possible individual rewards variables that went into that "rewards index" in chapter 5 and look at means for men versus women, as in table 6.3, some clear differences jump out.

TABLE 6.1. Costs Variable Means and Overall Index, by Sex (with Each Cost Cariable Constrained to a Binary)

| Perceived Cost | Mean for Men (percent) | Mean for Women (percent) |
|---|---|---|
| It is important to me that I can "[Be] sure of always having a relatively well-paying job" | 87.1* | 89.9 |
| I would be more likely to run if "It would not interfere with [my] family's privacy" | 81.1** | 75.3 |
| I would be more likely to run if "Campaigns were fully publicly financed, so [I] would not have to raise money for [my] campaign" | 78.0 | 77.5 |
| I would feel negative about "Calling people to ask for donations" | 72.1 | 75.2 |
| I "Hate to lose at anything" | 71.2*** | 56.0 |
| I "Avoid conflict whenever possible" | 51.3 | 47.0 |
| The consideration of being expected to contribute financially to my family of origin is "very or somewhat important to [my] choice of future job(s)" | 44.0 | 49.1 |
| I "will be expected to contribute financially to [my] parents, siblings, or other relatives in the future" to a large or moderate extent | 43.4 | 48.7 |
| I would feel negative about "Dealing with the media" | 31.2*** | 46.5 |
| I would feel negative about "Facing hostile questions" | 24.8*** | 50.1 |
| I am not "Thick-skinned" and I believe "It takes a thick skin to survive in politics" | 26.8*** | 47.6 |
| "In today's media environment, you'd have to be crazy to run for office" | 33.7 | 40.1 |
| I would feel negative about "Dealing with party officials" | 34.5 | 32.3 |
| I am not "Willing to take risks" | 27.9*** | 37.6 |
| I believe that politicians often "lie" | 28.4 | 29.3 |
| I do not fit into either major political party | 30.6 | 26.2 |
| I would feel negative about "Going door-to-door to meet constituents" | 26.7 | 29.3 |
| I would feel negative about "Making public speeches" | 12.4*** | 24.6 |
| I think politicians often "Act immorally" | 15.8 | 13.5 |
| I would be more likely to run if "[I] had fewer skeletons in [my] closet" | 13.9** | 8.2 |
| **Overall Costs Index Score** | .318*** | .355 |

Source: LPS-PAS, Survey Sample; N = 764
Sex Difference Significance: * $p<.1$, ** $p<.05$, *** $p<.01$

TABLE 6.2. Regressions with Costs Index Predicting Political Ambition, and Other Factors Predicting Costs

| Independent Variables/Controls | Model 1 (Logistic) Dependent Variable: Had thought seriously of running for office (binary) | Model 2 (OLS) Dependent Variable: Costs Index (continuous) |
|---|---|---|
| Female | −.898*** | 0.034*** |
| Nonwhite | .311 | 0.012 |
| In public policy program (versus law) | .194 | −.023* |
| At either Harvard School (versus Suffolk) | .397 | 0.011 |
| Family income at about age 16 | −.041 | −.004 |
| COSTS INDEX | −4.188*** | — |
| Constant | −.338 | .330*** |
| N | 748 | 758 |
| R-Sq | .07 | .12 |

Source: LPS-PAS, Survey Sample; N = 764
* p<.1, ** p<.05, *** p<.01

As before, with costs, this is not a story purely about gender difference; there are several questions on which men and women as groups did not disagree much, or at all. But there are also some rewards to running that men as a group saw far more than women did, such as thinking that politics solves problems. To put it another way, if we look only at those people who agreed strongly with the statement "The problems I most care about can be solved through politics" and break down those strong-agreers by sex, the group is 80 percent male.[22] On the other side, if we look only at those who disagreed with that statement, the disagreers group is 57 percent female.[23] Those two groups, however, may overstate the case, as they are only those who feel most strongly. What about those who agreed or disagreed, but not strongly? The same gendered pattern shows up, although less starkly; women, even though they are exactly half of the sample as a whole, are less than a majority of those who think that politics solves important problems, and a majority of those thinking it does not.[24]

TABLE 6.3. Rewards Variable Means and Overall Index, by Sex

| Perceived Reward | Mean for Men (percent) | Mean for Women (percent) |
|---|---|---|
| Considers self "Good at being in charge" | 86.5 | 88.5 |
| Would feel positively about "Being a part of history" as a candidate^ | 85.6 | 84.3 |
| Considers "Feeling useful, doing something good in the world" an important life goal^ | 73.1 | 87.8 |
| Considers self "A good public speaker" | 80.8*** | 69.2 |
| Would be more likely to run if "Cared about an issue and knew [I] could make a difference if [I were] in office" | 56.3 | 61.7 |
| Would feel positively about "Going door-to-door to meet constituents" | 56.7 | 52.1 |
| Would be more likely to run if thought "Could help [my] community" | 52.1 | 53.4 |
| Would be more likely to run if thought "It would help [me] get a better job later"^ | 47.4 | 44.2 |
| Thinks "The problems I most care about can be solved through politics" | 48.5*** | 30.5 |
| Considers self "Very competitive"^ | 59.0** | 29.9 |
| Would feel positively about "Attending fundraising functions" | 27.7 | 34.0 |
| Has strong opinions on policy issues | 22.6** | 28.7 |
| Believes one person can "make a difference in politics" | 26.0 | 21.4 |
| Thinks politicians often "work for the public good" | 25.7* | 21.7 |
| Would be "very likely" to interrupt professor in a class | 26.6*** | 14.6 |
| Thinks politicians often "help people with their problems" | 21.0*** | 14.2 |
| Considers becoming "famous" an important life goal | 16.6*** | 8.4 |
| **Overall Rewards Index Score** | **.370***** | **.315** |

Source: LPS-PAS, Survey Sample; N = 764 (for most questions)
Sex Difference Significance: * $p<.1$, ** $p<.05$, *** $p<.01$
^ These questions have a low n (around 47 responses each), as they were asked only in the final survey wave.

The interviews and survey data both suggested in chapter 4 that believing that politics is useful to solving problems is a key reward component of running for office. The fact that young women are significantly less likely than men to believe that politics has this kind of reward potential is an important reason why women as a group perceived fewer rewards when thinking about running for office, as compared with similarly situated men. But other variables show large differences as well, including thinking that politicians "often help people with their problems," which men believed far more than women. Men were also about twice as likely to want to be famous, to be ready to interrupt, to think themselves good at public speaking, and more likely than women to see rewards from the competition inherent to politics. On the other hand, women were somewhat more likely to have strong policy opinions. But overall, men were far more likely to see politics, and running for office, as potentially rewarding than women were.

Charlotte, a white female MPP candidate at Harvard's Kennedy School of Government, mused on several of the costs at once, saying:

> I'd hate [running]. Just because I think that there's such a good chance you could lose. I'm a pretty risk-loving person, but I wouldn't enjoy that kind of a risk . . . for the most part, it's just going to be really hard to get the work done once you're in there. And so, I mean it doesn't pay well, it's—you're frustrated all of the time, you've got no job security 'cause you have to think about getting elected again, and running just seems miserable, having to knock on a million doors, convince people that you're awesome and the other guy sucks, even if that's not necessarily true, and then promising change that you probably can't bring, because it's not just you in office, it's you plus like 50 other people, so, just because you're elected doesn't mean things are necessarily going to change, even with your best efforts. I just feel I can effect a lot more change and do good work from the outside and find it much more satisfying.

Charlotte was one of a number of what we might call "refusers"—those who absolutely disliked the idea of running, no matter how I asked about it. It wasn't that she hadn't thought it through. Being a student at the Kennedy School, surrounded by politicians and former politicians and future politicians, she had thought about it quite a lot. But put together, the high costs and low rewards that she perceived were pretty darn deterring.

## Levels of Office, by Sex

Figure 4.1 showed the proportions of all respondents in the sample who said they could imagine themselves running for different types of office at different levels of government. When we look at the sample as a whole, we see a good level of interest across multiple levels, without much of a pattern, except that the lowest number of people wanted to run for president and the highest for city council. If we now go back to that chart and break down the responses by sex, a different pattern emerges, only for women. Figure 6.2 shows the percent of men versus women who said yes, they could imagine themselves maybe running for that type or level of office at some point in the future.

If we look only at the darker bars (men), the levels of possible interest in all offices is relatively high and pretty constant, with a dip in wanting to run for president (although more than 20 percent of men in this sample seemed ready to consider it!). And men's level of "No interest in any office," shown in the far-left bar, is quite low compared with women's. Women, on the other hand, seem more interested in local legislative offices (school board and city council had the most interest) and show more interest in the legislative rather than executive options at both the

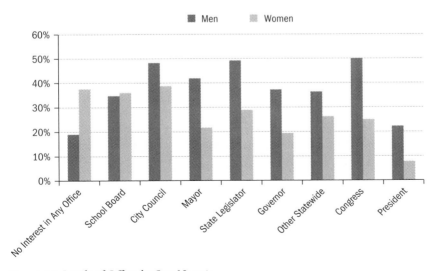

Figure 6.2. Levels of Office, by Sex; N = 764

state and national levels, preferring state legislator to governor and Congress to president. Indeed, a dummy variable testing for female sex was strongly and negatively associated with a variable testing for interest in higher levels of office.[25] And women were far more likely than men to be in that "never want to run for anything" category, the "refusers."[26]

## Costs versus Rewards Distributions, by Sex

The data presented thus far suggest that for otherwise ambitious women as a group, political ambition is simply—and rationally—lower than for similarly situated men. This does not mean that women are not ambitious; they are. And it does not mean that women do not want to change the world—the interviews and survey evidence strongly suggest that they do. In fact, women were significantly more likely than men to rank "improving life in my community" as an important life goal.[27] Men too wanted to change the world yet were far more likely to think that they could do so through politics. Not every man was more politically oriented than every woman, but the distributions speak to an important pattern: those who believe they could change the world through politics were far more likely to be men than women.

Earlier, figure 5.4 showed the distribution of rewards-minus-costs scores for the sample as a whole as one distribution curve. Now, in figure 6.3, I show the curves for men and women separately. As the figure makes clear, the curves overlap more than they diverge—women and men are more alike than they are different.[28] But on the whole the men's curve is shifted to the right of the women's, further toward the rewards side and away from the costs side. The bulk of people, in other words, both male and female, hover around the 0-line when costs are subtracted from rewards. But in this rare activity, running for office, where it is the far-right tail that likely matters most and not the great bulk in the middle, that far-right tail (where rewards far outweigh costs) has far more men than women. Small but powerful marginal differences in the means can add up to large differences in the tails.[29]

But that is not the end of the story. It turns out that in addition to seeing higher costs and lower rewards on average, women also saw a whole other important cost that affected the sexes differently: discrimination. Some people were vague about where the bias might come from, while

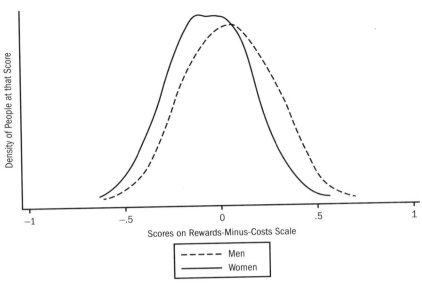

Figure 6.3. Distribution Curves of Rewards-Minus-Costs Index Scores, by Sex (Kernel density estimates). Source: LPS-PAS, Survey Sample. N = 764.

others were quite specific, naming a variety of actors who could show bias (voters, party leaders or other gatekeepers, recruiters, funders, and journalists). Many of my interviewees seemed to agree with the famous sentiment of comedian Elayne Boosler from the 1980s, that she was "just a person trapped in a woman's body." Yet being so trapped, they expected to be treated like women rather than like people. And taking this factor seriously as a cost further shifts women's scores both away from men's and away from wanting to run.

## Role Incongruity

I think it's harder for women than it is men to run. Not only because of the way they approach problems . . . , but also because of the way they're able to deliver a message, the problem is if they're too staccato or too hysterical about it, it sounds like you want to get away from it, it sounds like an angry woman sounds. Whereas a yelling man is like, "holy

crap," and you at least acknowledge that something is going
on, so it's hard for [women].
—Ben, white male student at Suffolk Law School

In an interview long after her race, Bonnie Campbell, the former attorney
general of Iowa and the Democratic Party candidate for Iowa governor
in 1994, recounted the difficulty she had simply in getting dressed each
morning of the campaign. If she wore pants, she said, she feared criticism for trying to imitate men. (This was before Hillary Clinton popularized the black pantsuit for political women.) But if she wore a skirt,
she thought she risked looking weak to potential voters. If she wore no
makeup or jewelry, she knew the media would comment on their absence, perhaps suggesting that she did not care enough about her appearance or was a lesbian. But if she wore makeup and jewelry, she feared that
commentators or voters would think she had something to hide. She said,
"Sometimes I would just stand in front of my closet, paralyzed."[30]

Campbell doubted that her male opponent had the same problem,
instead linking her experience to the difficulties women have when running for political office. She said her opponent used her sex against her
in underhanded ways, including saturating the radio airwaves of the
state with negative ads featuring the sounds of a lion roaring with a male
announcer saying, "It's a jungle out there." The ads implied that the female Campbell was not tough enough to be governor (despite her years
of experience as a lawyer and attorney general of the state). "Running a
political campaign is often antithetical to what it means to be a woman,"
she reflected several years after losing that race.[31]

Women seeking leadership roles, as with Campbell, often feel that
being visibly different from the male norm affects them in some way.
When reporters asked veteran Representative Pat Schroeder (D-CO) if
she was "running as a woman" in her 1988 presidential bid, she responded,
"Do I have an option?"[32] Her levity in no way detracts from the power
of this message. She clearly felt she would be perceived as a woman,
whether or not she wanted to be, and therefore as different.

In some cases, difference can be a helpful attribute, as when "insiders"
are seen as corrupt, incompetent, or even just "business as usual," in a
time when the public is fed up with such. In these cases, "outsider" status
is a positive, and insiders may even attempt to emulate it.[33] In general,

however, and especially in cases of crisis, military conflict, or a poor economy,[34] scholars of gender suggest that the gendering of leadership as masculine, and the conflation of politics with war, conflict, and/or force, all of which are historically masculine rather than feminine pursuits, presents challenges for women.[35]

The dilemmas detailed by Bonnie Campbell in her gubernatorial race reminiscences are described by scholars of women and leadership as "gender role incongruity."[36] While gender roles have been changing rapidly in the past few decades, the preponderance of evidence suggests they are still strong influences in most people's lives.[37] Gender identity is one of the earliest things we learn about ourselves and those around us; most children begin defining themselves and others in gendered ways at age two if not before.[38]

Certain features of gender roles have proven immune to the feminist challenges of the past century. As a society, we still associate masculinity with authority, leadership, and aggressiveness, while we link femininity with compassion, nurturance, and subservience and still assume women to be primary caregivers for children and the elderly.[39] In a speech in 2002, U.S. Representative Rosa DeLauro (D-CT) suggested that a woman running for office was and still is something of a gender paradox: "Think about the attributes of someone running for office—smart, tough, knowledgeable in foreign policy. And if you do have all these things, my God, are you really a woman?"[40]

Scholars of women and politics agree that the gendering of the public leadership as masculine creates challenges for women candidates. Susan Carroll writes, "Although socialized to exhibit values and behaviors considered appropriate for females, in running for office women enter a sphere of life dominated by masculine values and behavior patterns."[41] Georgia Duerst-Lahti and Rita Mae Kelly, in their study of gender power, say, "Our review of the literature on power and leadership reveals how rarely the words *women* and *feminine* are associated with them and how heavily men and masculinity saturate our understanding of power and leadership."[42] Likewise, Cheryl King cites a "preference for masculine" in our cultural definitions of leadership, and writes that leadership and governance "[bear] an explicit masculine identity."[43] Lyn Kathlene says bluntly, "Few social and occupational domains are more masculinized than politics."[44]

One result is the necessity for women to prove they can do the job as well as the men. Political scientist Sue Thomas has written, "Women legislators often find themselves continuously in a position to prove themselves to be every bit as competent, knowledgeable, dedicated, serious, and ambitious as their male counterparts."[45] In several over-time studies of women and men who hold the same jobs, women indicate that they have to work harder. The researchers argue that "the association between sex and reported required work effort is best interpreted as reflecting stricter performance standards imposed on women, even when women and men hold the same jobs."[46] Noting the findings from experimental research showing that people rate work more highly when told it was done by a man, one researcher (Gorman) explained, "This is what women are up against. They have to prove themselves."[47] The prospect of additional hurdles to surmount because of one's sex or race may make the idea of competing for leadership, and particularly against a white male (the vast majority of incumbent office holders[48]), less appetizing than it might be for another white male.

Research on gender and political ambition has found that women who have not themselves run for public office anticipate that female candidates as a group will face sexism. In a 2008 study by political scientists Jennifer Lawless and Richard Fox, fully 87 percent of women agreed that it would be "more difficult" for a woman to be elected to high-level public office compared with a man.[49] "Women are nearly twice as likely as men to contend that it is more difficult for women to raise money for a political campaign, and only half as likely to believe that women and men face an equal chance of being elected to high level office (13 percent of women, compared to 24 percent of men)."[50] Women in their sample (adult professionals in the fields leading to political candidacies) were far more pessimistic about the possibility of female candidates' ability to raise as much money and gain as many votes as male candidates, and they were more skeptical than the men about their own chances of winning. Many of their female respondents connected these negative assessments to their sex.[51] Lawless and Fox conclude, "The perceptual differences we identified translate into an additional hurdle women must overcome when behaving as strategic politicians and navigating the candidate emergence process."[52]

## The Cost of Being a Token

One additional factor, which some interviewees raised, was the idea of not wanting to enter an institution where they would be in the minority. This could certainly make sense in the sense of partisanship—individuals' political ambition could rationally wax and wane depending on whether their party is in the majority or minority. But this kind of minority-anticipation could also play a role in terms of race, gender, or other identity factors (possibly sexual orientation, religion, or others, although my research did not examine these).

In terms of gender, research on participation (and to some extent political ambition) has found that young women are far more likely to consider politics as a possible career choice when they see women role models serving in office.[53] This may be due, as other research and theory has suggested, to an expansion of the social definition of who can rule.[54] But what of the related idea that women may be more likely to want to serve in office if they didn't think they would just be the "token woman"?[55] Public policy student Esther certainly talked about how much she admired the pathbreaking women currently serving in Congress. Yet her description, however laudatory, did not suggest that that kind of pathbreaker role was one she necessarily wanted for herself. She said, "There are some fabulous women leaders in Congress, but they are certainly not the majority. So it's a brave thing for a woman to have to do, to . . . go down that path where not many others have, it's hard." Recent research suggests that where more women run, more women will run[56]—but that doesn't make it any easier for the individual pathbreaker who must go first or alone.

## Women in the Sample

The Millennial women in my study were, for the most part, extremely aware of their difference from the male norm in politics, and most considered it a disadvantage. In general, these women already perceived higher costs and lower rewards from running than did the men. Adding in perceptions of discrimination and double standards appears to have further weighted the scales against running for the women studied.

Charlotte, the white female MPP student quoted earlier, explained her perceptions of gender and racial bias in this way:

> I think it's a lot harder for a person of color to be elected, and I think it can be harder for a woman to be elected also. I think a white male is perceived to be genderless and colorless, so his gender and color just [don't] enter the picture, whereas the fact that someone is a woman or a person of color, those are things to think about and so that enters the picture in a way that being a white male doesn't. And I think it also affects your access to those resources we were talking about. I think you have a lot less access to resources when you're a person of color or a woman.

Similarly, Liz, the public policy student quoted at the start of this chapter, gave an explanation of why more women might not want to run that begins to link (gender-related) experiences to expectations of future discrimination. She said she thought that "[w]omen are taught to be less publicly opinionated in a lot of ways, so to have to stand up and proclaim what you think on any issue under the sun all the time . . . ." This thought led her to another: "And ambition. You don't get rewarded for it on lower levels, so to suddenly decide you have this burning fire, or want power, it's less commonly found." Women's expectations of being treated differently were, to her mind, perfectly rational given experiences of being expected to act differently from men.

This kind of anticipation of discrimination could be seen as an additional "cost" to running that affects women far more than men. Women in general, and especially women who had already experienced discrimination, were very likely to anticipate it in the future. The result was that both men and women anticipated discrimination against women in politics, but women more so. This pattern, as it turns out, applied to many of the other costs of running that were explicated in previous chapters. While most people seemed affected by these costs, women in the sample were often more sensitive to them than the men.

By the time they reach their mid-twenties, the mean age of the sample, men and women have had more than two decades of gender-differentiated experiences to draw upon. Most of the women and some of the men in my study appeared to have thought a great deal about gender, both in their own lives and as a concept more broadly. Many (including men) talked in interviews about having taken women's studies or gender studies classes, or having encountered this subject matter in other classes in college. And fairly large proportions, especially of the women, had had what scholars believe to be critical gender-consciousness experiences (discrimination, harassment, or assault based on sex, gender, or sexuality).[57]

Women were far more likely than men to report experiences of all forms tested except religious discrimination. Nearly half of the women (46.0 percent) and 12.1 percent of the men said they had faced discrimination because of their sex. Similarly, 45.9 percent of the women and 7.3 percent of the men reported having been sexually harassed. Sexual violence was not as widespread but had still touched the lives of many in the sample: 13.3 percent of the women and 1.8 percent of the men.[58] Such experiences, particularly sexual harassment and assault, are described as "gender-motivated violence" by those who study them. Such experiences can have a "consciousness-raising"[59] effect, leading those who connect their experience to larger gender trends to see the "personal as political," in the words of a famous slogan of the 1970s women's liberation movement.[60] As Simone de Beauvoir famously wrote in *The Second Sex* in 1949, "One is not born but rather becomes a woman."[61]

Women were also far less likely to have lived a life free of experiences of discrimination. Overall, fully half of the men (52.2 percent), and 64.6 percent of white men, reported that they had never experienced discrimination in any of the listed forms. Conversely, only 28.0 percent of women (33.7 percent of white women) reported no experience of discrimination, a strongly significant difference statistically, by both race and gender.[62] Figure 6.4 shows these gender differences graphically, comparing the proportions of women versus men within those saying they have experienced any of the listed forms of discrimination, and, in the final column, showing the percentage of men versus women reporting no experience of discrimination. In short, the cumulative effects of discrimination fell far harder on women in the sample than men, particularly when the discrimination was based on sex, gender, or sexual orientation/gender identity.

These experiences of discrimination strongly predict expectations of future discrimination. Respondents who had experienced discrimination, in other words, were more likely to expect that the political world

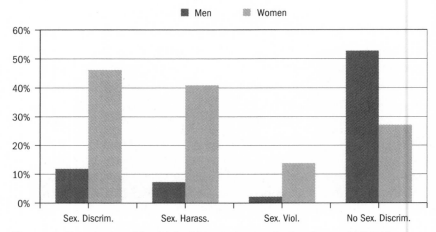

Figure 6.4. Experiences of Sex-Linked Discrimination, by Sex. Source: LPS-PAS, Survey Sample. N = 764.

was unfair. Scholars of identity, particularly relating to race, gender, and sexuality, suggest that experiences of discrimination can "teach" individuals to expect more of the same in the future.[63] Causality, however, could run in another direction; it might be that those who are aware of or sensitive to discrimination are more likely to view experiences in that light. Either way, experiences of discrimination correlated strongly with expectations of it.

Large majorities in the survey sample expected that whiteness and maleness provided a professional advantage. Both men and women expected women to face bias in the working world and in the media; 67.2 percent agreed with the statement "Men get more opportunities than women for jobs that pay well, even when women are as qualified as men for the job." Similarly, 91.8 percent of agreed that "Women are judged for their appearance more than men are."

Not surprisingly, given this set of expectations about gender in the wider world, politics as a specific domain was considered strongly biased in favor of men. Only 7.4 percent of the sample agreed with the statement "It is just as easy for a woman to be elected to high-level political office as a man."[64] These kinds of "anticipation-of-discrimination effects" are shown graphically in figure 6.5, which gives average answers

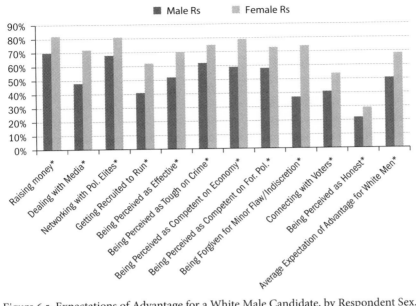

Figure 6.5. Expectations of Advantage for a White Male Candidate, by Respondent Sex. Survey instructions: "Please mark which of the following type of candidates you think would have an advantage in the following list of campaign activities, if any." Answer choice gave respondents a matrix of types of candidates (white male, white female, black male, black female, Hispanic male, Hispanic female, Asian American male, and Asian American female) and a series of campaign activites (listed along the X-axis). The chart gives the weighted average of a "yes" response for the white-male-candidate category, by respondent sex, for that type of campaign activity. The stars indicate statistically significant differences between the answers of male versus female respondents. Source: LPS-PAS, Survey Sample. N = 713.

by respondent sex to a series of questions about who might have an advantage in campaign activities. The survey asked respondents to mark the type of candidates they thought would have an advantage in each type of campaign activity in a matrix of types of candidates by race and sex: white male, white female, black male, black female, Hispanic male, Hispanic female, Asian American male, and Asian American female. The campaign activites asked about are along the X-axis. The chart gives the average for male and female respondents, respectively, who anticipated that a white male candidate would have an advantage in these aspects of a campaign.

As the figure shows, large proportions of both male and female respondents anticipated that a white male candidate would have an advantage in most activities, but women thought so more than men. On
average, women were nearly 20 percentage points more likely than men
to think a white male candidate would have an advantage in these campaign activities. The gap wanes, as with "being perceived by voters as
honest," and waxes, with the largest gap showing up in "being forgiven
for a minor character flaw or indiscretion." In few activities did the majority of women agree with the majority of men; all of these averages are
statistically significantly different by sex,[65] with women always anticipating more advantage for a white male candidate.

Factors other than previous discrimination may also give rise to expectations of bias against women in the political world, on the part of
a number of political actors (voters, media, funders, and party leaders).
Even without experiencing it oneself, one could observe and "read" discrimination in current U.S. politics. For example, although only a few
in my survey sample knew the exact number of women in Congress,
almost all (98 percent) believed that women were under-represented.
(They were right—the current figure is 19 percent women in Congress,
despite 51 percent of the U.S. population's being female.[66]) And a majority
of the sample (53.4 percent) believed that a specific woman, Hillary Clinton, was treated unfairly when she ran for the Democratic presidential
nomination in 2008.[67] A plurality of men thought this too, but women
believed it more: 39.8 percent of the men thought Clinton was treated
unfairly, compared with 67.6 percent of the women (and the difference
between the sexes was strongly statistically significant).[68] These sample
means and others along this vein are displayed in figure 6.6.

Women in this sample, in other words, saw the political world as
pretty strongly biased in favor of men.[69] They saw race as well as sex
bias, thinking for example that Hispanics/Latinos are generally por-
trayed negatively in the media. Men agreed, just not seeing quite as much
bias. Almost no one thought that running for office was gender- or
race-neutral.

To test this idea further, I created an index of expecting discrimation,
which aggregated into one scale all the survey questions about discrimination (both race and gender) and standardized the index by dividing
by the number of questions, as I had done before for both the costs and

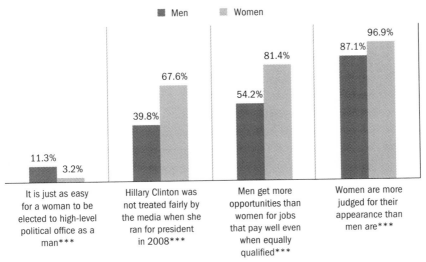

Figure 6.6. Expectations of Gender Bias: Percent Agreeing with the Statement, by Sex. Source: LPS-PAS, Survey Sample. * *p<.1,* ** *p<.05,* *** *p<.01* (for difference between sexes). N = 763 (for all question except job opportunities). N = 716 (for Q on men versus women and job opportunities).

rewards indices. When the index was standardized by my dividing by the number of points possible, each person could score between 0 and 1 on this "expecting political discrimination" scale. Those scoring 1 or close to it expected a whole lot of bias in political campaigns, while those scoring around 0 saw little. As we would expect from the data given thus far, men and women both expected that those who are not white or male would face political discrimination, but women expected it more. On average, male respondents scored .37 on this index, while the corresponding figure for females was .52.[70]

Having already experienced discrimination seems in the survey data to have heightened women's perceptions of it in politics, but even those women who reported no personal experiences of discrimination expected that women would face it as candidates. Relatedly, men who had experienced some form of discrimination (racial, religious, or gender/ sexual orientation) were more likely to see bias in U.S. politics. To give a simple illustration of how gender and discrimination experiences intersect in these kinds of expectations of discrimination, consider figure 6.7,

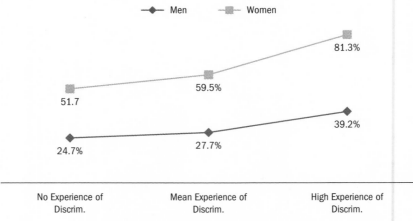

Figure 6.7. Predicted Probabilities of Expecting Discrimination, by Sex and Experience of Discrimination. Source: LPS-PAS, Survey Sample. N = 764.

giving means for different groups. This figure gives predicted probabilities of how likely one would be to expect discrimination against women and racial/ethnic minorities, based on whether one has already experienced discrimination. And the figure gives the probabilities separately for men versus women. It tells us that both one's sex and one's experiences of discrimination matter strongly in predicting how likely one will be to expect discrimination. Men who have not themselves experienced bias have about a 25 percent probability of expecting discrimination against women and minorities in politics and other realms. Men who have some experience with discrimination themselves are more likely to expect it for others (about 28 percent), while men who have faced a lot of bias have nearly a 40 percent probability of expecting discrimination.

Meantime, women as a group are already very likely to expect bias, but having already experienced discrimination is a very strong predictor of expecting it even more. Women with no experience of discrimination have about a 52 percent probability of expecting it, and women who have experienced some discrimination have about a 60 percent probability. Women who have had many experiences of discrimination have an 81 percent probability of expecting that women and racial/ethnic minorities will face bias. The upshot is that both gender and previous discrimination are significant predictors of expecting political discrimination, in other words—and those who expect it most are women who have faced it before.

## Perceptions versus Reality

Whether the costs actually are higher for women as candidates is subject to debate; plenty of research has found that gender discrimination continues to exist on the part of voters, party leaders, media, and campaign donors, although recent research also finds that these biases are far smaller than they used to be (and are perhaps smaller than most people think).[71] We know, for instance, that female candidates now regularly raise the same amounts of money as male candidates—although it also appears that women may have to work harder than men to raise that same amount of money, such as by making twice as many phone calls to donors.[72] Research on media treatment of women as candidates finds that they are more likely than men to find themselves discussed in terms of their appearance (what Marie Wilson, formerly president of the Ms. Foundation for Women and the White House Project, has famously called "hair, hemlines, and husbands" coverage), less likely to be quoted in their own words, and more likely to be paraphrased.[73]

It appears that gender biases in recruitment of candidates persist, although in some places far more than others, and often because of social network effects rather than conscious discrimination.[74] Researchers of women in business call these "second generation" discrimination effects and find them in recruitment for leadership in business as well.[75] The model is that people in leadership (mostly white men) tend to mentor, support, and recruit people they already know, and/or with whom they feel most comfortable, who are often though not always similar to the existing leaders in terms of gender and race.[76] Gender quotas, often within parties, have been effective in increasing the recruitment of women in more than one hundred other countries, including most of those in Europe, but are resisted strongly in the United States and would not make as much sense within our "candidate-centered" system here, where candidates often must self-recruit.[77]

In terms of voters, good research tells us that, in surveys, very few people admit to outright bias against voting for women as candidates.[78]

Indeed, political scientists Lawless and Fox use these figures to suggest that female candidates should just get out there and run[79] more often, as they are over-expecting gender discrimination. However, think of it this way: if women are far less likely to run, and less likely to feel confident about and qualified to run, as these researchers have found, then generally only the most qualified and confident women end up as candidates, which helps explain why women tend to be higher-quality legislators[80]—social scientists call this a major selection bias. If what we see is mostly high-quality women running, but men of all candidate-qualities feel qualified to run (even if they are not),[81] we should indeed see voter bias, just the other way. The rates of voting for women as candidates should be higher than the rates of voting for men, but they are not. Mere equality of voting rates for both types of candidates, then, is not really evidence of a lack of voter discrimination; indeed, it may be the opposite.

Biases continue to exist, in other words, but perceptions of discrimination among the sample may overestimate the extent of these biases. Or maybe not, if you believe (and some of the research is quite convincing on this point) that "second generation" discrimination is still pretty powerful. And more important, in the case of political ambition, as researchers have pointed out, perceptions are more powerful than reality.[82] How and why respondents *perceive* gender biases in the acts of running for and/or holding political office—and how such expectations affect their political ambition—is what is most relevant. And the answer is that they perceive a whole lot of bias, and it seems to have quite a large effect.

## Cumulative Effects: Women More Deterred

When added to the perceived costs one might face in running for office, anticipation of discrimination further led women (and especially women of color, whom I will discuss specifically in the next chapter) to see more costs than benefits. Why play a game when the deck is stacked against you, and especially if you do not much like what you may get if you win?

Three related but theoretically distinct mechanisms are thus at work in creating the difference we observe between women's and men's political ambition. The first is that for women, the costs of running for office just seem higher (even before adding in expectations of bias). On average, if we look at the sexes separately on the costs index from chapter 5, we see that men scored .32 and women .36.[83] Women on average saw higher costs, in other words, and the difference is strongly statistically significant.[84] The second mechanism is that women on average saw lower rewards. On the "rewards index," men on average scored .37 and women .32, with the difference again being strongly statistically significant.[85]

The third mechanism is that women as a group, and especially those who had already faced discrimination, expected that as candidates they would face a whole set of costs relating to gender bias. Many expected fairly high levels of bias and double standards, particularly thinking that women would be more likely to be judged by their appearance, that white men would have advantages in most aspects of campaigning, and that Hillary Clinton was treated unfairly in her 2008 run for the Democratic presidential nomination.

Let's add data on that third mechanism to the previous costs-rewards integrated framework of analysis. Expecting to face discrimination as a candidate could be thought of as a cost to running. In line with the way the costs index was constructed, we can give those expecting some discrimination a 1, while those who expect a lot of discrimination get a 2. (This will also change the denominator of the ratio, that calculation of how many points are possible overall, so I will adjust the formula accordingly.) The addition of this new cost to running also affects the overall score we get when we subtract total costs from total rewards, so I will recalculate that score for each person as well.

If we re-map the distribution curves of men's versus women's perceptions of rewards-minus-costs, as in figure 6.8, we see that adding in perceptions of a biased political world exacerbates yet furthers the existing gender split on costs and rewards. These curves still overlap, but not quite as much as before. Now, as figure 6.8 shows, the average of the summary measure (rewards minus costs) falls further behind the 0 line for women. Taking seriously the expectation of gender bias, in other words, makes costs more clearly outweigh rewards for women as a whole.

Figure 6.9 revisits the 2x2 matrix of costs and rewards developed in the previous chapter, this time looking at the distribution of men and women across the four cells. Looking at the distributions of men versus

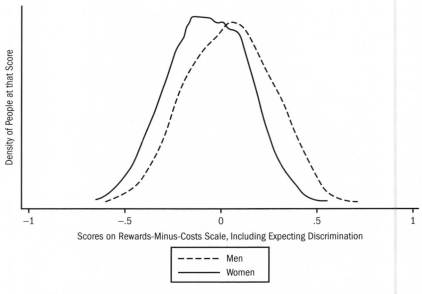

Figure 6.8. Revised Distribution Curves of Rewards-Minus-Costs Index Scores, by Sex. Source: LPS-PAS, Survey Sample. N = 764.

Figure 6.9. 2x2 Matrix: Costs Dummy versus Rewards Dummy, by Sex. Source: LPS-PAS, Survey Sample. N = 763. Notes: "Low" here signifies falling below the sample mean for that index. "High" signifies above the sample mean. Chart gives distribution of women versus men in each cell.

women in each cell of the matrix in figure 6.9 is instructive. Women are most plentiful in the two low-rewards boxes and are least likely to be in the box of those seeing high rewards but low costs.

## Summary

The men and women in this elite sample should be, and in many ways are, more alike than they are different. However, certain items show very strong differences between men and women, and many of these relate to running for public office. From the evidence presented here, it appears that women in general are less likely than men to think that politics is of use in solving the problems they care about—and this correlates strongly with political ambition.[86] Also, women have been far more likely than men to have experienced discrimination and are much more likely to expect to face it in the electoral arena, should they run. Women, more than men, see running as a game that is stacked against them.

Differing perceptions of the usefulness of politics by sex and differing experiences with discrimination both seem extremely related to the disparate levels of political ambition between men and women. Even before we add the expectation of discrimination as a cost, women saw higher costs and lower rewards to candidacy than did men. However, the vehemence with which interview respondents spoke about bias in the electoral arena and the high numbers of the survey sample expressing concerns about such biases together suggest that such expectations should indeed be considered as part of a rational cost-benefit analysis. When they are added to the rewards-minus-costs index, women as a whole fall far below the zero-line. And women, despite being fully half of the sample, were only 38 percent of the people in "high rewards, low costs" box of the 2x2 matrix. Instead, they were disproportionally clumped in the "low rewards" boxes (see figure 6.8).

As studies have found, certain personality characteristics, such as confidence, differ across men and women as groups. Such characteristics may partially account for women's relative reluctance to run for office.[87] But the larger story is that almost everyone in the sample saw costs to running for and holding office, and only a narrow slice saw compensating rewards. For women as a group compared with men as a group, the costs just seem higher and the rewards seem lower. On the other hand, those who did have high political ambition—both women and men—were very likely to see politics as useful in solving important problems. Future research should investigate this connection more thoroughly, and the origins of positive perceptions of politics more generally.

# 7

# Not Our Kind of Game

## *Women of Color and the Impact of High Costs and Low Rewards*

I think it's a shame that I would feel personally like there's just no way that world [electoral politics] would be open to me right now, but I know that's how I feel.
—Tomo, female Asian American student, Harvard Law School

It is no secret that wealthy white men dominate U.S. politics, even though they are a minority of the country's population. This continued dominance derives from a long history of exclusions, by key characteristics (class, race, and sex). The discrimination was not just social but legal; it took state- and eventually national-level constitutional amendments to get the right to vote (and therefore count in politics) for, first, non–property-owning white men, then black men, then women. Formal political inclusion, however, did not lead automatically to full representation, and the categories of people who had been excluded—women, racial minorities, and poorer whites—are still under-represented in officeholding.[1]

One common trope is that these representational differences will simply fade over time, as women and minorities accrue more of the educational and professional qualifications that underpin political careers. But this easy expectation of future political equality is belied by the numbers: women are getting more education than men now, and have been for a while, but their numbers in elective office are stagnating. Women of color get more education than their male minority counterparts but have not seen a corresponding increase in political power. And, for racial minorities in general (who on the whole have less access to both wealth and income than whites), as well as poorer whites, the role of resources is growing more rather than less important in U.S. politics.

Time alone is not a panacea to the problem of political under-representation. Instead, what is needed is greater diversification of the candidate pool, by multiple identity factors. The 2012 pool, for instance, as measured in the first-ever National Candidate Survey, was 72 percent male and 81 percent white, with an average income of $96,000.[2] Our candidates right now, in other words, look a whole lot like our elected officials.

What, then, are the prospects for greater diversity, by race as well as by gender, of the candidate pool in the future? Not great, I predict, given the data I will present in this chapter—and especially for women of color, who stand out as the subgroup most deterred from the idea of running, unless we can change a lot of their minds about what politics and its potential can be. On the other hand, women of color are the most community-minded of the subgroups; my hypothesis, from the data I present in this chapter, is that far more women of color could and would run if they could see politics as rewarding.[3]

Again, the analysis I present does not find such candidate deterrence irrational. Instead, women of color simply see higher costs and lower rewards than anyone else and also perceive additional costs that further skew their cost-benefit analyses. Men of color, on the other hand—at least in this elite sample—were not so deterred. Largely this appears to be because of differing perceptions of rewards, with the men of color being the group most likely to see rewards from politics, while women of color saw the fewest. And while all racial minority subgroups in the sample were very likely to anticipate discrimination, the women of color carried the additional weight of expecting sex as well as race bias.

## Equal Ambition but Unequal Political Ambition, by Race and Sex

Figure 6.1 showed unequal political ambition by gender. Figure 7.1 replicates this analysis, adding race as well as gender. As the figure demonstrates, and as we would expect given the elite nature of this sample, the large majority (85 percent or more) of every race–gender subgroup said they were ambitious or very ambitious. There were no significant differences in describing oneself as ambitious between whites versus nonwhites.[4] But again, this general ambition did not easily translate to political ambition and does not show a consistent effect of being in

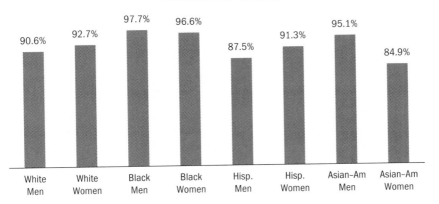

**Describes self as "ambitious"**

90.6% White Men, 92.7% White Women, 97.7% Black Men, 96.6% Black Women, 87.5% Hisp. Men, 91.3% Hisp. Women, 95.1% Asian-Am Men, 84.9% Asian-Am Women

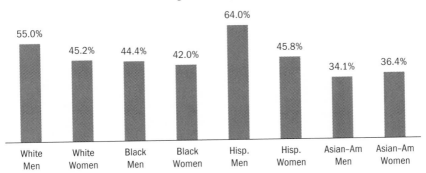

**Has thought of running, in passing**

55.0% White Men, 45.2% White Women, 44.4% Black Men, 42.0% Black Women, 64.0% Hisp. Men, 45.8% Hisp. Women, 34.1% Asian-Am Men, 36.4% Asian-Am Women

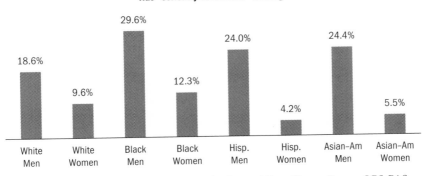

**Has "seriously considered" running**

18.6% White Men, 9.6% White Women, 29.6% Black Men, 12.3% Black Women, 24.0% Hisp. Men, 4.2% Hisp. Women, 24.4% Asian-Am Men, 5.5% Asian-Am Women

Figure 7.1. Ambition and Political Ambition, by Sex and Race Group. Source: LPS-PAS, Survey Sample. Ns by race/ethnicity = 435 white, 137 black, 74 Hispanic, 97 Asian American. Note that the black and Hispanic male samples have relatively low Ns, making the variability higher within these groups.

one racial group. The differences are more about gender than race, but the charts in this figure now shows that even within the group "women," there are some substantive differences in having thought seriously about running for office.

The students are well matched in terms of demographics and education, although the family incomes of black men as a subgroup were significantly lower than those of other students. Again, this sample selection design does not erase class differences across racial groups, but as much as possible it minimizes them. In regression analyses, class measures like parental education levels and family income when the student was about sixteen consistently show no effects on political ambition, and race by itself was never significantly related to one's wanting or not wanting to run for office. Nor were the individual racial groups (black, Hispanic, Asian American) significant predictors of either high or low political ambition when tested separately. The race–gender differences displayed in figure 7.1 thus require explanation beyond income or education, or even nonwhite race itself.

Based on the race–gender analyses I will present in this chapter, I argue a series of complex propositions. These come directly from the data I collected but tap into far longer-standing debates about race and gender and how they intersect.[5] First, in certain ways gender appears to play a far larger role than race, at least for nonwhite women. On many of the variables relating to political ambition, women look more alike—no matter their race—than they look like men of their individual racial groups. But for certain other questions, situations, or contexts, particularly relating to economics and faith in the political system, race may trump gender. And then sometimes, as with thinking about whether politics can solve important problems, race and gender appear to "stack up," making women of color look different from both white women and nonwhite men.

Altogether, if we add up the perceived costs and benefits using the tools and framework established in previous chapters, even before looking at what additional costs students of color might see when contemplating candidates, women of color stand out as the most deterred subgroup. When we add in additional costs and take seriously the differences in perceptions in rewards, women of color (especially black and Hispanic women, but also Asian American women, for some different reasons) are especially deterred from the idea of candidacies. With women and people of color already under-represented in U.S. politics, this finding does not bode well for a more diverse cadre of future candidates.

## Men of Color and Political Ambition

One of the most interesting differences is that men of color, collectively, seem more rather than less interested in possibly running for office. They are certainly more politically ambitious than their female minority counterparts and show somewhat more political ambition (in the sense of their having thought seriously of running for office) than white men.[6]

This could possibly be an "Obama effect," wherein the election of our country's first black president shifted the perceptions of young men of color about the costs and benefits of politics. Unfortunately, all data for the LPS-PAS were collected post-2008, so I have no way of testing for such an effect.[7] It could also be because much of what we know about race is really about race-plus-class, as these factors—while theoretically distinct—are deeply intertwined in people's lived experiences. This high political ambition, then, may not be true of all young men of color but may have a distinct class bias, as even the lower-income black, Hispanic, and Asian American men in my sample were still students at elite graduate schools. Relatedly, it may be, as other work has suggested, that extremely high-SES people of color like those in my sample have had different experiences of race from those of their counterparts in the general population.[8]

In interviews, both of these possible explanations—an "Obama effect" and an "elite effect"—find support, although more for the men than the women of color. In broad, open-ended questions about the role of their race and gender in their path through life, the men of color (especially the Asian Americans and Hispanics) mostly told me they had not felt discrimination to be a problem in their lives. The black men were more likely to say they thought they had been treated differently but did not feel that the different treatment had deeply affected their lives. On the whole, the men of color in the sample seemed fairly positive about politics and government, and even if they expected to face some differential treatment, that expectation did not seem to deter them much. As the data will show, this was in stark contrast to the experiences, expectations, and political ambition expressed by the women in these racial minority groups.

As noted previously, although countless studies have examined the political participation of racial subgroups in American politics, only a few have looked specifically at race and candidate ambition.[9] Those few had suggested to me that race, and its attendant socialization and ongoing differential treatment, might operate in much the same way as gender seems to, in the more extensive literature on women and political ambition—as a depressant, in other words. But this appears to be the case only for the women of color—the African American, Hispanic, and Asian American men were not deterred any more than the white men were, and they were perhaps even more politically ambitious.

In the rest of this chapter, I turn to women of color, trying to explain why their political ambition is lower than that of both their white female and their nonwhite male counterparts. The explanation is an extension of the gender-linked candidate-deterrence effects argument described in the previous chapter. For black, Hispanic, and Asian American women, the costs of politics seem higher and the rewards lower than for white women and men of all races. Notably, the reasons for such deterrence appear to differ across subgroups of women of color, which this chapter will also investigate.

"Women of color" is a useful category at times, but at other times we must disaggregate that group. Because with each further axis of identity we need to further divide the data, we have fewer and fewer respondents in both the survey and interview samples. This lessens our ability to reach statistically significant conclusions but gives us more particularity about these complicated students and the ways in which their identities overlap and intersect. If we do find statistically significant results even in these small samples, we can assume they are meaningful—and if we see large differences, we can flag them as interesting even if they do not reach conventional levels of statistical significance. And again, I will do my best to illustrate the statistical trends with some of the more powerful language from the interviews.

## Costs Seem Higher

Table 7.1 shows the individual cost-factors discussed previously, but now looking only at female respondents, and at the differences between white women versus women of color. Generally, all women agreed that nearly all of these costs mattered to some degree; the similarities in table 7.1 are in many ways more important than the differences. As noted earlier in this chapter, the largest differences in my sample are by sex rather than race; these costs as a whole turned off women far more than men. But a sex-plus-race lens still turns up some significant differences among women, as the table shows.

The most noticeable race gaps in table 7.1 are about economics; women of color are far more likely to think that they will need to contribute financially to their families of origin (parents, siblings, etc.) in the future, and these expectations weigh more heavily on them in choosing a career than seems to be true for white women.[10] As this is the most significant difference, I will explore it in more depth shortly.

Beyond economics, some of the largest differences have to do with perceptions of corruption or immoral behavior among politicians. Women of color, for instance, were significantly more likely than white women to think that politics corrupts good people into doing bad things.[11] When we dig further into this data by racial subgroup, we find that the means did not differ meaningfully for black, Hispanic, and Asian American women but were substantially higher for white women compared with any of these groups. Relatedly, women of color collectively were more likely than white women to think that politicians "often lie" and "often act immorally."[12] The women of color also appeared to be more concerned by the idea of privacy invasion, both in the sense of being more likely to run "if I had fewer skeletons in my closet" and being more likely to run if it "would not interfere with my family's privacy."[13] This may also relate to women of color's somewhat greater concern about "dealing with the media."[14]

An additional potential cost arose in my quantitative analysis, one that appears to connect both to sex and to sex-plus-race. This is the idea of "authenticity," which came up in the "personality self-assessments" section of the survey and also in my "costs coding" of the interview data. The survey asked respondents how well a set of terms described

TABLE 7.1. Costs Variable Means and Overall Index for Women, by Race (with Each Cost Variable Constrained to a Binary)

| Perceived Cost | Mean for White Women (percent) | Mean for Women of Color (percent) |
|---|---|---|
| It is important to me that I can "[Be] sure of always having a relatively well-paying job" | 89.1 | 92.5 |
| I would be more likely to run if "It would not interfere with [my] family's privacy" | 40.5* | 43.8 |
| I would be more likely to run if "Campaigns were fully publicly financed, so [I] would not have to raise money for [my] campaign" | 51.5 | 55.9 |
| I would feel negative about "Calling people to ask for donations" | 79.4* | 68.0 |
| I "Hate to lose at anything" | 55.7 | 56.5 |
| I "Avoid conflict whenever possible" | 49.0* | 59.5 |
| The consideration of being expected to contribute financially to my family of origin is "very or somewhat important to [my] choice of future job(s)" | 38.2*** | 67.6 |
| I "will be expected to contribute financially to [my] parents, siblings, or other relatives in the future" to a large or moderate extent | 37.5*** | 66.2 |
| I would feel negative about "Dealing with the media" | 45.4* | 49.9 |
| I would feel negative about "Facing hostile questions" | 47.8 | 54.4 |
| I am not "Thick-skinned" and I believe "It takes a thick skin to survive in politics" | 48.6 | 48.0 |
| "In today's media environment, you'd have to be crazy to run for office" | 44.6** | 33.9 |
| I would feel negative about "Dealing with party officials" | 29.6 | 37.6 |
| I am not "Willing to take risks" | 41.0 | 33.2 |
| I believe that politicians often "lie" | 26.1** | 34.4 |
| I do not fit into either major political party | 26.0 | 27.2 |
| I would feel negative about "Going door-to-door to meet constituents" | 33.1 | 24.5 |
| I believe politics "corrupts even good people into doing bad things" | 35.0*** | 49.6 |
| I would feel negative about "Making public speeches" | 21.9* | 29.3 |
| I think politicians often "Act immorally" | 10.5** | 18.4 |
| I would be more likely to run if "[I] had fewer skeletons in [my] closet" | 6.0* | 12.2 |
| **Overall Costs Index Score** | **.346*** | **.374** |

Source: LPS-PAS, Survey Sample; N = 389
Race Difference Significance, within women as a group: $* p < .1, ** p < .05, *** p < .01$

them, one of which terms was *authentic/sincere*. If we look only at the top-most category ("very well"), we see a large and statistically significant gender difference, with 70.0 percent of women and 54.0 percent of men saying the term *authentic/sincere* describes them very well.[15] There is a further difference in means by race among women, with 67.0 percent of white women and 73.1 percent of women of color saying the term describes them very well, although the difference is not statistically significant. This idea (being authentic) came up in fully one-third of the interviews as well, in all cases as a "cost" to a life in politics; as Sting sings, "You could say I'd lost my belief in our politicians; they all seem like game show hosts to me."[16]

Finally, women of color were also more somewhat more likely than white women to say that they prefer to avoid conflict, which is a factor predicting lower political ambition. The desire to avoid conflict could come from any number of factors, but some works suggest it may be shaped, at least in part, by one's race and gender.[17] In other words, in saying that they avoid conflict whenever possible, these women of color may be expressing internalized social gender and race roles about who is allowed to express strong opinions and argue strenuously rather than expressing some innate, unchanging personality aspect. Either way, however, the desire to avoid conflict seems notably related to political ambition, both in a correlational test (the absolute value of the correlation coefficient is low, at 0.07, but p = .04) and in an ordered logistic regression controlling for race and gender (p < .07).

White women, on the other hand, were significantly more likely than women of color to agree with the statement "In today's media environment, you'd have to be crazy to run for office." Among white women, 42.6 percent agreed or strongly agreed, compared with almost a third (31.2 percent) of women of color. White women were also somewhat more likely to be bothered by the idea of calling people up to ask for donations (mean of 79.2 percent among white women versus 71.0 percent among women of color).[18] For both of these, though, it is fair to say that a substantial portion of all women were bothered by these things, with white women being a little more concerned.

As an example of how these concerns are arrayed in the minds of individuals, consider the words of Sofia, a Hispanic female student also at Harvard Law, who thought that the political system would be constraining, and possibly corrupting. She noted, on running for and holding office: "[It is] good people with ideals usually that do it, but also people with really big egos. . . . Then also there's something about the process itself, for better or for worse, where, no matter how you go into it, once you're in the system, you have to play by certain rules, and they're not necessarily aligned with those ideals, or like the original reasons you went in." Sofia's words here express the sentiments that seem to underlie some of the major concerns that young people, especially women, and especially women of color, have about life in politics. In her mind, many of these concerns are stacked up rather than separate. You might go on for good reasons ("ideals," "original reasons"), but those can get lost when you have to "play by certain rules." She went on:

> There's so much, what's it called, the tabbing your special interest money, like I'll vote for your thing if you vote for my thing, where I get this much money for my community and it's all this game, and also how much they have to spend fundraising and campaigning, and how that's naturally going to lead to groups with money being able to influence what happens. It's just, like, there's not really clear—there's no real way to fix that, and it's very few people who can try to play against that and stay in office for long. I mean, you can't without fundraising at all.

Politics, to her mind, is deeply entwined with fundraising and therefore special-interest money and therefore the need to make deals that might compromise morality, authenticity, or other personality features important to her and those like her. As she spoke, it was as if she were feeding on her own negative impressions, sometimes contradicting herself by bringing in something positive, but ultimately ending on a negative note. It is not pure negativity but deep ambivalence that she seems to feel. One could, after all, get "money for my community" through this process, but it kind of feels like a rather dirty "game," and one in which the deck is rigged from the start.

## Financial Opportunity Cost Matters More for Women of Color

The economic costs involved in candidacy deserve special mention, as on this set of cost variables, white students looked quite different from

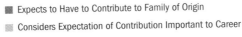

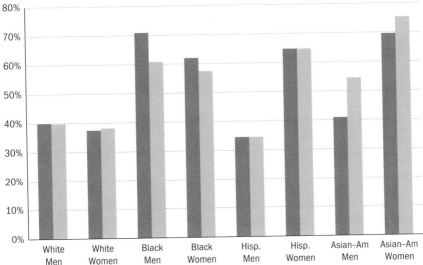

Figure 7.2. The Economic Costs of Running, by Race and Sex. Source: LPS-PAS, Survey Sample. Ns by race/ethnicity, on these questions=291 white, 129 black, 51 Hispanic, 67 Asian American. Note that the black and Hispanic male samples have relatively low Ns, making the variability higher within these groups.

those of color. In my data, these were some of those rare questions where one's race seemed to matter far more than one's sex. Some of the sex differences within racial groups (for Hispanic women versus men, and for Asian American women versus men) are statistically significant, but the larger story is that students of color in general looked different from white students on these questions.[19]

Overall, as figure 7.2 shows, the subgroups most affected by the opportunity cost of a forgone private-sector salary were black men and women, Hispanic women, and Asian American women. Particularly, the Asian women and the black men were significantly more likely to care about contributing to relatives in the future, when compared with all other survey respondents, with Hispanic women also coming close to statistical significance on this comparison.[20] In looking at the data more broadly, we see that people of color as a group attached far more importance than whites to the expectation of future financial contributions to relatives and said this would be important or very important to their choice of careers.[21] On average, fewer than half of whites (39.5 percent) but more than half of all people of color (62.9 percent) say they will be expected to contribute, and that such an expectation is important to their choice of future careers/jobs (40.3 percent for whites versus 60.9 percent for nonwhite students).[22] Given the relatively low pay of elective office, these data suggest that it is worth considering the opportunity cost of high salaries as an additional cost that disproportionately affects the students of color in the sample and, in some race groups, the women more than the men.[23]

## Potential Rewards from Politics Seem Lower

Looking at table 7.2, on perceived rewards, also shows some interesting and important differences, although again these are mostly smaller than the male–female disparities from chapter 6.

Some of the largest differences between white women and women of color have to do with differing perceptions of rewards about solving problems, helping communities, and interacting with people. Compared with white women, women of color were significantly less likely to think that politics can "solve important problems," and less likely to think that politicians often "work for the public good."[24] On the other hand, they were significantly more likely than white women to say they would run if they thought their doing so could "help their community" and were far more positive about the prospect of "going door-to-door to meet constituents." Finally, they were somewhat more likely to prize "becoming famous" as a goal in life. (Feeling useful, as a reward, seemed important to women as a whole, but more important to women of color, although because this was asked only in the final wave, there was a very low sample answering this question and the difference was not statistically significant. Conversely, far more women of color than white women said they would be more likely to run if doing so would help them get a "better job" in the future, but again, this was in the final wave of the survey and had a low sample size, and the difference was not significant statistically.)

Of these factors, perceptions about politics' not solving problems are the most critically related to political ambition; here, women of

TABLE 7.2. Rewards Variable Means and Overall Index for Women, by Race

| Perceived Reward | Mean for White Women (percent) | Mean for Women of Color (percent) |
|---|---|---|
| Considers self "Good at being in charge" | 88.8 | 88.4 |
| Would feel positively about "Being a part of history" as a candidate^ | 75.0 | 86.5 |
| Considers "Feeling useful, doing something good in the world" an important life goal^ | 75.0 | 91.9 |
| Considers self "A good public speaker" | 73.1 | 62.7 |
| Would be more likely to run if "Cared about an issue and knew [I] could make a difference if [I were] in office" | 60.7 | 63.1 |
| Would feel positively about "Going door-to-door to meet constituents" | 47.1** | 58.6 |
| Would be more likely to run if thought "Could help [my] community" | 51.6** | 56.3 |
| Would be more likely to run if thought "It would help [me] get a better job later"^ | 25.0 | 56.9 |
| Thinks "The problems I most care about can be solved through politics" | 33.4** | 24.8 |
| Considers self "Very competitive"^ | 25.0 | 24.6 |
| Would feel positively about "Attending fundraising functions" | 32.0 | 37.1 |
| Has strong opinions on policy issues | 28.5 | 27.6 |
| Believes one person can "make a difference in politics" | 20.6 | 22.6 |
| Thinks politicians often "work for the public good" | 24.6* | 18.0 |
| Would be "very likely" to interrupt professor in a class | 14.9 | 13.2 |
| Thinks politicians often "help people with their problems" | 13.9 | 13.4 |
| Considers becoming "famous" an important life goal | 6.2* | 12.4 |
| **Overall Rewards Index Score** | **.319** | **.309** |

Source: LPS-PAS, Survey Sample; N = 389 (for most questions)
Race Difference Significance: * *p<.1,* ** *p<.05,* *** *p<.01*
^ These questions have a low n (around 47 responses each), as respondents were asked these only in the final survey wave. So even if there are large differences in means, they are not statistically significant.

color's lower levels of agreement that "politics can solve the problems I most care about" could have a large impact on their political ambition. Thinking that politics solves problems (or not) is one of the most important single predictors I found in this study of high versus low political ambition, second only to one's having been asked to run. In correlational tests, believing that politics solves problems is strongly related to all forms of political ambition, including having thought about running, having thought seriously about running, wanting to run for higher versus lower office, and wanting to hold office if one didn't have to run.[25] In regression analyses predicting political ambition, the "solves" variable is strongly significant even when controlling for school, program, race, gender, family income, and having been asked to run.[26]

Looking at this question of whether politics "solves important problems" by race as well as sex is therefore critical. As figure 7.3 shows, white, black, and Hispanic women are less likely than their male counterparts to see politics as useful in solving important problems. The difference between Asian American men and women was not statistically significant but was 10 percentage points, suggesting that this difference too may have been significant with a larger sample. Additional tests, not shown in the figure, show that women of color as a group (aggregating black, Hispanic, and Asian American women) were less likely than white women to believe that politics solves problems.[27] In particular, black women as a group were significantly less likely to think that politics solves important problems, compared with all other female respondents.[28]

Consider the words of Maya, a black female Harvard Law student, in response to my question about whether politics can solve problems. She said, "I initially thought that, but I don't think so any more. I don't feel like the politicians have the power to get things through, nor do they have the knowledge to make substantive changes and there are just so many things fighting against them." Politicians, in her view, may have been trying hard but lacked both knowledge and power, meaning that she (and, apparently, other black women as a whole) was the least likely to see politics as problem solving. Not only did women of color see the highest costs, in other words, but they also saw the lowest rewards from holding office.

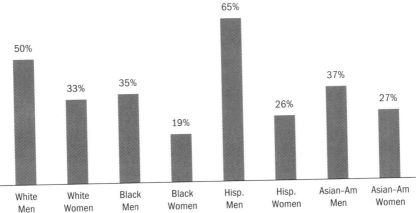

Figure 7.3. Believe Politics Can Solve Important Problems (Averages), by Race and Sex. Source: LPS-PAS, Survey Sample. Ns by race/ethnicity = 435 white, 137 black, 74 Hispanic, 97 Asian American. Note that the black and Hispanic male samples have relatively low Ns, making the variability higher within these groups.

## Women of Color and Levels of Office

Chapters 4 and 6 both looked at interest in running for office at different levels, finding that men overall showed high levels of interest in multiple types and levels of office, while women were more likely to prefer local and legislative offices. This is even more true for women of color as compared with men of color, as figure 7.4 shows. Men, whether white or not, look similar to one another and generally at least leave open the possibility of running for many of these types of offices. And just about everyone clumps together in terms of interest in school board, where there are no significant race or gender differences. Starting with city council, however, the men begin to pull away, showing more interest in every office north of school board, up to and including president (for which very few women, no matter their race, wanted to run). And for some of these offices/levels, women of color show somewhat less interest than white women, although the individual differences are not statistically significant. Looked at another way, women of color made up a disproportionate share (one-third) of the "refusers" category, those people who say they would never want to run for any of the listed offices, while being only a quarter of the sample as a whole.

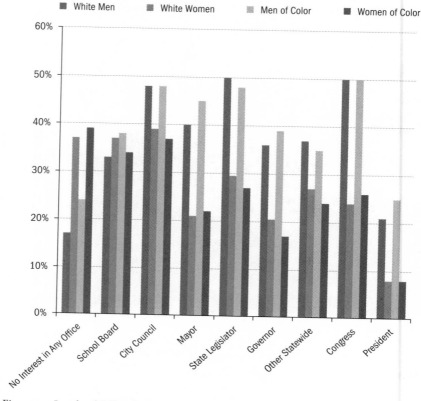

Figure 7.4. Levels of Office, by Race and Sex. Source: LPS-PAS, N = 764

## Where Are the Women of Color in the 2x2 Costs-Rewards Matrix?

Figure 7.5 presents again the 2x2 matrix of high-versus-low costs against high-versus-low rewards, now looking only at women of color. The figure gives the proportion of women of color as a group that ended up in each cell of the matrix, when costs and rewards were aggregated in the "costs" and "rewards" scales, and those scales were split at their means to produce this 2x2 matrix. The plurality of women of color is concentrated in the "high costs, low rewards" cell of the matrix—the cell most negatively correlated with political ambition. Few women of color (less than a quarter of the sample) fall into either of the two "high rewards" cells.

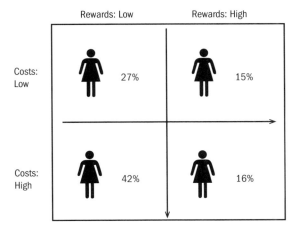

Figure 7.5. 2x2 Matrix: Costs Dummy versus Rewards Dummy, by Women of Color. Source: LPS-PAS, Survey Sample. N = 186 women of color. Note: "Low" here means below the sample mean for that index. "High" means above the sample mean. Chart gives the proportion of women of color in each cell.

And the smallest segment of women of color (15 percent) falls into the "high rewards, low costs" cell, from which we would expect the most future candidates. Before we even begin to look at expectations of discrimination, then, women of color were more likely to see costs and less likely to see rewards from the prospect of candidacy. But wait—it gets worse.

## Adding in a New Cost: Anticipating Discrimination Based on Race

Scholarship on race and racism by bell hooks, W. E. B. Du Bois, Michael Dawson, Audre Lorde, Richard Wright, and others describes a pernicious effect of racism: beyond its initial pain, it seems to teach individuals to expect further discrimination in the future. Consider the lessons Wright learned in "how to live as a Negro" in the Jim Crow South, foremost among them that he "must never again attempt to exceed my boundaries. When you are working for white folks . . . , you got to 'stay in your place' if you want to keep working."[29] He said he learned his "Jim Crow lessons" well: "The morning I applied I stood straight and neat before the boss, answering all his questions with sharp yessirs and nosirs.

I was very careful to pronounce my *sirs* distinctly, in order that he might know that I was polite, that I knew where I was, and that I knew he was a *white* man. I wanted that job badly."[30]

As Wright notes, people often learn to structure their lives so as to avoid having to experience this kind of pain; initial acts of racism, then, have ripple effects that persist far into the future.

Similarly, while attending Harvard for graduate school in the late 1880s, Du Bois deliberately avoided social interactions with his white colleagues, preferring instead to spend his nonclass time with non-Harvard black friends in Boston. Of this time, he wrote:

> I was happy at Harvard, but for unusual reasons. One of these was my acceptance of racial segregation. Had I gone from Great Barrington High School [in Massachusetts] directly to Harvard [rather than spending time in the South first], I would have sought companionship with my white fellows and been disappointed and embittered by a discovery of social limitations to which I had not been used. But I came by way of Fisk and the South and there I had accepted color caste and embraced eagerly the companionship of those of my own color.... In general, I asked nothing of Harvard but the tutelage of the teachers and the freedom of the laboratory and library. I was quite voluntarily and willingly outside its social life.[31]

The life experiences of the elite law and policy students in the LPS-PAS sample in the late twentieth and early twenty-first centuries were certainly very different from those of Wright (early twentieth century) or Du Bois (late nineteenth). More modern thinkers on race relations, however, suggest that at least vestiges of America's troubled history with race persist, especially for blacks in the United States. Beverly Tatum suggests self-protective self-segregation as a primary answer for a question that remains relevant in middle and high schools across the country in which black students are a minority: "[W]hy are all the black kids sitting together in [the] cafeteria?"[32] Tatum's answer, in short, is the greater ease and comfort of not having to face race-based assumptions, stereotypes, or differential treatment. Such avoidance of situations where racism could arise fits in well with hooks's understanding of many black people as suffering from a kind of "racialized post-traumatic stress disorder."[33]

For instance, two black women studying at Harvard Law, interviewed separately, used the same phrase to describe a shared experience. Both said they felt a constant need to prove themselves and used the expression "weight on your shoulders." Tamika said she felt more comfortable around other black people, explaining, with real pain, "It's kind of hard. I feel like even as a woman too I can sort of let my guard down and be who I actually am when I'm with a group of black people, so I don't know. It definitely changes it. I feel like I have to put on less of a front and sort of be 'I'm at Harvard Law School, I'm Tamika Jackson, I'm going to conquer the world.' I can just be myself."

Invoking the same idea in a much later interview, Maya said:

> I've always had this . . . I don't know if it is self-imposed or imposed from life circumstances, where we kind of represent the race, or you represent black women. What you do represents the abilities of other black people. It is a burden. I have to show them I got where I am through merit, being genuinely intelligent and capable and a lot of the stereotypes you see are not true. It feels like I'm carrying things on my shoulders. I don't know if that's self-imposed or because we do tend to be representative for a lot of people who haven't interacted with black people on a regular basis or grown up around a lot of us, or whatever it may be.

This experience was not true for all or even most of the black students I interviewed—or, if it was, they did not tell me about it. Most, especially the men, said it didn't matter, or didn't matter much. For some, this was not because they didn't feel race-related pressures but because they had already made some decision about how to think about and handle such expectations or differential treatment. Jasmine did not share Tamika's distress, even if race (and the expectations associated with it) remained a part of her life. In answer to my question about expecting people to treat her differently, she explained:

> Oh, absolutely [laughs]. Absolutely. I mean I'm not naïve to that fact. I certainly don't try to find a racial incident or a gender incident in every interaction I have with people. Are there times though when I feel there could be a racial or gender incident? Absolutely. It's like the antenna is up enough so that if something happens it's like wait a minute; but it's not up

so much that I'm actually seeking something if the [radio] station is clear. But I absolutely feel that out in the world I will deal with people who have stereotypes about people of color or women.

No one likes playing a game that is rigged against them. People who feel they may face a negative and potentially painful experience like discrimination may logically avoid putting themselves in that situation, unless they really think it is worth their while. This does not have to be limited to race or gender (although those came up most often in the data)—it could be discrimination based on religion, language, sexual orientation, or any other number of characteristics. Straight, Christian, cisgender[34] white men in this country generally have the great advantage of not having to think of themselves as being any of these things (which is often referred to as "white privilege," "male privilege," "straight privilege," and so on).[35]

Meanwhile, people outside this narrow "norm" are often very aware of their difference(s). In terms of race, Du Bois famously wrote of "double consciousness," wherein blacks in America are constantly forced to see themselves as white people see them. This awareness can factor into their anticipation and decision-making about all kinds of behaviors, politics included.[36] At the extreme, this may take the form of black mothers in the Jim Crow–era South teaching their children to fear and kowtow to whites so as to avoid potentially life-threatening conflicts.[37] In a less severe and more recent context, the black law students I interviewed spoke candidly of their constant awareness of their own race and of the ways in which race often affected how they behaved.[38]

Such perceptions are fully rational; to put it in the language of game theory, if one learns something from a previous game, such as discrimination on the basis of race, then one will logically expect to face the same thing in future games. As Jasmine put it, in response to another question: "This isn't my first time on the merry-go-round; this is my life." She did not appear deeply upset as she said this; racism was simply a fact of life, around which she had learned to navigate.

But if the biases of the political world are just a reality one must face, this may at least in part have some further deterrence effects for those who already feel a little different, a little (or a lot) outside the norm.[39] Who wants to play a game in which the deck is stacked against you?

Whether entirely accurate or exaggerated, perceptions of bias in the political world may have independent effects on certain types of would-be candidates, and these may come into operation long before someone makes a conscious decision not to run. Expectations of discrimination, by race as well as gender, are thus another potential "cost" to which we should be sensitive in analyzing rational candidate deterrence.

The survey data support the dual suggestions from the interviews. First, expectations of discrimination were more prevalent among and seemed more important to black and Hispanic women than to white or Asian American women. Second, survey data confirm that such expectations matter far more for some black and Hispanic women than for others. Some individuals appeared to care deeply about the race and gender biases they expected to encounter should they become candidates. Others, like Jasmine, may have believed they would face discrimination, but they didn't let that deter them. Jasmine, for instance, had her "racial antenna" up but also wanted to run for office. For individuals like her, high perceptions of the rewards of politics may help overcome negative expectations of bias. As a group, though, women of color already showed the strongest candidate-deterrence effects, as in seeing the highest costs but the lowest rewards. Adding in expectations of both sex and race discrimination further exacerbated the deterrence.

Figure 7.6 gives the means for the various race–gender subgroups on the index (developed in the previous chapter) testing for expectations of political discrimination. As the figure shows, high proportions of all race–gender subgroups seem to expect politics to be a discriminatory environment, by race as well as gender—but again, the effects are stronger for women than for men, and strongest for women of color. White women, black women, Hispanic women, and Asian American women all expect significantly more race and gender discrimination in politics than their male counterparts. And women of color as a group expect significantly more bias than white women.[40] Black women were particularly likely to expect bias by both race and gender.

The interview evidence can help shed some light on how perceptions and expectations of both race and sex bias might manifest. I remember in particular talking to Dominique, a black female Harvard Law student with ethnic roots in the Caribbean. She was particularly aware of not only her skin color and its difference from the white norm in politics

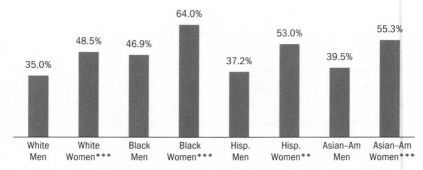

Figure 7.6. Means of Expecting Discrimination, by Race and Sex. Source: LPS-PAS, Survey Sample. N = 764. Sex Difference Significance within Racial Groups: * $p < .1$, ** $p < .05$, *** $p < .01$.

but also other race-linked body features like weight, curves, and kinky hair.[41] She explained, "In terms of the weight and appearance . . . [I] realized that society expects women, and thus female politicians, to look a certain way. Society expects them to be skinny, have straight hair, not curly, and generally do not have curves. Even the minority female politicians, or minority female political figures, generally do not have curves."

Sofia, a Latina originally from Washington Heights in New York City, spoke about being a major feminist (she was very active in campus women's groups) but also part of the Hispanic law students association. Awareness of multiplicity of identities (not just female and Hispanic, but national origin divisions among Latinos like Puerto Ricans versus Dominicans versus Mexicans, etc.) made her sensitive to the expectations of her not just as a woman but as a Latina. She said, "[A]s Latinos, we're all conscious of that we're all connected, but we're all really different. So it's very strange, at least in the way it's played out in the Hispanic group here. So when I'm here with a Hispanic group, I feel like I'm always trying to prove that I'm enough of a Hispanic person to be in that group and talking for that group, and there's more of a sensitivity to not thinking that you're speaking for everyone at the table." Sofia was particularly concerned about eventually giving back to her original community. The issue of affirmative action had recently come up in one of her law classes, and she recalled for me a conversation she had had with a friend about how easy it would be for someone like her to basically become white— just, as she put it, "tanner."

[We] were talking after class, and he was like, "Sometimes I think that affirmative action is this brilliant white power plan because you take the best people and you take them out of your communities and you make them part of white community." Like, you take people like me out of Washington Heights and maybe I'll go back, but I'll have to consciously think, "I'm going to have to go back to Washington Heights and make it better." Yeah, because I could really easily just go to the East Side and live there. You know, I just happen to be a tanner person. But, in all other respects, I'm into and hip with white culture and elitism. It is kind of brilliant—he was making fun of me because my fiancé's last name is Cole, so I'll be Sofia Cole. He was like, "You, you're the perfect example!" I was like, "I guess it is kind of true." It is difficult. I guess that's how it starts and then hopefully enough people give back and you build up. Like, I always like to think that if I ever become mega-rich, I'm going to have scholarships for Hispanic kids, stuff like that.

Sofia seemed pretty determined not to lose her ethnic identity, "difficult" as it was to always be thinking about it. For her, and for most of the nonwhite interviewees I spoke with, both male and female, growing up black, Hispanic, or Asian was an important piece of their sense of selves. It conferred advantages in the sense of confidence in one's identity[42] but also came with this added awareness of the possibility of discrimination. For women who already expected some bias based on sex, this often meant double the expectation.

Interestingly, however, women of different racial groups expected to face different stereotypes, and not all negative. Kim, an Asian American female student at Suffolk Law, noted that people often assume she is good at math (even though, as she said, all she does is "pull out my calculator!"). Even though Kim herself made it clear she never wanted to run for office (she hated public speaking), a presumption of intelligence or particular expertise based on race could in certain contexts be helpful rather than harmful.[43] And again, several interviewees noted that being racially like constituents in a majority–minority area, town, city, or district could be a plus rather than a minus in running. Sofia had noted that even though she was Puerto Rican, she felt that other Hispanics would recognize her as a Latina, which would be a positive. When expecting to face a white electorate, however, generally people of color and women of color especially expected disadvantages by both race and gender.

## Putting It All Together

One last useful tool to look at women of color in comparison both with men of color and with white women is the Rewards-Minus-Costs index, developed in previous chapters. As the data suggest that women of color strongly expect bias, I here use the "Rewards-Minus-Costs" scale to which I have added the "expectation of political discrimination" costs, as described in the previous chapter.

As chapter 6 showed, women as a whole had a distribution curve that was offset from men's distribution curve on this scale, with women seeing in general more costs and fewer of the possible rewards. The curves pull yet further apart if we add race as well as sex to the analysis, as shown in figure 7.7. In the curves shown in the figure, women of color stand out as the race–gender group most deterred, as in seeing the highest costs without seeing compensating rewards from politics.

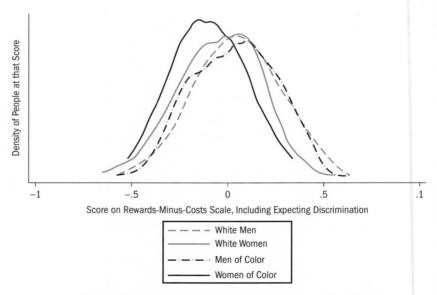

Figure 7.7. Revised Distribution Curves of Rewards-Minus-Costs Index Scores, by Sex and Race. Source: LPS-PAS, Survey Sample. N = 764.

TABLE 7.3. Regression Models on Political Ambition, by Women of Color

| | Model 1 (Ordered Logistic) | Model 2 (Ordered Logistic) | Model 3 (Ordered Logistic) |
|---|---|---|---|
| | Dependent Variable: Three levels: had not thought of running, had thought but not seriously, had thought seriously | (same as in Model 1) | (same as in Model 1) |
| **Independent Variables/Controls** | | | |
| Female | −.707*** | −.437** | −.309 |
| Nonwhite | .297 | .213 | .208 |
| Woman of color | −.574** | −.686** | −.591* |
| In public policy program (versus law) | .383** | .155 | −.023 |
| At either Harvard School (versus Suffolk) | .471** | .209 | .284 |
| Family income at about age 16 | −.053 | −.066 | −.080 |
| Mom's level of ed. | .128 | .111 | .082 |
| Dad's level of ed. | −.097 | −.029 | −.005 |
| Has been asked to run | — | 2.212*** | 2.039*** |
| Expects Discrimination Index | — | — | .049 |
| Rewards-Minus-Costs Index | — | — | 3.505*** |
| Constant | 1.78 | 3.20 | 3.359 |
| N | 728 | 728 | 728 |
| R-Sq | .043 | .169 | .223 |

Source: LPS-PAS, Survey Sample; N = 764
* $p < .1$, ** $p < .05$, *** $p < .01$

To analyze this further, and to see if these results about women of color hold up to regression analyses, I created a series of models. Table 7.3 presents results, putting together as many of the above-discussed elements as possible. To see if there are differences among race–gender subgroups in the operation of certain of the regressor variables, I include in the regressions separate variables for race and gender. Models test the same set of regressor variables, including gender (being female), having been recruited/asked to run in the past (which research finds to be perhaps the most important predictor of political ambition), and my scales of perceived discrimination and rewards-minus-costs.

To ensure there are no lurking SES effects, I also include in each model R's family income (when R was about sixteen years old) and the levels of education of both of R's parents. And, as always, because the majority of the students of color come from Harvard Law School, I test for school- and program-specific effects.

Table 7.3 reports on three different models, one in each column, testing whether women of color are significantly different from other women and from other students of color. ("Women of color" acts as an interaction term in this regression, and its components, female and nonwhite, are also included.) In the first column, I give results from a standard demographics-based model, predicting individuals' level of political ambition using only demographic features like race, gender, school, program, family income, and parents' levels of education. In this model, being female and being a woman of color are both strongly significant predictors of one's having thought of running for office. In the second column, I keep those same demographic factors in the model but also add in a major variable that previous literature has found important—having been recruited (asked to run for office). As we might expect, this appears to have a major impact on the political ambition of individuals, but as I have said earlier, this could merely be the effect of correlation rather than causation. Those who are asked to run are likely those who are already involved, such as by volunteering on a campaign, and those who volunteer probably already think that politics is worth their time. Either way, in the model it does indeed help predict political ambition.

In the final column of table 7.3, however, I offer my own, much more complete model of political ambition, which now takes into account both the costs-rewards score and to what degree individuals are expecting to face political discrimination. The score that people get on the Rewards-Minus-Costs scale developed in previous chapters is very strongly significant as a predictor of political ambition—and, once it is added to the model, being female is no longer by itself a predictor of political ambition, and the significance has decreased for the coefficient on women of color from what it was in Model 2. Taking into account the costs and rewards that people see, in other words, helps us explain far more about their political ambition than mere demographics or even demographics plus one's having been asked to run. Costs and rewards perceptions, this tells us, are a deeply important part of the story of why someone would or would not want to run for office. And as an added bonus, they help us explain these other demographic puzzles. It is not that sex by itself or race by itself necessarily causes anything; it is that women, and especially women of color, are more likely to see costs to than rewards from running.

## Summary

On the whole, the interview data suggest three main conclusions about women of color specifically, when compared with either men or white women. The first is that they show greater sensitivity to many of the already-discussed costs to running for or holding office. The second is that women of color perceive additional barriers to candidacy. Third, and perhaps most important, women of color are the group least likely to think that politics can solve important problems.

When we combine these factors, it is no wonder that the political ambition of women of color falls below that of both white women and of men generally. This group of bright, ambitious, and thoughtful young women saw with the "clear eyes" that Liz said women in general had about politics, and many also possessed the "second sight" discussed by Du Bois in reference to American racial minorities.

Yet this was also an extraordinarily strong and inspiring group, deeply committed to helping their communities. I got the feeling that, had they truly believed politics was the sphere in which they could make a difference to the world, they would have lined up to run. What was most damning for their political ambition was that the high costs were not counterbalanced by perceptions of high rewards.

8

# Change the System, Change the Candidates

In the three years encompassed by this research, negative portrayals of politics abounded. There were media frenzies over at least a dozen major and innumerable minor political scandals, at all levels of government. The federal government spent two weeks shut down over budget negotiations in October 2013 and came close to doing so again several times. Popular fiction is filled with portrayals of politicians as power-hungry, dishonest, ruthless, and/or corrupt; consider some of the most popular television shows in the past year, which feature such characters centrally, including ABC's *Scandal*, Netflix's *House of Cards*, and CBS's *The Good Wife* (to say nothing of HBO's *Game of Thrones*)—contrast these characters with the respected "noble public servant" characters of 1990s political dramatizations like *The West Wing* or *The American President* (or, to reach back to a far earlier era, Jimmy Stewart's "Mr. Smith" in Frank Capra's 1939 classic *Mr. Smith Goes to Washington*). There are few revered figures in today's electoral politics (beyond perhaps the First Lady, who is political but unelected), as news services continue to broadcast coverage of gridlock, hyperpartisanship, incivility, and the many other aspects of political life that feed into young eligibles' negative perceptions of politics and its ability to produce positive change.

In the interviews, even those who felt that politics could have the potential to produce what they saw as positive change were skeptical of its ability to do so right now. Many who saw high costs explained their perceptions in more depth. Some felt that the level of partisanship, gridlock, and negativity would interfere with the ability of politics to produce what they saw as positive change. Melody, a law student who had previously held an internship in a government office, said definitively that she did not like politics. She clarified: "I liked my experiences working for the government, but I did not like politics. And there's a strong distinction for me. I like doing things for my community and for my

Figure 8.1. "American-ish Government," *FoxTrot* Comic Strip, September 29, 2013. Source: *FoxTrot*, by Bill Amend. Used by permission of Bill Amend and Universal UClick/Andrews McNeel Universal.

country . . . but to me politics is kind of what gets in the way some-times." Elena, another law student, did not see politics as being useful and wanted to do something that for her felt more connected to solving problems: "I just realized I wasn't going to be happy unless I was doing something that felt socially important."

The law and policy students in my study were on the whole an ex-tremely public- and civic-minded bunch. Their survey answers showed a deep level of concern about their country and their communities and about the public good in general. Talking with more than fifty of them in person, for about an hour each, and with some for up to two hours, I was impressed with their compassion and their desire for creating positive change in the world. They had already chosen a career path related to law, public policy, and/or politics and were in competitive institutions that are major breeding grounds for future politicians. So among Millennials, this is a reasonably good sample of eligible candidates—these should be the young people most interested of their peer group in possibly run-ning. It is, as we say in social science, a "hard case"—if these particular

Millennials seem deterred from running, we can probably expect the effects to be greater for the larger group.

With a few notable exceptions, however, a large portion of the sample did not see politics as the best path toward helping people or communities. Many saw politics as being ineffective or inefficient or both and thoughtfully enumerated for me the many rational reasons for their mostly low levels of political ambition. Many also saw great rewards in politics, but those who saw more rewards than costs were a small and unrepresentative group. They tended to be men rather than women and were already in a positive feedback loop of political participation and interest in politics.

On an individual level, it is fully rational for those I surveyed and interviewed not to want to run. As they could clearly see, campaigns today at almost any level of government are expensive in lots of ways. Campaigns are financially costly as well as being time-consuming and energy-intensive. An increasingly intrusive news media can make running quite uncomfortable, not only for the candidate herself but also for her family, friends, children, and neighbors. As a voting public, we often seem hostile to those who offer to represent us, distrusting them and/or their motives; the respect once accorded to public service seems all but lost. Unless some damn good rewards can compensate for these costs, it would be unreasonable to expect individuals to want to run. Yet the rewards are even more subjective than costs; one of the greatest rewards seems to be whether one thinks politics can solve important problems. That perception has motivated movements but seems mostly missing among most of those I studied. And with politicians generally held in low regard, the personal rewards (respect, power) are unable to compensate for the perceived lack of social usefulness of politics.

On a system-wide level, however, individually rational behavior is producing a larger irrational outcome. It is irrational on a societal level to be turning off those who could be excellent public office candidates and instead sending them running for the hills (that is, the private sector). The kinds of professions they sought to join instead of electoral politics—NGOs, think tanks, consulting, law firms, private-sector businesses—do noble and important work. Yet none of them can replace the state. Government is, Jane Mansbridge tells us, the only source of the kind of "legitimate coercion" we need to solve our large and persisting collective action problems.[1]

Other research has found that young people are generally "turned off" by the incivility, the gridlock, and other negative features of current hyperpartisan politics.[2] Political scientists Lawless and Fox found the same in a massive study of high school and college students. They note the danger for democracy of alienating a whole generation: "With more than half a million elected positions, the US political system will thrive only if a large number of people aspire one day to run for office."[3] They suggest some important solutions, including encouraging young people to see politics as a "vibrant, effective way to engage with and improve their communities and society," such as through political leadership programs, smartphone apps, and political video games.[4] Generally, these researchers have given up hope that current generations of adults can change the way we do politics and are looking ahead to Millennials as the eventual solution.[5]

I think otherwise. It is up to us, I believe, to radically change their calculations about joining the system. My hope, in other words, is that if we know "the kids are watching," perhaps we can begin to act more like adults.

The young people I surveyed and interviewed were smart, savvy observers of our current political, legal, and social systems and did not express only negativity. More than anything else, their words and definitions of politics expressed ambivalence. Several called it a "necessary evil," or terms to that effect, and disliked the incivility and lack of compromise in current politics but thought that representative democracy was deeply important. I believe that the best way to make them think that politics is meaningful is to make current politics more meaningful. And that is up to us, not to them. They are not incorrect when they see high costs or middling rewards, but both of those can change.

We could lower the costs of running by putting into place reasonable campaign finance spending limits and public funding schemes, as most other advanced democracies already use. We could overturn *Citizens United* with a constitutional amendment saying corporations are not people and strictly limiting their ability to affect political races. We could give our leaders some leeway in terms of being human, needing time off, making slips of the tongue, and so forth, so that those contemplating candidacy did not have to think they would be facing "gotcha" media surveillance 24/7. We could accept that while some people like to argue and speak loudly, others don't, and often the quiet ones have good things to say too—this would require the louder and more argumentative folks to keep quiet now and then, which would not be a bad thing (they might learn something).

On the rewards side, we could shun those who, like Donald Trump or Ted Cruz in the 2016 Republican presidential primary, show blatant disrespect for others. High-quality young people would recognize and reward a renewed era of respectful politics, even (or perhaps especially) when we disagree. As Voltaire famously said, "I may not agree with a word you are saying, but I will fight to the death to defend your right to say it." Simple respect and civility would go a long way.

But even more important is showing that politics can actually solve problems. As I am writing this, the city of Flint, Michigan, is suffering from lead-contaminated water that has been making children (and others) there sick. One set of solutions is nongovernmental, and the response has been heartening; Little League teams and other nonprofits around the country have been sending bottled water to Flint. On the other hand, heartwarming as these efforts to help may be, they are unfortunately not equal to the long-term task. No celebrity[6] or nonprofit can send enough bottles of water to actually sustain a city.[7] This is a problem necessitating a governmental solution, and currently the Flint mayor is fighting with the Michigan governor over the cost of replacing the city's water pipes. Water, to my mind, is a classic public good—this is why we, the people, create and institute government. This is exactly the kind of problem that government should solve, but when politics (especially of the hyperpartisan variety) gets in the way of attempts at solutions, young people rationally see rewards that do not balance out the often-high costs.

## The Big Picture

Imagine what would happen if, one Election Day soon, all the polling places were set up but everybody decided simply not to vote. Can't you just see all those empty voting booths? Our democracy would collapse. Sovereign citizenship has its price as well as its privileges!

Now think, what if it weren't everyone who decided to abstain, but just certain groups? Democracy would not fall apart if it were mostly older white men who voted, but its claims to legitimacy, justice, and representation would no longer hold in such a diverse country, in this twenty-first-century context. (As Canadian Prime Minister Justin Trudeau said, when asked to explain why he wanted fully half of his cabinet to be women, "Because it's 2015.") We would be extremely concerned if women, racial minorities, and young people were mostly absent from the voting public, even if such exclusion stemmed from their own choices. Together, these are the rather large majority of our country's citizens, after all.

We should be just as concerned when the political participation in question is running for office rather than voting. Democracy in the context of an extremely diverse population requires a diverse group from which we can draw representatives, but our candidate pools are very skewed by race, gender, class, and age.

I maintain strongly that political ambition is not something one is born with. I believe instead it is malleable and depends to a large extent on the perceptions people have about the kinds of goods and bads they might face if they were to run for office. Not surprisingly, in my qualitative and quantitative evidence from a group of highly ambitious, passionate, and intelligent young people, I found that those who seemed to see higher rewards and lower costs were more likely to want to run. Conversely, those who saw high costs and low benefits from running or serving in office did not (for some very good reasons) want to throw their hats into the ring anytime soon.

This understanding of political ambition is, I believe, more hopeful than previous versions. It means that if we could find a way to lower the costs and/or raise the perceived rewards of running, we could get to a more diverse and high-quality candidate pool. Perhaps most important, we need to find a way to help bright, community-minded Millennials think that politics is a good way to solve important collective problems.

My analysis has also shown that "candidate deterrence" effects are stronger for some types of candidates than others; in particular, women are currently more averse to running than men, and women of color (especially black women) are the least likely to want to run of all subgroups. Most of the under-representation of people of color comes from under-representation of women of color; this, to my mind, is the group to whom the greatest efforts should be targeted. With the future of the United States increasingly racially diverse, it is essential that women, and especially women of color, be at the policymaking tables. As is commonly said in Washington, D.C., "If you are not at the table, you are on the menu."

Young people, women, and people of color are hardly genetically averse to politics; rather, these groups led the major social movements of the twentieth century. What the black civil rights, feminist, LGBT, and other movements managed to do was make politics seem important and useful to those who had been too long excluded from that arena. In a time of "anti-politics,"[8] however, we must work doubly hard to overcome the (unfortunately reasonable) cynicism I saw in the graduate students I studied about politics, electoral politics in particular, and to rehabilitate the notion of politics as "public service."

The data I have presented in this book paint a picture of candidate deterrence, where the bulk of those I surveyed and talked to want little to do with electoral politics. But the effects are not evenly dispersed; women are harder hit than men, and women of color are least likely to want to run. While everyone saw relatively high costs to running, women saw higher costs, both because they were more sensitive to the base level of costs and also because they saw additional costs that men did not see. The effect was exacerbated for women of color, who strongly expected to face racial as well as gender discrimination and who were least likely to think that politics could solve important problems.

This is likely no surprise to anyone who studies politics, race, or gender, yet I hope it can become a call to arms. At some indeterminate tipping point in this negative-feedback cycle we are in, the public sector will lose so much respect and legitimacy that it will no longer have the ability to address the kinds of long-term and overarching problems to which Mansbridge referred.[9] We still have a chance to revive our democracy, to make it more fully representative and also stronger and healthier. For this to happen, we need new blood, of all different kinds. And the best way I can see to get it is to convince a new, diverse, and entrepreneurial generation that this system of government that it has taken us hundreds of years to set up and institute is worth their time, effort, and input. We need to decrease the costs of running, by constitutional amendment (if necessary) and also through revising social norms about privacy and respect for those who dedicate their lives to such public service.

Above all, we must convince young people, and especially young women, that without their voices and their support, true change in the system can never be possible. Despite the costs, politics needs them; politics matter. I firmly believe that our future depends on this.

# APPENDIX

*Methodology*

## THE LAW AND POLICY STUDENT POLITICAL AMBITION STUDY (LPS-PAS)

The goal of this project's methodology was to find a subset of the population that would be well-positioned to run for office but who had not (yet) run. I hypothesized that whatever "candidate-deterrence effects" exist would be visible earlier in life than previous samples have tested (more details on previous samples/surveys will follow). I therefore sought young adults, but ones who had already made key decisions about their career directions by choosing a graduate school program in law or policy. The ideal sample would therefore come not just from law and policy schools but also from high-ranking programs.

The use of students from top-tier law and policy schools equalizes to a large degree (although certainly not entirely) the structural factors that tend to give certain candidates (and especially white men) a competitive edge. Yet this project hypothesizes that gender and race differences should still persist, even among elites. The design chosen minimizes SES effects in the attempt to isolate effects of race, gender, and then race–gender intersectionality. The data in this sample allow me to investigate the multiple factors working simultaneously that correlate with depressed political ambition among women in general, and women of color in particular, through comparisons with similarly situated men.

## SITE SELECTION

The three specific schools chosen for sample recruitment were Harvard Law School and Harvard's Kennedy School of Government (which together produce a number of national political leaders) and Suffolk Law School (which produces many Massachusetts political leaders). The Harvard schools were a natural choice, given their reputations and the likelihood that these schools would attract extremely ambitious students across race and gender. Harvard Law and Harvard's Kennedy School are also well known as conduits into national-level governmental positions. Harvard sends a significant number of its graduates into politics and government in the United States. More U.S. presidents have attended Harvard than any other university; seven presidents, including current President Barack Obama, attended Harvard Law School.[1] Currently, 47 Harvard affiliates hold U.S. congressional seats, constituting slightly less than 9 percent of the congressional body and more than double that of any other university.[2] Each Congress for the past two decades has had at least 34 Harvard alumni in its ranks, peaking at 48 in 1995.[3] Twelve percent of U.S. attorneys general have been Harvard graduates (more than any other single university).[4] At the state level, Harvard has the largest number of alumni in legislative statehouses across the country (totaling 104 in number).[5]

Looking specifically at graduates from Harvard's Kennedy School: a substantial portion of its graduating classes each year enters the public sector. Between 2001 and 2012, of those who reported employment, the Kennedy School sent an average of 46 percent of its graduates into government jobs, with a low of 38 percent in 2011 and a high of 59 percent in 2002.[6]

I chose Suffolk Law after collecting data on current state legislators in Massachusetts and finding that Suffolk Law is the modal degree: forty-two percent of Massachusetts state legislators with a JD come from Suffolk, a far higher proportion than the next closest competitors, New England School of Law and Boston College Law.[7] (Not all state legislators have a JD, but it was the most common form of graduate degree, held by 47 percent of Massachusetts state legislators.[8]) Suffolk Law, then, is the largest "feeder" of graduates into state-level politics, just as Harvard—specifically Harvard Law and Harvard's Kennedy School—is the largest "feeder" of graduates into national-level politics. The Suffolk data also serve as a check on the Harvard data, to test which effects might be Harvard-specific and which may be more generalizable to the population of elite law students. Likewise, the Harvard Kennedy School data serve as a check on the data from the two law schools, to test for differences between highly ambitious JD students and their non-JD but still policy-minded counterparts.

Together, these students from elite law and policy schools constitute an ideal sample; they are, on the whole, relatively high-SES young people, who are mostly unmarried and childless (thus minimizing the effects of work–family conflict). Most notably, the work of the admissions committees of these schools ensures a far closer "match" between men and women, and between whites and nonwhites, than we would find in a representative sample from the general population or in many other institutional settings.

## SURVEY RECRUITMENT

Between 2011 and 2014, I conducted an original web-based survey of law and policy school students from the three previously-described campuses. Of the 777 collected surveys, 764 were usable; the rest were omitted because of incomplete responses or because the respondents were not U.S. citizens (a prerequisite of sample inclusion). I supplemented the survey data with one-hour interviews with more than 50 survey respondents, varied by race, gender, year, and school, to further understand respondents' interest in and reactions to politics and to a possible political candidacy.

I began the project by launching the survey in April 2011 at Harvard's Kennedy School, with a sampling frame of 330 students, from which I had a 60 percent response rate, resulting in a sample of 217 students who took the survey. I then replicated the process at Harvard Law (with a response rate of about 62 percent, resulting in a sample of 330) and Suffolk Law (sample of 150 respondents).[9]

Recruiting only from uncompensated volunteers for this survey could skew the results, as it might mean that only students already interested in politics would take the survey. Because I wanted to capture the politically uninterested as well as the interested, and the politically unambitious as well as the ambitious, I used funding from several grants to provide incentives to all respondents. Funding for survey recruitment incentives was generously provided by grants from IQSS (The Institute for Quantitative Social Science at Harvard), CAPS (the Center for American Political Studies at Harvard), the Ash Center for Democratic Governance at Harvard's Kennedy School, and Marie Wilson. With this assistance, I was able to promise each survey respondent a $10 reward (in the form of a coupon for Amazon.com or Starbucks) for taking the fifteen-minute survey.

A reward of this magnitude for this amount of time works out to a rate of $40/hour, which is a competitive wage for law and policy students, and it ensured a good participation rate in my study. It is, however, neither coercive nor out of line with the kinds of salaries such students might expect from summer jobs with law or consulting firms. The incentive should make us trust the data more, as it maximized participation from those who might otherwise have passed over a survey request with "politics" in the title. Table A.1 gives basic demographic data about the sample from each campus, compared with the known demographics of the students at that campus as a whole.

Overall, both Harvard's Kennedy School and Suffolk Law underrepresent domestic minorities as students, making an intersectional race–gender analysis more difficult because of a low-n problem. However, Harvard Law School has a relatively large proportion of black American students, and I oversampled these, which greatly increased the number of black respondents in my survey sample. My sample also includes a fairly good proportion of Asian American students, and a lower but still testable number of Hispanic students, allowing some comparisons to whites and to other minority groups. Regarding gender, the sample is 51 percent female at both of the law schools, and 46 percent female at Harvard's Kennedy School. This percentage is comparable to the student populations at all three schools.

TABLE A.1. Demographics of Survey Sample by Race/Ethnicity, Compared with Race/Ethnic Demographic Information from Campuses

| | HKS (percent) | HKS Sample (percent) | HLS (percent) | HLS Sample (percent) | SLS (percent) | SLS Sample (percent) |
|---|---|---|---|---|---|---|
| Female | 41.0 | 46.2 | 47.0 | 53.7 | 51.0 | 51.0 |
| White | 67.0 | 68.3 | 70.0 | 44.0 | 79.1 | 76.7 |
| Black | 5.1 | 3.8 | 11.3 | 31.5 | 2.6 | 2.0 |
| Hispanic | 11.4 | 10.9 | 7.9 | 10.5 | 3.9 | 6.0 |
| Asian Am. | 14.8 | 14.2 | 5.0 | 12.8 | 7.5 | 10.7 |
| Other Race/Ethn. | 1.7 | 2.8 | 5.8 | 1.3 | 6.9 | 4.7 |
| Sample N | — | 217 | — | 402 | — | 150 |

Sources: *U.S. News & World Reports* 2010, 2012;
HKS Office of Registrar;
LPS-PAS Survey Sample

## WEIGHTING DATA BY RACE

The survey design called for stratified sampling. Where possible (which turned out to be only at Harvard Law), I collected the names and e-mail addresses of every student and information about each student's racial/ethnic background. Race was observer-coded by me and checked by at least one research assistant, to divide the sample into two major groups: those who we were pretty sure were white/Anglo/Caucasian, including Jewish, and those who appeared to have some other kind of racial or ethnic background (East or South Asian, Native American, black, Hispanic). I drew a random sample from the list of white students and Asian, of whom there were many to choose, for sampling, and included the entire list of black and Hispanic students in the sampling frame. The response rate for this campus was 62 percent, resulting in a sample of 402 responses.

For the Harvard Kennedy School sample, as the MPP program was much smaller (I received one list of all 330 students then enrolled), I included the entire list of both white and minority students as the sample for that campus. I received a 60 percent response rate at this campus, resulting in a sample of 217 students who took the survey (211 of which resulted in usable responses).

At Suffolk, where names and e-mail addresses were not available because I was not a student at that university, I recruited through three methods: (1) an e-mail request that the Dean of Students sent as part of a weekly newsletter (which included for several weeks/issues my announcement of paid survey recruitment); (2) posters I put up all around the Suffolk Law campus with pull-off tabs announcing the survey and payment, with my e-mail address on each poster and each pull-off tab (those interested e-mailed me and once I ensured from their e-mail addresses that they were Suffolk Law students, or asked them to write from their official Suffolk Law addresses if they had not done so at first, I sent them a web link for the survey); and (3) I hired a Suffolk Law student to recruit participation in the survey through the race- and ethnicity-based student clubs, like the Black Law Students Association. This resulted in 150 usable responses from this campus.

The resulting survey sample as a whole (for all three campuses) contains a good oversample of minority students, such that the sample is 57.2 percent white and 42.8 percent minority. But the large bulk of the black and Hispanic students come from Harvard Law and were recruited in a different manner than the white and Asian American students in that sample. I therefore calculated and applied sample weights.

## CALCULATING AND APPLYING SAMPLE WEIGHTS

Because not every student had had an equal chance of being included in the sample, in the interests of achieving black and Hispanic oversamples, I calculated sample weights to be applied only to those who were oversampled (black and Hispanic students at Harvard Law School). The calculation allowed me to underweight the responses of black and Hispanic students from Harvard Law School (who were oversampled), and overweight the responses of black and Hispanic students from Suffolk Law and Harvard's Kennedy School. This necessitated knowing the proportions of both of these groups not only in my sample but in the overall school populations from which the sample was drawn. Having obtained these figures about each school's population from their admissions offices or outside sources, I calculated sample weights ("pweights") by dividing the population percentage by the sample percentage.[10] I then applied these pweights to each analysis where possible (means, correlations, and regressions). In the book text, the first time I refer to a sample mean, I use the term *weighted*, with a footnote to explain, and to indicate that from then on all means would actually be weighted means, without my saying so each time.

## INTERVIEW METHODOLOGY

Interview respondents (n = 53) were recruited from those who took the survey. A "thank-you" screen at the end asked those interested in discussing these questions further, for an additional $20 incentive, to contact me. With interviews that usually took forty-five minutes to one hour, this worked out to compensation at a rate of between $20 and $27 per hour—not as high as for the survey, but still a reasonable rate of pay for their time.

I selected the interviewees from among those survey respondents who, after taking the web-based survey, responded to a request to talk with me further about the questions in the survey. In that choice, I considered gender, race/ethnicity, school, and year in the school's program, to

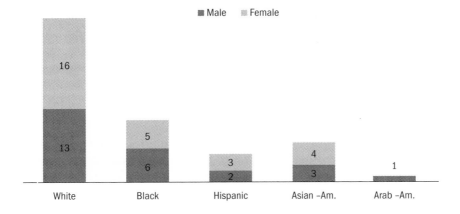

Figure A.1. Interview Sample, by Sex and Race/Ethnicity (n = 53). Source: LPS-PAS, Interview Sample.

achieve a diverse mix. I ended up interviewing more than 70 percent of those who volunteered for an interview, with the interviewees I passed up being mostly white in my quest for racial diversity. Figure A.1 presents demographics from the interview sample.

I generally met interviewees at a coffee shop on or close to their campus, or in my office or a room in their campus's library if they asked for more privacy. With respondents' permission, I audiotaped each interview and transcribed the full file, then deleted the audio recording to preserve respondents' confidentiality.[11] I coded each transcript and analyzed the quotes for each code, as well as analyzed the transcripts more holistically. Figure A.1 gives demographic (race and gender) information about the sample of interviewees for this project.

SAMPLE VERSUS GENERAL POPULATION
The students of the two Harvard schools and Suffolk Law School constitute an elite sample; as much as possible, this project attempts to minimize the role of SES (which previous studies have shown to be perhaps the most powerful factor in explaining political participation) so as to study the effects of other factors—in particular, race, gender, and perceptions/expectations of elections and holding office. The sample is

representative of U.S. political candidates—who, as research has documented, are more educated, wealthier, more partisan, and more politically active than those in the general population.

Several studies have conducted surveys of elite populations of eligible candidates, in the same vein as the LPS-PAS. Two of the most notable come from Lawless and Fox (2005) and Stone and Maisel (1997–98). Recently, Broockman and colleagues have collected data from the first-ever "National Candidate Study" (2012), drawing from 10,000 declared state legislative candidates. Table A.2 gives demographic and political engagement information about each previous study's sample in the first three columns and the LPS-PAS sample in the fourth column.

Previous samples of potential candidates have tended to be whiter and more male than the general population (which is also true of actual candidates—see the National Candidate Study data from Broockman et al.). The LPS-PAS sample of eligibles, however, intentionally over-represents people of color and women, as the project's original questions centered on these groups. My sample is also intentionally younger than other samples in this vein, to look for effects "upstream" of earlier research. Relatedly, the LPS-PAS sample is more Democratic than previous samples of candidates and potential candidates, as is true of this age group more generally. Otherwise, as table A.2 shows, my sample is in line with previous samples of eligibles and declared candidates in terms of unusually high incomes and levels of education.

SURVEY AND INTERVIEW INSTRUMENTS

The original survey and interview questionnaires for this project were approved by Harvard's IRB (Institutional Review Board) in December 2010 and reapproved each year up to 2014 while I collected several rounds of data to ensure a sizeable and diverse sample. Both instruments were beta-tested extensively among then-current Harvard students of various schools. The survey instrument (available from the author upon request) contained many original questions and also replicated questions from several previous surveys, including the ANES (multiple years); Verba, Schlozman, and Brady's "Citizen Participation Study" (1990), and Lawless and Fox's "Political Ambition Study" (2005). The instrument contained items testing for:

TABLE A.2. Selected Characteristics of Potential and Actual
Candidate Samples

| | Maisel & Stone "Potential Candidates" Study (1997–98) | Lawless & Fox "Eligibles" Study (2001–2) | Broockman et al., "National Candidate Study" (2012) | Shames LPS-PAS (2012–14) |
|---|---|---|---|---|
| **Demographic Background** | | | | |
| Male | 77% | 53% | 72% | 50.5% |
| White | 92% | 83% | 81% | 66.1% |
| Graduate or Professional Degree | 63% | (see Note 1) | 45% | (all pursuing one) |
| Age | 47% aged 50 or more | 48.5 (mean) | 55–64 (median range) | 27 (median) |
| Family Income $90,000 or Higher | 54% | (see Note 2) | $96,000 mean income for sample | 46% (see Note 5) |
| **Political Background** | | | | |
| Identify with Democratic Party | 59% | 45% | 55% | 61.3% |
| Identify with the Republican Party | 41% | 30% | 45% | 10.1% |
| Identify as Liberal | 30% | NA | 37% | 63.6% |
| Identify as Moderate | 19% | NA | 18% | 23.6% |
| Identify as Conservative | 51% | NA | 45% | 12.8% |
| Active in Political Campaigns | 54% | (see Note 3) | 67% | 23.6% |
| N | 1,708 (see Note 4) | 3,614 | 10,000 | 763 |

Sources: LPS-PAS, Survey Sample;
Maisel and Stone 1998 (see Note 4); Lawless and Fox 2005; Broockman et al 2012
Note 1: Lawless and Fox 2005 does not publish this percentage, but the "average education score" for their sample was a 5.4 out of a possible 6, suggesting that most of their sample had postcollege education.
Note 2: Lawless and Fox 2005 does not publish this percentage, but the "average income score" for their sample was a 4.6 out of a possible 6, suggesting (as with the other samples) a family income significantly higher than for the U.S. population average.
Note 3: Lawless and Fox 2005 does not publish this percentage, but the "average participation score" for their sample was a 5.5 out of a possible 9, drawing on a list of nine possible political activities.
Note 4: For this sample, table only gives data for first-time "named candidates," not the state legislators who were positioned to move up to Congress.
Note 5: The LPS-PAS instrument gave income categories rather than allow students to enter their family income manually, in the interest of accuracy and response rate. However, the income categories do not exactly match up with those given in the other surveys listed here. This percentage for the LPS-PAS sample gives the percentage of people whose families earned $100,000 or above rather than $90,000 or above.

a) *Education factors*: current program, parents' education levels, subjects' high school experience(s) (such as whether the high school was single-sex and how racially mixed it was);

b) *Demographics*: race, gender, citizenship, religion/religiosity;

c) *Childhood and background factors*: family income, whether subject grew up in a rural, suburban, or urban environment; how racially mixed the subject's neighborhoods and high schools were; R's history of participation in high school and college activities;

d) *Personality and psychological self-assessments*: how subject identifies on a number of traits linked to gender and/or race, including ambition, confidence, competitiveness, and willingness to take risks;

e) *Political socialization factors*: parents' political and civic activity; subjects' child and early adulthood political engagement and participation;

f) Experiences of *discrimination*, based on race and/or gender (including harassment).

g) Current *political factors and engagement*: interest and participation in political activity; party affiliation and ideology self-placement scale;

h) *Policy stances* on two major political issues (abortion and income inequality);

i) *Perceptions of politics, politicians, and officeholding*: whether subject thinks politics is useful to solve problems, trusts government, and thinks politicians can make positive change;

j) *Running-for-office variables*, including: willingness to consider running (even at some point in future); level of office in which subject might ever be interested; and reasons why subject would or would not run; and

k) *Perceptions of discrimination/disadvantage* in politics: whether subject anticipates barriers/burdens; does subject think whites versus minorities and men versus women have advantages or disadvantages in campaigns.

To categorize subjects racially, I used the current U.S. Census series of questions on race/ethnicity. I first asked respondents to identify as ethnically Hispanic or not, and then (if yes) what type of Hispanic origin (with great detail in answer choices). I then asked their racial category (black, white, Asian, with a fine degree of detail under Asian). For purposes of analysis, I folded all Asian respondents into a category I call "Asian American," and respondents with Hispanic ethnicity origins into the category "Hispanic."[12] If respondents self-identified as being both white and of a nonwhite race, I classified them for data analysis purposes into the nonwhite group.

This combination of survey and in-depth interview data makes possible an analysis of young elite eligible candidates' expectations of both positive and negative factors in the electoral environment and legislative institutions, including those relating to race and gender, and their expectations about the usefulness of politics to effect positive change. The data shed light on the ways in which structural barriers and perceptions of political usefulness shape eligible candidates' willingness to consider a political campaign seriously.

For those interested in using the survey dataset, it will soon be available for public use from the Harvard Dataverse, through the Harvard Institute for Quantitative Social Science (IQSS), at https://dataverse.harvard.edu/.

# NOTES

CHAPTER 1. GOOD REASONS NOT TO RUN

1  All interviewee names have been changed to protect confidentiality. All interviews were one-on-one and lasted about an hour. I recorded and transcribed each, then destroyed the recordings and worked from anonymous transcripts, knowing only the interviewee's school, race, gender, and whatever he or she chose to disclose to me in the interview itself.

2  Downs 1957.

3  Lawless and Fox 2015 find the same, studying high school and college students nationally.

4  I collected 777 surveys between 2012 and 2014 but eliminated several that were unusable, either because they contained too many missing answers or because the respondents said they were not U.S. citizens, a requirement for inclusion in the sample. Some 764 of the surveys were usable, although N's vary by question, as not all questions were asked of each respondent. In particular, I added several questions between the Harvard Kennedy School (HKS) and Harvard /Suffolk Law Schools versions of the survey, based on the initial data from the HKS group. I also collected several rounds of data from Harvard Law School (HLS) students, as each new HLS class entered each year. For the final wave of the survey, collecting data only from the first-year law students (1-Ls) at HLS, I subtracted several questions from the survey instrument that had not shown good variation in answers from the data collected thus far and added a few new questions to test new hunches based on the data collected up to that point. Each table thus gives the N for each question, and I will give Ns in endnotes each time I give statistical data in the text of this book.

5  The schools from which I recruited my survey and interview samples were Harvard's Kennedy School and Harvard Law School, chosen because these together are major feeders into national-level politics, and Suffolk Law School, which at the time was (and probably still is) the largest feeder into state-level politics in Massachusetts, where I was based. I am grateful to all three of these schools for permission to conduct research on their campuses. Full methodology details are available in the appendix, along with demographic information about the samples.

6  Lawless and Fox 2005, 2010.

7  Ibid.; see also Fulton et al. 2006; Carroll and Sanbonmatsu 2013; Political Parity 2014.

8 Gaddie 2004, 9.

9 Ibid.

10 Gaddie 2004.

11 Ibid, 10.

12 Carroll and Sanbonmatsu 2013, 61.

13 Lawless and Fox 2005, Fulton 2005.

14 Definition is from Lawless and Fox 2004, 2010, informed by Fowler and McClure 1989; Schlesinger 1966; Black 1972.

15 Box-Steffensmeier 1996.

16 See, for example, Green 1968 and Powell 1990.

17 Lawless and Fox 2015; Harvard IOP 2012–15.

18 Lawless and Fox 2015.

19 Unfortunately few (twelve) law and policy school students in my samples identified themselves as Native American, making it impossible for me to draw generalizations about this group beyond its relative dearth within these elite institutions, which is in itself problematic. Three of these Native American students also identified themselves as another nonwhite category (two black and one Asian American), and the other nine were categorized in the survey data as "other nonwhite." I also depart from the current U.S. Census method of categorizing black and Asian as "races" while Hispanic is considered an "ethnicity." Instead, here, I consider race and ethnicity as deeply related concepts, with "people of color" here meaning black, Hispanic, and Asian American. Following Du Bois and hooks, I do not capitalize *black*, but following general practice in ethnic studies, I capitalize *Hispanic* and *Asian American*. The Hispanic category includes all those answering yes to a question about Hispanic origin ("Are you of Spanish, Hispanic, or Latino descent?"), asked prior to the question of race (as with current U.S. Census survey practice). The Asian American category includes all those who identified themselves as any of a number of Asian subcategories, including Chinese, Filipino, Japanese, Korean, Vietnamese, Other Asian, or Other Pacific Islander. However I use the term *Asian American* to describe my respondents as all respondents were U.S. citizens (those of any race who reported they were not U.S. citizens were removed from the survey sample).

20 Verba, Schlozman, and Brady 1995; Rosenstone and Hansen 1993.

21 For those interested, I explain my recruiting procedures and samples in detail in the Methodology appendix.

22 Lawless and Fox 2015 also finds higher political ambition among the blacks and Hispanics in their sample (twenty-nine).

23 Hibbing and Theiss-Morse 2001.

24 Patterson 2003.

25 Kamber 2003.

26 Mutz and Reeves 2005, Mutz 2007.

27 Murray 2014.

28 Pew 2014; on primaries, see Brady, Han, and Pope 2007; Bartels 2000; Thomsen 2014; Hall 2014.

29  Neustadt 1997, 187.

30  Gallup 2014.

31  Ibid.

32  Public Policy Polling 2013.

33  Smith and Roberts 2016.

34  Gallup 2015a.

35  Nye, Zelikow, and King 1997; see also Hibbing and Theiss-Morse 2001; Hofstadter 1965, however, suggests that the "paranoid style" is a constant in American politics.

36  Gallup 2015a.

37  Ibid.

38  Hofstadter 1965, 3.

39  Kamber 2003.

40  Indeed, my previous work suggests that the popularity of outsider status can benefit women as candidates, who are immediately marked by their gender as being "un-candidates" (Shames 2001; Shames 2003).

41  Fenno 1975.

42  Hibbing and Theiss-Morse 2001; Nye, Zelikow, and King 1997; Gallup 2015.

43  Mutz 2005; Mutz and Reeves 2007.

44  Gallup 2013.

45  Nye 1997, 3.

46  Ibid., 5.

47  Hibbing and Theiss-Morse 2001, 1.

48  Alsop 2008.

49  Lopez et al./CIRCLE 2006.

50  Pew 2014b.

51  Alsop 2008.

52  Pew 2014b.

53  Ibid.

54  Lopez et al./CIRCLE 2006.

55  Pew 2014b.

56  Harvard IOP Poll 2014.

57  Harvard IOP Poll 2012.

58  Harvard IOP Poll 2015.

59  See Gilman 2016 for other positive examples of inspired participation.

60  Lawless and Fox 2010, 2005; Maisel, Stone, and Maestas 2008; Fulton et al. 2006; Maisel and Stone 1997; Fowler and McClure 1989.

61  Data analysis by the author, based on data in the *Almanac of American Politics 2010* and website of the Massachusetts General Court (state legislature).

62  *Harvard Gazette* 2008; *Liberty Voice* 2014.

63  *Liberty Voice* 2014.

64  *Harvard Magazine* 1995, 1997, 1999, 2001, 2005, 2009, 2011, 2012, 2014.

65  Based on author coding of the biographies given in U.S. Department of Justice 2014.

66 Hu 2011 (although this article notes that for the most part state legislatures are not Ivy League–dominated as Congress is—instead, often key local schools within a state become "feeders" for the state legislature, as with Suffolk Law and Boston College Law in Boston).

67 Harvard's Kennedy School 2012.

68 Figures derived from author analysis and coding of member biographical data from the website of the Massachusetts General Court (state legislature), at https://malegislature.gov/People/House/ (accessed May 10, 2010).

69 Ibid.

70 As in Lawless and Fox 2012.

71 As in Fulton et al. 2006; see also Hochschild 2003.

72 Eight of the 716 students in the sample (1 percent) had previously sought political office (not including student government).

73 As in Fulton et al. 2006; see also Niven 2006, although this is less relevant as it looks at candidates who drop out of a race (but after having declared candidacy, which is further along than most of the students in my sample, only eight of whom had previously declared a candidacy for public office).

CHAPTER 2. POLITICAL AMBITION

1 See Polity IV Project 2016 and Freedom House 2016.

2 Schattschneider 1942, 52.

3 Wattenberg 1991, 1996.

4 Schumpeter 1976 [1942].

5 Schlesinger 1966.

6 Fowler and McClure 1989.

7 Thomas 1994, 87.

8 Schlesinger 1966, 2.

9 Kazee 1994, 5.

10 Mansbridge 1999a; Phillips 1995; Phillips 1991.

11 Broockman et al. 2012; note that Lawless and Fox 2004 and 2010 and Maisel and Stone 1997 find the same types of gaps in their surveys of eligible candidates.

12 McGlennon and Mahoney 2012.

13 Keohane 2001, 4.

14 Ibid.

15 Arnold 1990, 68.

16 Downs 1957, 5.

17 Riker and Ordeshook 1968.

18 Box-Steffensmeier 1996.

19 Branton 2009.

20 Maisel and Stone 1997, 79.

21 Fulton et al. 2006, 235.

22 Lawless and Fox 2005.

23  Downs 1957; on political participation models, see Verba, Schlozman, and Brady 1995 and Rosenstone and Hansen 1993.
24  U.S. Census 2014.
25  CAWP 2016.
26  U.S. Census 2014; NCSL 2009.
27  NCSL 2009.
28  CRS 2016.
29  CAWP 2013; NCSL 2009; Carroll 2001.
30  NCSL 2009.
31  CAWP 2016.
32  CAWP 2010.
33  Carroll 2001; Carroll and Jenkins 2005, 2001.
34  Ibid.
35  Lawless and Fox 2005.
36  Lawless and Fox 2005, for instance, posits that women's lower levels of confidence, including feeling qualified to run, is a big part of the story. I do not disagree, but I frame this in terms of rationality; if one knows one will be subjected to double standards and other biases, I believe it is fully rational to not feel as confident.
37  Marschall, Ruhil, and Shah 2010; Shah and Marschall 2011.
38  Branton 2009, 459.
39  Kaufmann 2003, 1998; Bobo and Gilliam 1990; see also Barreto et al. 2004 on the same effect for Hispanics; although for a contrary perspective see Gay 2001. If there are empowerment effects by race, the literature thus far suggests they are more likely to occur at the local level than in higher levels of office. The effect may also be moderated by ideology; see Griffin and Keane 2006.
40  Htun 2004.
41  Carnes 2013.
42  Verba, Schlozman, and Brady 1995; Rosenstone and Hansen 1993.
43  Earlier research supports this idea, although I study it in a new way and with a new population; see Lawless and Fox 2010, 2005; Fulton et al. 2006; Niven 2006.
44  On this point, see the discussion in Mansbridge (1999) about why women representing women, or blacks representing blacks, is unlike "morons representing morons."
45  Kymlicka 2002, 381.
46  Mansbridge 2003, 1999, 1983.
47  Kymlicka 2002; Mansbridge 1999a; Phillips 1995; Phillips 1991; Young 1994, 1990.
48  Lawless and Fox 2008, 3.
49  Kymlicka 2002; Phillips 1994. Schlozman, Verba, Brady, and Shames 2012 makes this same point, but in the context of the unequal political voice of citizens rather than the unequal participation of groups in leadership.
50  Mansbridge 1999a, 628.
51  On gender of legislators and policy outputs, see Swers 20013, 2002; Reingold 2006; Thomas and Wilcox 2005; O'Connor 2003; Caiazza 2002; Rosenthal 2002;

Carroll 2001; Rosenthal 2002, 1998a, 1998b; Kathlene 1999; Little, Dunn, and Deen 2001; Thomas 1994. On the need for race- as well as gender-descriptive representation, see Brown 2014; Hardy-Fanta 2011; Montoya, Hardy-Fanta, and Garcia 2000; Tate 2003; Hawkesworth 2003. On race of legislators and policy outputs, the question is more complex because of geographical and partisan clustering by race/ethnicity. Some studies suggest that the formation of majority–minority districts is essential to increasing the racial diversity of legislative bodies (see, e.g., Lublin 1999). Another strain of research suggests that such districts end up polarizing the surrounding districts in a way that makes the legislature as a whole more conservative and less likely to pass policies in the interests of greater racial equality (see Cameron, Epstein, and O'Halloran 1996). Both camps agree, however, that having some mix of nonwhite legislators along with white legislators increases substantive representation of nonwhite citizens.

52 Osborn 2012; Karpowitz, Mendelberg, and Shaker 2012; Rosenthal 1998a and 1998b; Thomas 1994; Kathlene 1994; see also Eagly, Johannesen-Schmidt, and van Engen 2003 and Eagly and Johnson 1990, two rare meta-analyses of men's and women's leadership styles, which both find more similarities than differences overall between men's and women's leadership style but also find some key differences, even controlling for level and position of leadership.

53 Lawless and Fox 2004, 2010, Phillips 1995; Shah and Marschall 2011; Tate 2003.

54 The prime example is Schlesinger 1966; see also Fowler and McClure 1989; Mandel 1981.

55 For example, Lawless and Fox 2010, 2005; Fulton et al. 2006; Fulton 2005; see also Maisel, Stone, and Maestas 2008 for an innovative research design in studying nonvisible candidates.

56 Hewlett 2007; Lawless and Fox 2005; Hochschild 2003; Crittenden 2002; Thomas 2002; Williams 2000; Goss 2013.

57 Chang 2010; Burns, Schlozman, and Verba 2001; Conway 2001; Williams 2000; Blau and Kahn 2000; Waldfogel 1994.

58 Palmer and Simon 2006.

59 Palmer and Simon 2006; Fox and Lawless 2010; Sanbonmatsu 2006; Dolan 2004; Baer 2003, 1993; Shames 2003, 2001.

60 U.S. Census 2012 shows that more women than men are enrolled in college and graduate schools. ABA 2013 reports that law school enrollment currently stands at 53 percent men, 47 percent women and that women are nearly half (45 percent) of both associates and summer associates in law firms now.

61 Lawless and Fox 2005; author coding from the *Almanac of American Politics 2010*.

62 IWPR 2014.

63 Chang 2010.

64 See, for example, Hawkeworth 2004; McDonagh 2009; Goss 2013; Duerst-Lahti and Kelly 1995; see also Dittmar 2015 for an excellent exploration of how campaign professionals working for female candidates navigate institutional gender norms and stereotypes.

65  Atkeson and Carrillo 2007; Atkeson 2003; Burns, Schlozman, and Verba 2001.

66  Stout and Tate 2013; Kaufmann 2003, 1998; Bobo and Gilliam 1990.

67  See Paumgarten 2007 for an example.

68  Norris and Lovenduski 1995; Norris 1997; Davidson-Schmidt 2006; Ashe and Stewart 2012.

69  Ashe and Stewart 2012; Dahlerup and Leyenaar 2013; Krook 2009; Davidson-Schmidt forthcoming, 2008, 2006; Dahlerup 2006, 2003.

70  Ashe and Stewart 2012; Hinojosa 2012; Norris 2007, 1997; Norris and Lovenduski 2010, 1995.

71  Ashe and Stewart 2012; Norris and Lovenduski 1995.

72  Lawless and Fox 2010, 2005, and 2008; and Maisel, Stone, and Maestas 2008, along with other research from Maisel and Stone (1997 and others), focus on individual attributes; as Lawless and Fox 2005 states, "Our research debunks the literature that purports to explain women's numeric underrepresentation on the grounds of structural impediments and institutional inertia alone" (14). Carroll and Sanbonmatsu 2013 emphasizes the interplay between institutional factors and individuals' will to run.

73  See Political Parity 2014; Carroll and Sanbonmatsu 2013; Schneider et al. 2015; Sanbonmatsu 2006; Niven 2006; Fulton et al. 2006; and Fowler and McClure 1989 for good models linking institutions to individuals.

74  Lawless and Fox 2010, 2005.

75  Lawless and Fox 2012, 2010, 2005; Hochschild 2003; Crittenden 2002; Williams 2000; Valian 1999; Phillips 1991; Bem 1988; Sapiro 1983; Jennings 1983; Duverger 1955; see also endnote 56 on work/family conflict for women.

76  Atkeson and Carrillo 2007; Campbell and Wolbrecht 2006; Burns, Schlozman, and Verba 2001; Kahn 1996; Phillips 1991; Sapiro 1983.

77  See, for example, Fulton et al. 2006. Also, Lawless and Fox 2005 finds that women are more likely to judge the districts they live in as more competitive, and therefore harder to enter, than men.

78  On biases in parties and media, see Falk 2008; Sanbonmatsu 2006; White House Project 2005, 1999; Baer 2003, 1993; Burrell 1993. On expecting sexism or double standards, in politics and in other workplaces, see Lawless and Fox 2010, 2008, 2005; Babcock and Laschever 2007; Fulton et al. 2006; Bowles et al. 2005; Fletcher 1999.

79  Jenkins 2007.

80  Anzia and Berry 2009.

81  Political Parity 2014; Carroll and Sanbonmatsu 2013.

82  See, however, Platt 2008 for an investigation of policy-motivated political activism.

83  Schlozman, Verba, Brady, and Shames 2012.

## CHAPTER 3. THE COSTS OF RUNNING

1  Downs 1957.

2  Verba, Schlozman, and Brady 1995; Rosenstone and Hansen 1993.

3   *The Onion* 2008.

4   Follow the Money 2012 (giving figures for 2009–10 races); see also Campaign Finance Institute 2016.

5   Ibid.; New Hampshire is highly unusual in this regard as there are far more seats available in the New Hampshire House ("General Court") than in any other state (400 members).

6   OpenSecrets.org 2014.

7   Metcalfe 2012.

8   Ibid.

9   *National Post* (Toronto, Canada) 2013.

10  *Time Magazine* 2014.

11  Ibid.

12  Ibid.

13  Wattenberg 1995, 1991.

14  International IDEA 2003, 4.

15  International IDEA Political Finance Database 2012. See also IFES 2009.

16  International IDEA 2012.

17  The statewide exceptions, particularly in Maine and Arizona, while possibly imperiled by recent Supreme Court decisions, are important and are described in the excellent overview given by the NCSL, the National Conference of State Legislators (NCSL 2016). At the presidential level, also, matching funds are available to presidential candidates who agree to limit spending, but this did not apply to either major-party candidate in 2012, and then-candidate Barack Obama opted out of public funding, so as not to be bound by the spending limits, in 2008.

18  Clements and Moyers 2014; Lessig 2015.

19  See in particular the U.S. Supreme Court decisions in *Free Enterprise Club of Arizona v. Bennett* (2011), *Citizens United v. FEC* (2010), *First National Bank of Boston v. Bellotti* (1978), and *Buckley v. Valeo* (1976).

20  OpenSecrets.org 2010.

21  Conley 2009; see also Chang 2010. The major racial/ethnic exception here is Jews, who are vastly overrepresented among the rich and also among candidates and elected officials. Jewish Americans make up about 2 percent of the U.S. population but 7 percent of the House of Representatives and 12 percent of the Senate (Pew 2011, 2009; JTA 2009).

22  Carnes 2013; see also Gilens 2012.

23  Each campaign operation that intends to raise and spend more than $1,000, for instance, must create and maintain a separate bank account only for campaign expenses, which must be tracked carefully in case of audit. Individual candidates must also file numerous forms to announce their intention to run and their financial interest. Starting a new campaign operation is very much like starting a brand-new business. For more information, see Trost and Grossman 2005.

24  Ibid., 76.

25 Ibid., 36.

26 Professionalization of campaigns has increased greatly in the past few decades, especially at higher levels of government but increasingly in lower-level campaigns as well (Strachan 2002; Dittmar 2015).

27 Interview for Shames 2014. Subject was a campaign manager for a recent major-party gubernatorial campaign. (Name kept confidential.)

28 Stevenson and Vavreck 2000. This average is only for what the authors call "unscheduled campaigns," wherein Parliament is dissolved and elections are scheduled without a standardized electoral timetable. They code "scheduled elections," which are a minority in their dataset, as having campaigns of 6 months (180 days) on average, which is still far shorter than the U.S. average (see Table 1, 224).

29 CBC News 2015.

30 Parlapiano 2015.

31 See, for example, Polsby 1983; Bartels 1998.

32 Respondents were allowed to skip questions, but only if they bypassed an auto-mated reminder asking them to complete each question before submitting. Of the 777 completed surveys, 763 respondents answered most of the questions, although some people skipped one here or there, leading to a few scattered missing values throughout the dataset. But to get their survey incentive reward ($10, generally as a coupon at Amazon.com or Starbucks, or as a check or cash if desired), respondents had to e-mail me a "survey completion code" that they would receive only after the survey was submitted.

33 The need for analysis by race necessitated an oversample of people of color in the survey data, which necessitated a different type of survey recruitment. Because the minorities were generally recruited in different ways, throughout the book I give averages weighted by race and use sample weights for analyses like correlation and regression testing, to re-weight sample means to what they would be if black and Hispanic respondents were the same proportion in the sample that they are in the population of the schools from which they were recruited. The method of sample recruitment and calculating sample weights by race and school is described in the Methodology appendix. From now on, all sample and subgroup means should be assumed by the reader to be weighted means.

34 N = 761 for this survey question.

35 N = 761.

36 Because this question was asked only in the final wave of the survey sample, which primarily surveyed students of color, it is possible that race/ethnicity differences between the final-wave survey respondents and the rest of the sample could bias the mean. Given the data from other questions about raising money, however, these data do not appear out of proportion. And weighting the data by race raises rather than lowers the value of the mean, from 83.0 percent unweighted to 88.2 percent weighted.

37  N = 760.

38  N = 760.

39  N = 761.

40  N = 760.

41  Patterson 2003, especially chapter 3.

42  Which apparently is where a large proportion of young people get their news information (see CBS News 2004).

43  N = 761.

44  N = 761.

45  N = 760.

46  Thomsen 2014.

47  Congressional Research Service 2014b.

48  Calculated from the data given in NCSL 2014.

49  Smith 2012.

50  N = 761.

51  N = 550.

52  N = 546.

53  Lawless and Fox 2005, 2010.

54  N = 760.

55  N = 761.

56  N = 713.

57  N = 763.

58  Jews in my survey sample were somewhat more likely than non-Jews to say they would interrupt. The number in the sample was small (23), but the z-value of a Wilcoxon rank-sum test comparing Jews with all others on the binary likelihood of choosing "very likely" or not on this question had a value of .064.

59  Question wording: "Have you ever thought about running for office, not including student government?" Answer choices were: "Yes, I have seriously considered it," "Yes, it has crossed my mind," or "No, I have not thought about it." Question and answer wording similar to key political ambition measure used in Lawless and Fox 2005, 2010. N = 753.

60  Interestingly, though, in the survey data it was men who said they would be more likely to run if their families' privacy could be ensured ($p < .05$, N = 761).

61  Lawless and Fox 2005, 2010.

62  On such clustering, see Einstein forthcoming.

63  Lawless and Fox 2010, 2005; Fulton et al. 2006; Fowler and McClure 1989.

64  Lawless and Fox 2010, 2005.

65  $R = .36$, $p < .001$.

66  $R = .11$, $p < .003$.

67  $R = .13$, $p < .0005$.

68  N = 179.

69  Carroll and Sanbonmatsu 2013; see also Fowler and McClure 1989, and the description of nascent versus expressive political ambition in Fox and Lawless 2005.

## CHAPTER 4. THE REWARDS OF RUNNING

1 Eight of the 763 usable survey responses indicated that the respondent had already run for some form of elective office beyond student government, although this overstates the case, as the free-response text following a follow-up query ("What office?") showed that several of these had misunderstood the question and entered things like "class president." But at least two of the interviewees, who were all survey respondents before being interviewed, told me about running for public office that was not school-based (city council, mayor), so at least a handful did not misinterpret the survey question. There were not, however, enough to analyze statistically, and not being able to link the anonymous survey data to specific interviewees, I cannot tell from just the survey data who actually ran for a nonschool public office. All eight in the survey who said they had run, however, indicated the highest possible level of political ambition, saying they had "thought seriously of running," so I simply treated them as part of that high-political-ambition group.

2 Boren, in Foreword to Gaddie 2003, vii.

3 Lawless and Fox 2015, 143.

4 $N = 713$.

5 LatinasRepresent is a joint initiative of Hunt Alternatives and the National Hispanic Leadership Agenda.

6 LatinasRepresent 2014.

7 The variable "solves," measured as a 5-point agree/disagree scale in response to the statement on whether politics solves problems, has a correlation coefficient of 0.092 ($p = 0.011$) with a binary variable coding for whether or not the respondent has strong policy opinions. Each respondent got a 1 in the binary "strong opinions" variable if he or she had a strong opinion (in either the pro- or con- direction) on both of two policy-issue questions in the survey: should abortions be allowed in the first trimester, and should the government help reduce income differences between the rich versus the poor. Respondents who did not have a strong opinion on both of these questions received a 0 in the "strong opinions" binary variable.

8 Fulton et al. 2006.

9 Lake Research Partners/Hunt Alternatives 2012.

## CHAPTER 5. WEIGHING THE COSTS AND REWARDS OF POLITICAL CAREERS

1 Quoted in Long 2012.

2 *National Journal* 2015.

3 Gaddie 2003.

4 Thanks to Lawless and Fox 2005 for question wording.

5 To test the reliability of this index as a scale, I computed a Cronbach's alpha coefficient, measuring how much the items (variables) that went into this index "hang together" as a group. Generally the reliability is a little lower than what we would want to see in a reliable scale (0.7 or above), but it comes close ($a = .675$).

6　Pearson's R = −.198, p < .001, N = 753.

7　Pearson's R = −.222, p < .001, N = 746.

8　Using an ordered logit regression model with robust standard errors, N = 753, p < .001.

9　R-sq = 0.026.

10　The coefficient is still relatively large and negative, and its p-value is still less than .001.

11　See, for example, Zaller 1992; Haidt 2001.

12　Also as before, I tested the scale reliability of the rewards index with a Cronbach's alpha test (a = .733). I had to exclude the few questions that were asked only of the final wave because of very low n for these questions as compared with the rest of the questions.

13　To get technical, the indices are indeed correlated, but not at all perfectly in a 1-to-1 way; the Pearson's R correlation coefficient between the two scales has an absolute value of 0.39, with p < .0001. So there is a strong correlation here, as in the indices are negatively related, but they are not tapping exactly the same thing.

14　Carroll and Sanbonmatsu 2013; Political Parity 2014.

15　Weighted mean, N = 763.

16　Lawless and Fox 2015, xi.

17　N = 763.

18　I chose 0.45 as a cutoff point on this 0–1 scale as it is a full standard deviation below the mean.

19　And other recent research, like Schneider et al. 2015, suggests that women are more likely to be politically ambitious when they perceive politics as being useful and communal rather than egotistical or self-serving.

## CHAPTER 6. INEFFICIENT AND UNAPPEALING POLITICS

1　Carroll and Sanbonmatsu 2013, 125. Emphasis in original.

2　And, as Carroll and Sanbonmatsu 2013 finds, an essential component of women's political ambition. Putting their findings alongside mine suggests that perceiving politics as useful is more important to the political ambition of women than to that of men, but that (absent support, encouragement, recruitment, or other messages about the usefulness of politics) women are less likely to see politics as useful.

3　See especially Lawless and Fox 2004, 2010.

4　Ibid.

5　This means there were no significant differences comparing white students with minority students as a whole. Black students, however, were significantly more likely than all other groups to call themselves "ambitious," with the difference mostly coming in putting themselves in the "very ambitious" category. This may relate to Mansbridge's interesting discussion of black women's having been frequently told they were "too independent" (Mansbridge 1999b).

6　Weighted averages given for both sex groups, N = 355 men and 356 women.

7 Ibid.; question derives from Lawless and Fox 2005.

8 N = 114 who had seriously considered running.

9 Lawless and Fox 2015; Carroll and Sanbonmatsu 2013.

10 Lawless and Fox 2013.

11 N = 753, p = .554.

12 N = 758, p = .350.

13 Lawless and Fox 2005.

14 Ibid.

15 Fulton et al. 2006.

16 Lawless and Fox 2005, 2010.

17 Kanthak and Woon 2014.

18 Fulton et al. 2005; Lawless and Fox 2005.

19 See also Schneider et al. 2015.

20 P < .001.

21 Unrelated to the gender point, students at Harvard's Kennedy School were somewhat more likely to see fewer costs than students in law schools. This is probably what we should expect, given that the public policy students had already chosen politics/public policy as a career path. It is also a good reminder to keep controlling for type of school and program in future regression analyses.

22 N = 50.

23 N = 222. (The "strong-disagreers" group is 49.3 percent female but with a far smaller N.)

24 The gender difference is strongly statistically significant whether measured with the "strongly agree/disagree" group or the simple "agree/disagree" measure. It shows up both in correlation and regression testing and is not sensitive to any demographic controls.

25 Pearson's R = -.27, p < .0001; N = 380 women.

26 p < .05, N = 389 women.

27 N = 761, p < .005.

28 Sapiro and Shames 2008.

29 Special thanks to Jane Mansbridge for pointing this out to me.

30 Shames 2001.

31 Campbell 2001.

32 Schroeder 1998, 183.

33 Shames 2003; Kamber 2003.

34 Ibid.

35 Pearson and Dancey 2011; Dittmar 2015; Dolan 2004; Matson and Fine 2006; Eagly and Karau 2005; Beckwith 2005; Hawkesworth 2003; Williams 2000; Kahn 1996; Duerst-Lahti and Kelly 1995; Witt, Paget, and Matthews 1994; Thomas 1994; Eagly and Johnson 1990.

36 Eagly and Karau 2005.

37 See the numerous studies cited in Babcock and Laschever 2007; see also Rosenfeld 2008; Hewlett 2007; Campbell and Wolbrecht 2006; Bowles et al. 2005; Fels

2004; Ferree 2004; Hochschild 2003; McGlen et al. 2002; Burns, Schlozman, and Verba 2001; Fausto-Sterling 2001; Carli and Eagly 2001; MacKinnon 2001; Williams 2000; Fletcher 1999; Kahn 1996; Phillips 1995, 1991; MacKinnon 1991; Young 1994, 1990; Goffman 1979; Beauvoir 1953.

38 Fausto-Sterling 2001.

39 Pearson and Dancey 2011; Dolan 2004; Matson and Fine 2006; Beckwith 2005; Hawkesworth 2003; Williams 2000; Kahn 1996; Duerst-Lahti and Kelly 1995; Boxer 1994; Witt, Paget, and Matthews 1994; Thomas 1994; Eagly and Johnson 1990; Carroll 1985; Sapiro 1983; Bem 1988; Goffman 1979; Beauvoir 1953.

40 DeLauro 2002; sociologist and expert in women's leadership Alice Eagly and various co-authors calls this "role incongruity" (see Eagly and Johnson 1990; Eagly and Karau 2005; Eagly and Carli 2007).

41 Carroll 1985, 94.

42 Duerst-Lahti and Kelly 1995, 9.

43 King 1995, 67–69; see also Ely et al. 2011.

44 Kathlene 1995, 167; see also Hawkesworth 2003 on "raced" and "gendered" political institutions.

45 Thomas 1997.

46 UVA Today 2007; see also Fletcher 1999.

47 Ibid.

48 Palmer and Simon 2006.

49 Lawless and Fox 2008, 13.

50 Lawless and Fox 2008.

51 Ibid.

52 Ibid.

53 Campbell and Wolbrecht 2006.

54 Mansbridge 1999; see also, for empirical tests of this idea, Stout and Tate 2013; Alexander 2012; Barnes and Burchard 2013; Beaman et al. 2012; Buhlmann and Schadel 2012; and Campbell and Wolbrecht 2006. For the same effect in a different context, see Djupe and Olson 2013.

55 Kanter 1977.

56 Hunt Alternatives 2012; see also Campbell and Wolbrecht 2006.

57 Rinehart 2013; MacKinnon 2001; Phillips 1995, 1991; Young 1994.

58 The religious discrimination item was the only one to show significant sex difference in the opposite direction, with 17 percent of men and 11 percent of women in the sample saying that they had had this experience ($p = .01$). The race-violence item also shows almost significant sex differences ($p = .1$), but the overall numbers involved are low (seven men and two 2 women reported this experience).

59 Schneir 1994; see also Hacker 1951.

60 See Schneir 1994 and the Redstockings 2016 materials sampling, as well as Brownmiller 1975.

61 Beauvoir 1953 [1949]; on this point, see also Moran 2012; Hacker 1951.

62 $p < .001$, for tests by both sex and race/ethnicity.

63 Rinehart 2013; Shelby 2005; MacKinnon 2001; hooks 1992; Du Bois 1909 [1903];
    Brownmiller 1975; Wright 2005; Hacker 1951.

64 N = 763. Question wording from Lawless and Fox 2005; means of responses are
    similar.

65 p < .001 or less for each.

66 CAWP 2016; U.S. Census Bureau 2014.

67 This study was being conducted between 2011 and 2014, so it does not include
    data on Hillary Clinton's 2016 presidential run.

68 Weighted averages: N = 369 men and 389 women. p-value for difference is <.001.

69 Lawless and Fox 2005 and 2010 found the same.

70 Weighted averages: N = 370 men and 389 women. Difference is statistically signifi-
    cant at p < .001.

71 Dolan 2004; see also Sanbonmatsu 2006, finding that biases vary across party
    leaders and states; and Mendelberg 2001 (on race rather than gender discrimina-
    tion), finding that well-meaning white people are likely to harbor implicit racial
    biases even as they object to outright (explicit) racism.

72 Jenkins 2007.

73 Lawrence and Rose 2010; Falk 2008; Norris 2007; White House Project 2005,
    2000, 1998; Kahn 1996.

74 Sanbonmatsu 2006; see also Eagly and Carli 2007 and Wilson 2004.

75 Strum 2001.

76 Ibid.; see also Eagly and Carli 2007.

77 Krook 2009; Dahlerup 2003, 2006; Norris 1997; Norris and Lovenduski 1995;
    Wattenberg 1991, 1996.

78 Dolan 2004.

79 Lawless and Fox 2005.

80 Anzia and Berry 2009.

81 Besley et al. 2013.

82 Lawless and Fox 2010, 2005; Fulton 2005; Niven 2006.

83 Weighted averages, N = 370 men and 389 women.

84 p < .001, N = 760.

85 p < .001, N = 760.

86 p < .001, N = 760.

87 Lawless and Fox 2010, 2005. My results on the confidence question align with the
    data presented in these works. We do not know, however, how much of women's
    lack of confidence may relate to their anticipation of discrimination and knowl-
    edge that they will likely be held to double standards (see, for more on this idea,
    Bowles et al. 2005). It is not irrational for women to undervalue their qualifica-
    tions if they believe the standards really are higher for them.

## CHAPTER 7. NOT OUR KIND OF GAME

1 Carnes 2013; CAWP 2016; Barreto 2004; Tate 2003.

2 Broockman et al. 2012.

3  On this point see also Carroll and Sanbonmatsu 2013, arguing that, indeed, "more women can run," and see Farris and Holman 2014 on black women, social capital, and political participation.

4  Black students, however, were significantly more likely than all other groups to call themselves "ambitious" (Pearson's R = .08, p < .05). On this idea, see Wilkins and Gulati 1996, as well as Mansbridge 1999b.

5  On intersectionality, see Hawkesworth 2003; hooks 2008; Crenshaw 1991; Combahee 1981. The term, created and popularized by black feminists, refers to the combined and synergistic effects of race and gender, which are incomprehensible if one is looking only at race or only at gender. (See also Frye 1983.)

6  p < .07 for difference between white men and men of color, N = 236 white men and 134 nonwhite men.

7  Although Lawless and Fox 2015 does find some suggestive evidence of such an effect for young people of color.

8  On the complicated ways in which SES and race interact, with political implications, see Shelby 2005; Dawson 1994; Conley 2009.

9  Shah and Marschall 2011; Marschall, Ruhil, and Shah 2010 in particular.

10  p < .001 for each question; N = 197 white women and 186 women of color.

11  p < .001, N = 197 white women and 186 women of color.

12  p < .05 for each; N = 197 white women and 186 women of color.

13  p < .1 for each; N = 197 white women and 186 women of color.

14  p < .1 for each; N = 197 white women and 186 women of color.

15  Sex difference significant at p < .001; N = 373 men and 389 women.

16  From "If I Ever Lose My Faith in You," on the album *Ten Summoner's Tales*.

17  Bowles et al. 2005; MacFarquhar 2007; hooks 2008, 1996, 1992; MacKinnon 2001; Bem 1988; Jennings 1983.

18  p < .05 for "crazy" question and p < .1 for "donations" question; N = 197 white women, 186 women of color.

19  Race differences between whites versus people of color significant at p < .005 for both questions.

20  For Asian American women, p < .001 and N = 38. For black men, p < .05, N = 50. For Hispanic women, p < .07, N = 37.

21  p < .001 for white versus nonwhite comparison; N = 259 nonwhite and 291 white.

22  p < .001 for difference on both questions; N = 259 nonwhite and 291 white.

23  On the other hand, for black students especially, see Downs 2016, reporting on a new report from the Center on Education and the Workforce at Georgetown University which found that African American college students "are more likely to pursue majors that lead to low-paying jobs," especially service-oriented fields like education and social work. My hypothesis about this finding, based on the data in my project, is that black college students, who are far more likely to be women than men, are more driven by their goals of "helping my community," which had significant differences in my survey between black women and black men as well as black women and white women.

24  p < .05 for difference between white women and women of color on "solves" question, and p < .1 for difference on the "public good" question. N = 197 white women and 186 women of color.

25  p < .001 for all correlations, with the absolute value of each correlation coefficient greater than .18.

26  This is true both in a logistic regression (with the dependent variable being simply having thought seriously of running or not) and in an ordered logistic regression, with a three-category dependent variable (having thought seriously of running, having thought in passing of running, never having thought of running). Having been asked to run is the strongest and most significant predictor variable in both models, but again, on a theoretical level, it may not make sense to include this in a regression model, as one is far more likely to have been asked to run if one is already deeply involved in politics—it is therefore endogenous. But believing that politics solves important problems is significant with a relatively large coefficient whether or not "asked-run" is included, for both models, and the p-value of the "solves" variable is always significant at p < .001.

27  P < .07, N = 186 women of color.

28  P < .001, N = 82 black women. Black women are also extremely significantly less likely to think politics solves important problems when compared with everyone else in the sample (including men as well, p < .001).

29  Wright 2005, 11.

30  Ibid., 7–8 (emphasis in original).

31  Du Bois 1909, 188.

32  Tatum 2003.

33  hooks 2008, 83–84; see also work by Steele and colleagues in sociology on "stereotype threat" for both race and gender, including Spencer et al. 1999 and Steele and Aronson 1995. Such works suggest that individuals in stigmatized groups often internalize the stereotypes they think others hold of them (such as that women are bad at math, or that blacks do poorly on the SAT test).

34  Where one's biological sex matches one's social gender presentation (the opposite of transgender).

35  hooks 2008; McIntosh 1989; see also Mansbridge and Shames 2008.

36  For instance, some strategic candidates can use their gender (or race) as a positive signal of "outsiderness" (Shames 2003).

37  Wright 2005; see also Mansbridge and Shames 2008.

38  See, for example, the explication by Wilkins and Gulati (1996) on black lawyers in corporate firms feeling a need to present as "superstars."

39  On gender and race in an institutional context, see Hawkesworth 2003.

40  p < .001, N = 389 women.

41  hooks 1999.

42  Carlton-Ford, Ender, and Tabatabai 2008.

43  Kim 1999.

CHAPTER 8. CHANGE THE SYSTEM, CHANGE THE CANDIDATES

1 Mansbridge 2014.

2 Lawless and Fox 2015; Harvard IOP 2012–2015.

3 Lawless and Fox 2015, 139.

4 Ibid., 143–63.

5 "[W]e are not naïve enough to believe that major changes to the performance of US government, or how the news media report on politics, are anywhere on the horizon," they write (Ibid., 144).

6 Associated Press 2016.

7 Owens 2016; and to boot, much of the water never made it to where it was most needed (see Karoub 2016).

8 Kamber 2003.

9 Mansbridge 2014.

APPENDIX

1 *Harvard Gazette* 2008; *Liberty Voice* 2014.

2 *Liberty Voice* 2014.

3 *Harvard Magazine* 1995, 1997, 1999, 2001, 2005, 2009, 2011, 2012, 2014.

4 Based on author coding of the biographies given in U.S. Department of Justice 2014.

5 Hu 2011 (although this article notes that for the most part state legislatures are not Ivy League–dominated as Congress is—instead, there are often key local schools within a state that become "feeders" for the state legislature, as with Suffolk Law and Boston College Law in Boston).

6 Harvard Kennedy School 2012.

7 Figures derived from author analysis and coding of member biographical data from the web site of the Massachusetts General Court (state legislature), at https://malegislature.gov/People/House/ (accessed May 10, 2010).

8 Ibid.

9 Because of federal restrictions on the sharing of student data (including names and e-mail addresses), I was not able to compile a "sample" of students at Suffolk Law or Boston College Law in the same way I was able to do at Harvard, where I myself was a student (and thus had access to other students' data). Instead, at Suffolk I took a "carpet-bombing" approach, doing my best to blanket the campus with requests. I put a notice in the "Deans Newsletter" (which was e-mailed to students each week) for three weeks in a row, I hung posters throughout the SLS building, I contacted student groups and asked them to send the notice of the survey to their members, and I hired an SLS student to e-mail the notice out to as many SLS students as she could. This process was less than ideal, but it was the best replacement for a list of students' e-mail addresses. I offered the same incentive ($10 for the survey, and an additional $20 for the interview) to students at all schools, which seemed a strong enough incentive to ensure a fairly good response rate at all the schools.

10  The method for this calculation **derived from** AppliedSurveyMethods.com 2016.

11  I transcribed several of the **interviews and** hired research assistants to transcribe the rest. When I was not the **transcriber,** I hired a second research assistant to listen to the tape and "verify" each written transcript to ensure an accurate transcription.

12  Current research in race/ethnicity suggests that multiracial individuals have complex understandings of **their identities** and may see themselves as "mixed" or "biracial" more than as either of their parents' races. Acknowledging that racial identity is complicated, **and following** current practices of the U.S. Census, I allowed respondents in my **survey to mark** as many races as they felt applied. But for statistical compilation **purposes, I wanted** to count each respondent only once. Thus if respondents **reported two** or more races, I sorted them into a single category as follows: if a respondent reported being both white and a member of a nonwhite group, I placed that **respondent** in the nonwhite group. If a respondent claimed to be Asian and black **or Hispanic,** I placed the respondent in the black or Hispanic group. If a respondent claimed to be black and Hispanic, I placed the respondent in the black **group. Because** there were not enough mixed-race respondents in the sample to **treat them** as a separate group and draw meaningful inferences, I needed either to **drop them** from the analysis or aggregate them into a single racial category. I chose **to place** them in the category to which I attributed more discrimination on the **grounds that** this process would produce the best possible test of the theory of **candidate deterrence.**

# REFERENCES

ABA: 2013. "Statistics from the ABA Commission on Women," American Bar Association Report. Available online at http://www.americanbar.org/groups/women/resources/statistics.html (accessed March 30, 2014).

Almanac of American Politics: 2010. *Almanac of American Politics*. Washington: National Journal.

Alsop, Rob: 2008. *The Trophy Kids Grow Up: How the Millennial Generation Is Shaking Up the Workplace*. San Francisco: Jossey-Bass.

Anzia, Sarah, and Berry, Christopher: 2009. "The Jackie (and Jill) Robinson Effect: Why Do Congresswomen Outperform Congressmen?," Working paper. Available online at: http://ssrn.com/abstract=1013443 (accessed June 2, 2010).

Applied Survey Methods: 2016. "Sample Weighting Adjustment," Applied Survey Methods, A Statistical Perspective. Available online at http://www.applied-survey-methods.com/weight.html (accessed February 15, 2016).

Arnold, R. Douglas: 1990. *The Logic of Congressional Action*. New Haven, Conn.: Yale University Press.

Ashe, Jeanette, and Stewart, Kennedy: 2012. "Legislative Recruitment: Using Diagnostic Testing to Explain Underrepresentation," *Party Politics* 18; 687–707.

Associated Press: 2016. "Cher Donates Thousands of Bottles of Water to Troubled Flint," *Washington Times*, January 16. Available online at http://www.washingtontimes.com/news/2016/jan/16/cher-donates-thousands-of-bottles-of-water-to-trou/(accessed February 22, 2016).

Atkeson, Lonna Rae: 2003. "Not All Cues Are Created Equal: The Conditional Impact of Female Candidates on Political Engagement," *The Journal of Politics* 65(4): 1040–61.

Atkeson, Lonna Rae, and Carrillo, Nancy: 2007. "More Is Better: The Influence of Collective Female Descriptive Representation on External Efficacy," *Politics and Gender* 3: 79–101.

Babcock, Linda, and Laschever, Sara: 2007. *Women Don't Ask: The High Cost of Avoiding Negotiation—and Positive Strategies for Change*. New York: Bantam.

Baer, Denise: 1993. "Political Parties: The Missing Variable in Women and Politics Research," *Political Research Quarterly* 46(3): 547–76.

———: 2003. "Women, Women's Organizations, and Political Parties," in *Women and American Politics: New Questions, New Directions*, ed. Susan J. Carroll. New York: Oxford University Press.

Barreto, Matt A.; Segura, Gary M.; and Woods, Nathan D.: 2004. "The Mobilizing Effect of Majority–Minority Districts on Latino Turnout," *American Political Science Review* 98(1): 65–75.

Bartels, Larry: 1998. *Presidential Primaries and the Dynamics of Public Choice*. Princeton, N.J.: Princeton University Press.

———: 2000. "Partisanship and Voting Behavior, 1952–1996," *American Journal of Political Science* 44(1): 35–50.

Beauvoir, Simone de: 1953 [1949]. *The Second Sex*. New York: Knopf.

Beckwith, Karen: 2005. "A Common Language of Gender?" *Politics and Gender Journal* 1(1): 128–37.

Bem, Sandra L.: 1988. *Psychology of Sex Roles, 2nd edition*. Littleton, Mass.: Copley Publishing Group.

Besley, Timothy; Folke, Olle; Persson, Torsten; and Rickne, Johanna: 2013. "Gender Quotas and the Crisis of the Mediocre Man: Theory and Evidence from Sweden," IFN (Research Institute of Industrial Economics) Working Paper No. 985. Available online at http://papers.ssrn.com/sol3/papers.cfm?abstract_id=2465902 (accessed February 20, 2016).

Biographical Directory of the United States Congress: 2014. "Biographical Directory of the United States Congress: 1774–Present." Available online at http://bioguide .congress.gov/biosearch/biosearch.asp (accessed March 30, 2014).

Black, Gordon: 1972. "A Theory of Political Ambition: Career Choices and the Role of Structural Incentives," *American Political Science Review* 66(1): 144–59.

Blau, F. D., and Kahn, L. M.: 2000. "Gender Differences in Pay," *Journal of Economic Perspectives* 14(4), Autumn: 75–99.

Bobo, Lawrence, and Gilliam, Franklin D.: 1990. "Race, Sociopolitical Participation, and Black Empowerment," *The American Political Science Review*, Vol. 84, No. 2. (June): 377–93.

Bowles, Hannah Riley; Babcock, Linda; and Lai, Lei: 2005. "Social incentives for gender differences in the propensity to initiate negotiations: Sometimes it does hurt to ask," *Organizational Behavior and Human Decision Processes* 103: 84–103.

Boxer, Barbara: 1994. *Strangers in the Senate: Politics and the New Revolution of Women in America*. Washington: National Press Books.

Box-Steffensmeier, Janet: 1996. "A Dynamic Analysis of the Role of War Chests in Campaign Strategy," *American Journal of Political Science* 40(2): 352–71.

Brady, D. W.; Han, H.; and Pope, J. C.: 2007. "Primary elections and candidate ideology: Out of step with the primary electorate?," *Legislative Studies Quarterly*, 32(1): 79–105.

Branton, Regina P.: 2009. "The Importance of Race and Ethnicity in Congressional Primary Elections," *Political Research Quarterly* 62(3): 459–73.

Broockman, David; Carnes, Nicholas; Crowder-Meyer, Melody; and Skovron, Christopher: 2012. Producers and distributors, National Candidate Study (unpublished datafile). Demographic statistics on sample provided by Broockman et al. to the author.

Brooks, Deborah Jordan, and Geer, John G.: 2007. "Beyond Negativity: The Effects of Incivility on the Electorate," *American Journal of Political Science* 51(1): 1–16.

Brown, Clifford W., Jr.; Powell, Lynda W.; and Wilcox, Clyde: 1995. *Serious Money: Fundraising and Contributing in Presidential Nomination Campaigns*. New York: Cambridge University Press.

Brown, Nadia: 2014. *Sisters in the Statehouse: Black Women and Legislative Decision-making*. New York: Oxford University Press.

Brownmiller, Susan: 1975. *Against Our Will: Men, Women, and Rape*. New York: Simon & Schuster.

Buhlmann, Marc, and Schadel, Lisa: 2012. "Representation Matters: The Impact of Descriptive Women's Representation on the Political Involvement of Women," *Representation* 48(1): 101–14.

Burns, Nancy; Schlozman, Kay; and Verba, Sidney: 2001. *The Private Roots of Public Action*. Cambridge, Mass.: Harvard University Press.

Burrell, Barbara: 1993. "John Baily's Legacy: Political Parties and Women's Candidacies for Public Office," in *Women in Politics: Outsiders or Insiders?*, ed. Lois Lovelace Duke. Englewood Cliffs, N.J.: Prentice-Hall.

Caiazza, Amy: 2002. "Does Women's Representation in Elected Office Lead to Women-Friendly Policy?" Policy Brief for the Institute for Women's Policy Research (IWPR), Publication #1910. Washington: IWPR.

Cameron, Charles; Epstein, David; and O'Halloran, Sharyn: 1996. "Do Majority–Minority Districts Maximize Substantive Black Representation in Congress?," *American Political Science Review* 90(4): 794–812.

Campaign Finance Institute: 2016. Tables, charts, and data on campaign finance. Available online at http://www.cfinst.org/ (accessed February 15, 2016).

Campbell, Bonnie: 2001. Interview with author via telephone, for use in Shames 2001 and 2003.

Campbell, David E., and Wolbrecht, Christina: 2006. "See Jane Run: Women Politicians as Role Models for Adolescents," *Journal of Politics* 68(2): 233–47.

Carli, Linda L., and Eagly, Alice, issue editors: 2001. "Gender, Hierarchy, and Leadership," *Journal of Social Issues*, Volume 57, No. 4: Winter.

Carlton-Ford, Steve; Ender, Morten G.; and Tabatabai, Ahoo: 2008. "Iraqi Adolescents: Self-Regard, Self-Derogation, and Perceived Threat in War," *Journal of Adolescence* 31: 53–75.

Carnes, Nicholas: 2013. *White Collar Government: The Hidden Role of Class in Economic Policy Making*. Chicago: University of Chicago Press.

Carroll, Susan: 1985. *Women as Candidates in American Politics*. Bloomington: Indiana University Press.

———: 1994. *Women as Candidates in American Politics, 2nd edition*. Bloomington: Indiana University Press.

———: 2001. "The Impact of Term Limits on Women," *Spectrum: Journal of State Government* (Fall): 19–21. Available online through the Center for American

Women and Politics, at: http://www.cawp.rutgers.edu/research/topics/term_limits .php#Impact (accessed June 4, 2010).

Carroll, Susan, and Jenkins, Krista: 2001. "Do Term Limits Help Women Get Elected?," *Social Science Quarterly* 82 (March).

———: 2005. "Increasing Diversity or More of the Same? Term Limits and the Representation of Women, Minorities, and Minority Women in State Legislatures," *National Political Science Review* 10: 71–84.

Carroll, Susan, and Sanbonmatsu, Kira: 2013. *More Women Can Run: Gender and Pathways to the State Legislature*. Oxford: Oxford University Press.

CAWP (Center for American Women and Politics): 2010. "Election Underscores Urgent Need for the 2012 Project: Women Suffer First Decline in Congress in Over 30 Years," CAWP Press Release (November 5). Available online at http://cawp.rutgers .edu/sites/default/files/resources/pressrelease_11–05–10–2012.pdf (accessed February 14, 2016).

———: 2016. "Facts and Findings," Fact Sheets from the Center for American Women and Politics. New Brunswick, N.J.: CAWP. Available at: http://www.cawp.rutgers. edu/ (accessed February 14, 2016).

CBC News (Canada): 2015. "Canada Election 2015: Stephen Harper confirms start of 11-week federal campaign," available online at http://www.cbc.ca/news/poli tics/canada-election-2015-stephen-harper-confirms-start-of-11-week-federal -campaign-1.3175136 (accessed February 15, 2016).

CBS News: 2004. "Young Get News from Comedy Central," available online at: http:// www.cbsnews.com/news/young-get-news-from-comedy-central/ (accessed March 30, 2014).

Chang, Mariko: 2010. *Shortchanged: Why Women Have Less Wealth and What Can Be Done about It*. New York: Oxford University Press.

Clark, Karen: 2004. Personal interview with author, May 1.

Clements, Jeffrey, and Moyers, Bill: 2014. *Corporations Are Not People: Reclaiming Democracy from Big Money and Global Corporations*. San Francisco: Berrett-Koehler Publishers.

Combahee River Collective: [1977] 1981. "Statement of the Combahee River Collective," in *This Bridge Called My Back: Writings by Radical Women of Color*, ed. Cherríe Moraga and Gloria Anzaldúa. Watertown, Mass.: Persephone Press.

Congressional Research Service: 2012. "African American Members of the United States Congress: 1870–2012," compiled by Jennifer E. Manning and Colleen J. Shogan. Congressional Research Service Report. Available online at http://www .senate.gov/CRSReports/crs-publish.cfm?pid=%270E%2C*PLW%3C%20P%20%20 %0A (accessed March 30, 2014).

———: 2013. "Asian Pacific Americans in the United States Congress," research report compiled by Lorraine H. Tong. Washington: Congressional Research Service. Available online at: www.fas.org/sgp/crs/misc/97–398.pdf (accessed March 30, 2014).

———: 2014. "Membership of the 113th Congress: A Profile," compiled by Jennifer E. Manning. Congressional Research Service Report. Available online at http://

www.senate.gov/CRSReports/crs-publish.cfm?pid=%260BL%2BR%5CC%3F%0A
(accessed February 15, 2016).

———: 2014a. "Membership of the 113th Congress: A Profile," research report compiled by Jennifer E. Manning. Congressional Research Service. Available online at: http://www.fas.org/sgp/crs/misc/R42964.pdf (accessed March 30, 2014).

———: 2014b. "Congressional Salaries and Allowances," research report compiled by Ida A. Brudnick. Available online at http://www.senate.gov/CRSReports/crs-publish.cfm?pid=%270E%2C*PL%5B%3D%23P%20%20%0A (accessed March 31, 2014).

Conley, Dalton: 2009. *Being Black, Living in the Red: Race, Wealth, and Social Policy in America, 10th anniversary edition.* Berkeley: University of California Press.

Conway, M. Margaret: 2001. "Women and Political Participation," *PS: Political Science and Politics* 34(2), June: 231–33.

Cook, Elizabeth: 1998. "Voter Reaction to Women Candidates," in *Women and Elective Office*, ed. Sue Thomas and Clyde Wilcox. New York: Oxford University Press, 56–72.

Cook, Elizabeth; Thomas, Sue; and Wilcox, Clyde: 1994. *The Year of the Woman: Myths and Realities.* Boulder, Colo.: Westview Press.

Crenshaw, Kimberlé. 1991. "Mapping the Margins": Intersectionality, Identity Politics and Violence Against Women," *Stanford Law Review* 43: 1241–99.

Crittenden, Ann: 2002. *The Price of Motherhood.* New York: Holt.

Dahlerup, Drude: 2003. "Comparative Studies of Electoral Gender Quotas," Paper Presented at International IDEA Workshop. Available online at http://www.quotaproject.org/CS/CS_Dahlerup_25–11–2003.pdf (accessed March 30, 2014).

———, ed.: 2006. *Women, Quotas, and Politics.* New York: Routledge.

Dahlerup, Drude, and Leyenaar, Monique: 2013. *Breaking Male Dominance in Old Democracies.* Oxford: Oxford University Press.

Davidson-Schmidt, Louise K.: 2006. "Gender and Political Ambition Revisited: What Questions Does American Politics Research Raise for Western Europeanists?" Paper presented at the annual meeting of the American Political Science Association (APSA), Aug. 31–Sept. 3, Philadelphia.

———: 2008. "Gender Quotas and Political Ambition: Evidence from Germany." Paper Prepared for the 2008 Midwest Political Science Association Annual Meeting, Chicago.

———: forthcoming. *A Glass Half Full: Gender Quotas and Political Recruitment.* Book manuscript in process.

Dawson, Michael: 1994. *Behind the Mule.* Princeton, N.J.: Princeton University Press.

DeLauro, Rosa: 2002. Public lecture for The White House Project, Washington.

Dittmar, Kelly: 2015. *Navigating Gendered Terrain: Stereotypes and Strategy in Political Campaigns.* Philadelphia: Temple University Press.

Djupe, Paul A., and Olson, Laura R.: 2013. "Stained-glass politics and descriptive representation: does associational leadership by women engender political engagement among women?," *Politics, Groups, and Identities* 1(3): 329–48.

Dolan, Kathleen: 2004. *Voting for Women: How the Public Evaluates Women Candidates*. Boulder, Colo.: Westview Press.

———: 2006. "Symbolic Mobilization? The Impact of Candidate Sex in American Elections," *American Politics Research*, Vol. 34(6): 687–704.

Downs, Anthony: 1957. *An Economic Theory of Democracy*. New York: Harper & Row.

Downs, Kenya: 2016. "African-Americans over-represented among low-paying college majors," *PBS.org* NewsHour story. Available online at http://www.pbs.org/newshour/rundown/african-americans-over-represented-among-low-paying-college-majors/ (accessed February 20, 2016).

Du Bois, W. E. B.: 1909 [1903]. *The Souls of Black Folk: Essays and Sketches*. Chicago: McClurg and Co.

Duerst-Lahti, Georgia: 1998. "The Bottleneck: Women Becoming Candidates," *Women and Elective Office*, ed. Sue Thomas and Clyde Wilcox. New York: Oxford University Press, 15–25.

Duerst-Lahti, Georgia, and Kelly, Rita Mae: 1995. *Gender Power, Leadership, and Governance*. Ann Arbor: University of Michigan Press.

Duverger, Maurice: 1955. *The Political Role of Women*. Paris: UNESCO.

Eagly, Alice, and Carli, Linda: 2007. *Through the Labyrinth: The Truth About How Women Become Leaders*. Cambridge, Mass.: Harvard Business Review Press.

Eagly, Alice, and Johnson, Blair T.: 1990. "Gender and Leadership Style: A Meta-Analysis," *Psychological Bulletin*, Vol. 108, no. 2: 233–56.

Eagly, Alice, and Karau, Steven J.: 2005. "Role Congruity Theory of Prejudice Toward Female Leaders," *Psychological Review* 109(3): 573–98.

Einstein, Katherine Levine: forthcoming. *Divided Regions: Racial Inequality, Political Segregation, and the Splintering of Metropolitan America*.

Elections Canada: 2015. "Political Financing Handbook for Candidates and Official Agents (EC 20155)," Elections Canada. Available online at http://www.elections.ca/content.aspx?section=pol&dir=can/man/ec20155&document=p3&lang=e#a (accessed February 15, 2016).

Elliott, Justin: 2012. "Vast Gender Disparity in Super-PAC Giving," Salon.com, available online at http://www.salon.com/2012/02/02/vast_gender_disparity_in_super_pac_giving/ (accessed April 1, 2014).

Ely, Robin J.; Ibarra, Herminia; and Kolb, Deborah: 2011. "Taking Gender into Account: Theory and Design for Women's Leadership Development Programs," Faculty and Research Working Paper, INSTEAD Working Paper Collection. Available online at http://bpwnz.org.nz/wp-content/uploads/2012/08/Taking-gender-into-account.pdf (accessed March 30, 2014).

Falk, Erika: 2008. *Women for President: Media Bias in Eight Campaigns*. Urbana: University of Illinois Press.

Faludi, Susan: 1991. *Backlash: The Invisible War Against America's Women*. New York: Crown.

Farris, Emily M., and Holman, Mirya R.: 2014. "Social Capital and Solving the Puzzle of Black Women's Political Participation," *Politics, Groups, and Identities* 2(3): 331–49.

Fels, Anna: 2004. *Necessary Dreams: Ambition in Women's Changing Lives*. New York: Anchor Books.

Fenno, Richard F., Jr.: 1975. "If, as Ralph Nader Says, Congress is 'The Broken Branch,' How Come We Love Our Congressmen So Much?," in *Congress in Change: Evolution and Reform*, ed. Norman J. Ornstein. New York: Praeger, 277–87.

Ferree, Myra Marx: 2004. "Soft Repression: Ridicule, Stigma, and Silencing in Gender-Based Movements," in *Research in Social Movements, Conflicts and Change*, ed. Daniel J. Myers and Daniel M. Cress. San Diego: Elsevier, vol. 25, 85–101.

Fletcher, Joyce: 1999. *Disappearing Acts: Gender, Power, and Relational Practice at Work*. Cambridge, Mass.: MIT Press.

Follow the Money: 2012. "An Overview of Campaign Finances, 2009–2010 Elections," research report, Follow the Money National Institute. Available online at http://www .followthemoney.org/press/ReportView.phtml?r=487 (accessed March 30, 2014).

Fowler, Linda L., and McClure, Robert D.: 1989. *Political Ambition: Who Decides to Run for Congress*. New Haven, Conn.: Yale University Press.

Fox, Richard L., and Lawless, Jennifer L.: 2005. "To Run or Not to Run for Office: Explaining Nascent Political Ambition," *American Journal of Political Science* 49(3): 642–59.

———: 2010. "If Only They'd Ask: Gender, Recruitment, and Political Ambition," *Journal of Politics* 72(2): 310–26.

Francia, Peter L., et al.: 2003. *The Financiers of Congressional Elections: Investors, Ideologues, and Intimates*. New York: Columbia University Press.

Frederickson, George M.: 2002. *Racism: A Short History*. Princeton, N.J.: Princeton University Press.

Freedom House: 2016. "Freedom in the World," Freedom House Report. Available online at https://freedomhouse.org/report/freedom-world/freedom-world-2016 (accessed February 14, 2016).

Frye, Marilyn: 1983. *The Politics of Reality: Essays in Feminist Theory*. Trumansburg, N.Y.: Cross Press.

Fulton, Sarah A.: 2005. "Perception Is as Powerful as Reality: The Impact of Anticipated Bias on Women's Office-Seeking Behavior," paper prepared for presentation to the Western Political Science Association's Annual Meeting, Oakland, California (March).

Fulton, Sarah A.; Maestas, Cherie D.; Maisel, L. Sandy; and Stone, Walter J.: 2006. "The Sense of a Woman: Gender, Ambition, and the Decision to Run for Congress," *Political Research Quarterly* 59(2): 235–48.

Gaddie, Keith: 2003. *Born to Run*. Washington: Rowman and Littlefield.

Gallup Poll: 2013. "Gridlock Is Top Reason Americans Are Critical of Congress," Gallup Report (June). Available online at http://www.gallup.com/poll/163031/gridlock -top-reason-americans-critical-congress.aspx (accessed February 14, 2016).

———: 2014. "Congressional Approval Languishes at Low Level," Gallup Report (July). Available online at http://www.gallup.com/poll/172859/congressional-approval-rating-languishes-low-level.aspx (accessed February 14, 2016).

———: 2015a. "Confidence in U.S. Branches of Government Remains Low," Gallup Report (June). Available online at http://www.gallup.com/poll/183605/confidence-branches-government-remains-low.aspx (accessed February 14, 2016).

———: 2015b. "U.S. Congress and Its Leaders Suffer Public Discontent," Gallup Report (August). Available online at http://www.gallup.com/poll/184556/congress-leaders-suffer-public-discontent.aspx?utm_source=Politicsandutm_medium=newsfeedandutm_campaign=tiles (accessed February 14, 2016).

Gay, Claudine: 2001. "The Effect of Black Congressional Representation on Political Participation," *The American Political Science Review*, Vol. 95, No. 3. (Sept.): 589–602.

———: 2002. "Spirals of Trust? The Effect of Descriptive Representation on the Relationship between Citizens and Their Government," *American Journal of Political Science*, Vol. 46, No. 4. (Oct.): 717–32.

Gay, Claudine, and Tate, Katherine: 1998. "Doubly Bound: The Impact of Gender and Race on the Politics of Black Women," *Political Psychology* 19(1): 169–84.

Gilens, Martin: 2012. *Affluence and Influence: Economic Inequality and Political Power in America*. Princeton, N.J.: Princeton University Press.

Gilman, Hollie Russon: 2016. *Democracy Reinvented: Participatory Budgeting and Civic Innovation in America*. Washington: Brookings Institution Press.

Goffman, Erving: 1979. *Gender Advertisements*. Cambridge, Mass.: Harvard University Press.

Goss, Kristin: 2013. *The Paradox of Gender Equality*. Ann Arbor: University of Michigan Press.

Green, P. 1968. *Deadly Logic: The Theory of Nuclear Deterrence*. New York: Schocken Books.

Greenwald, Anthony G., and Banaji, Mahzarin R.: 1995. "Implicit Social Cognition: Attitudes, Self-Esteem, and Stereotypes," *Psychological Review* 102(1): 4–27.

Griffin, John D., and Keane, Michael: 2006. "Descriptive Representation and the Composition of African American Turnout," *American Journal of Political Science* 50(4): 998–1012.

Hacker, Helen: 1951. "Women as a Minority Group," *Social Forces* 30(1): 60–69.

Haidt, Jonathan: 2001. "The Emotional Dog and Its Rational Tail: A Social Intuitionist Approach to Moral Judgment," *Psychological Review* 108(4): 814–34.

Hardman, Isabel: 2014. "It costs 34,000 British pounds to become an MP. No wonder they expect higher pay," *The Spectator* (UK), August 16. Available online at http://www.spectator.co.uk/2014/08/could-you-afford-to-become-an-mp/ (accessed February 16, 2016).

Hardy-Fanta, Carol: 2011. *Latina Politics, Latino Politics: Gender, Culture, and Political Participation in Boston*. Philadelphia: Temple University Press.

Harris-Lacewell, Melissa: 2005. "Contributions of Black Women in Political Science to a More Just World," *Politics and Gender* 1(2), June: 341–50.

*Harvard Crimson*: 1995. "Numbers of Harvard Grads in Congress Down," *Harvard Crimson* (January 6). Available online at http://www.thecrimson.com/article /1995/1/6/numbers-of-harvard-grads-in-congress/ (accessed March 30, 2014).

*Harvard Gazette*: 2008. "Obama joins list of seven presidents with Harvard degrees," *Harvard Gazette* (November 6). Available online at http://news.harvard.edu /gazette/story/2008/11/obama-joins-list-of-seven-presidents-with-harvard-degrees /(accessed March 30, 2014).

Harvard IOP (Institute of Politics): 2012–2015. "Survey of Young Americans' Attitudes Toward Politics and Public Service," across multiple years. Cambridge, Mass.: Institute of Politics, Harvard University. Available online at http://www.iop.harvard.edu /harvard-public-opinion-project-0 (accessed February 19, 2016).

Harvard Kennedy School: 2012. "Public Sector Employment Report for HKS Graduates," HKS Report. Available online at http://www.hks.harvard.edu/var/ezp_site /storage/fckeditor/file/pdfs/degree-programs/oca/employment_overview.pdf (accessed March 30, 2014).

*Harvard Magazine*: 1997. "John Harvard's Journal: Cantabrigians in the Capitol," *Harvard Magazine*. Available online at http://harvardmagazine.com/1997/03/jhj.capital .html (accessed March 30, 2014).

————: 1999. "Crimson in Washington," *Harvard Magazine*. Available online at http:// harvardmagazine.com/1999/01/jhj.crimson.html (accessed March 30, 2014).

————: 2001."Brevia," *Harvard Magazine*. Available online at http://harvardmagazine .com/2001/03/brevia.html (accessed March 30, 2014).

————: 2005. "Crimson on the Hill," *Harvard Magazine*. Available online at http:// harvardmagazine.com/2005/01/crimson-on-the-hill.html (accessed March 30, 2014).

————: 2009. "Crimson in Congress," *Harvard Magazine*. Available online at http:// harvardmagazine.com/2009/01/crimson-in-congress (accessed March 30, 2014).

————: 2011. "Crimson in Congress," *Harvard Magazine*. Available online at http:// harvardmagazine.com/2011/01/crimson-in-congress (accessed March 30, 2014).

————: 2012. "Crimson in Congress," *Harvard Magazine*. Available online at http:// harvardmagazine.com/2012/11/election-2012-crimson-in-congress (accessed March 30, 2014).

Haub, Carl. 2012. "Changing the Way U.S. Hispanics Are Counted," Population Reference Bureau. Available online at: http://www.prb.org/Publications/Articles/2012 /us-census-and-hispanics.aspx (accessed March 29, 2014).

Hawkesworth, Mary: 2003. "Congressional Enactments of Race-Gender: Toward a Theory of Raced-Gendered Institutions," *APSR* 97(4), November: 529–50.

Hetherington, Marc J.: 2001. "Resurgent Mass Partisanship: The Role of Elite Polarization," *American Political Science Review* 95(3): 619–31.

Hewlett, Sylvia Ann: 2007. *Off-Ramps and On-Ramps: Keeping Talented Women on the Road to Success*. Cambridge, Mass.: Harvard University Press.

Hibbing, John R., and Theiss-Morse, Elizabeth: 2001. *What Is It about Government That Americans Dislike?* New York: Cambridge University Press.

Hinojosa, Magda: 2012. *Selecting Women, Electing Women: Political Representation and Candidate Selection in Latin America*. Philadelphia: Temple University Press.

Hitchon, Jacqueline C., and Chang, Chingching: 1995. "Effects of Gender Schematic Processing on the Reception of Political Commercials for Men and Women Candidates," *Communication Research*, Vol. 22, No. 4 (Aug.): 430–58.

Hochschild, Arlie: 2003. *The Second Shift*, updated introduction. New York: Penguin Books.

Hochschild, Jennifer; Weaver, Vesla; and Burch, Traci: 2012. *Creating a New Racial Order: How Immigration, Multiracialism, Genomics, and the Young Can Remake Race in America*. Princeton, N.J.: Princeton University Press.

Hofstader, Richard: 1965. *The Paranoid Style in American Politics*. New York: Knopf.

hooks, bell: 1989. *Talking Back: Thinking Feminist, Thinking Black*. Boston: South End Press.

———: 1992. *Black Looks: Race and Representation*. Boston: South End Press.

———: 1996. *Bone Black: Memories of Girlhood*. New York: Holt.

———: 1999. *Happy to Be Nappy*. New York: Jump at the Sun Publishers (Hyperion/Disney).

———: 2008. *Belonging: A Culture of Place*. New York: Routledge.

Htun, Mala: 2004. "Is Gender Like Ethnicity? The Political Representation of Identity Groups," *Perspectives on Politics* 2(3): 439–58.

Hu, Winnie: 2011. "Many State Legislators Lack College Degrees," *New York Times* (June 12). Available online at http://www.nytimes.com/2011/06/13/education/13legis.html?_r=1and (accessed March 30, 2014).

IFES: 2009. "Political Finance Regulation: The Global Experience," report by the International Foundation for Electoral Systems. Available online at http://www.ifes.org/files/Political_Finance_Regulation_The_Global_Experience.pdf (accessed March 30, 2014).

International IDEA: 2003. "Funding of Political Parties and Election Campaigns," handbook produced by International IDEA. Available online at http://www.idea.int/publications/funding_parties/ (accessed March 31, 2014).

International IDEA Political Finance Database: 2012. Political Finance Database. Available online at http://www.idea.int/political-finance/index.cfm (accessed March 30, 2014).

IWPR: 2014. "Pay Equity and Discrimination," report by the Institute for Women's Policy Research. Available online at http://www.iwpr.org/initiatives/pay-equity-and-discrimination (accessed March 30, 2014).

Jamieson, Kathleen Hall: 1995. *Beyond the Double Bind: Women and Leadership*. New York: Oxford University Press.

———: 2000. *Everything You Think You Know About Politics . . . And Why You're Wrong*. New York: Basic Books.

Jenkins, Shannon: 2007. "A Woman's Work Is Never Done? Fund-Raising Perception and Effort among Female State Legislative Candidates," *Political Research Quarterly*, 60(2): 230–39.

Jennings, M. Kent: 1983. "Gender Roles and Inequalities in Political Participation: Results from an Eight-Nation Study," *The Western Political Quarterly* 36(3): 364–85.

JTA: 2009. "At least 139 of the Forbes 400 are Jewish," Jewish Telegraphic Agency. Available online at http://www.jta.org/2009/10/05/fundermentalist/at-least-139-of-the-forbes-400-are-jewish (accessed March 30, 2014).

Kahn, Kim Fridkin: 1996. *The Political Consequences of Being a Woman: How Stereotypes Influence the Conduct and Consequences of Political Campaigns.* New York: Columbia University Press.

Kamber, Victor: 2003. *Poison Politics: Are Negative Campaigns Destroying Democracy?* New York: Basic Books.

Kanter, Rosabeth Moss: 1977. "Some Effects of Proportions on Group Life: Skewed Sex Ratios and Response to Token Women," *American Journal of Sociology* 82: 965–90.

Kanthak, Kristin, and Woon, Jonathan: 2014. "Women Don't Run? Election Aversion and Candidate Entry," *American Journal of Political Science* 59(3): 595–612.

Karoub, Jeff: 2016. "A look at mass donations to Flint amid drinking water crisis," *Washington Times,* January 26. Available online at http://www.washingtontimes.com/news/2016/jan/26/a-look-at-mass-donations-to-flint-amid-drinking-wa/?page=all (accessed February 22, 2016).

Karpowitz, Christopher F.; Mendelberg, Tali; and Shaker, Lee: 2012. "Gender Inequality in Deliberative Participation," *American Political Science Review* 106(3): 533–47.

Kasinitz, Phillip et al.: 2008. *Inheriting the City: The Children of Immigrants Come of Age.* Cambridge, Mass.: Harvard University Press.

Kathlene, Lyn: 1994. "Power and Influence in State Legislative Policymaking: The Interaction of Gender and Position in Committee Hearing Debates," *American Political Science Review* 99 (3): 560–76.

———: 1995. "Position Power versus Gender Power: Who Holds the Floor?," in *Gender Power, Leadership, and Governance,* ed. Georgia Duerst-Lahti and Rita Mae Kelly. Ann Arbor: University of Michigan Press, 167–93.

———: 1999. "In a Different Voice: Women and the Policy Process," in *Women and Elective Office: Past, Present, and Future,* ed. Sue Thomas and Clyde Wilcox. Boulder, Colo.: Westview Press.

Kaufmann, Karen: 1998. "Racial Conflict and Political Choice: A Study of Mayoral Voting Behavior in Los Angeles and New York," *Urban Affairs Review* 33: 655–85.

———: 2003. "Black and Latino Voters in Denver: Responses to Each Other's Political Leadership," *Political Science Quarterly* 118(1): 107–25.

Kazee, Thomas A.: 1994. *Who Runs for Congress? Ambition, Context, and Candidate Emergence.* Washington: Congressional Quarterly Press.

Keohane, Robert O.: 2001. "Governance in a Partially-Globalized World: APSA Presidential Address," *The American Political Science Review* 95(1): 1–13.

Keyssar, Alexander: 2000. *The Right to Vote.* New York: Basic Books.

Kim, Claire Jean: 1999. "The Racial Triangulation of Asian Americans," *Politics & Society* 27: 105–38.

King, Cheryl Simrell: 1995. "Sex-Role Identity and Decision Styles: How Gender Helps Explain the Paucity of Women at the Top," in *Gender Power, Leadership, and Governance*, ed. Georgia Duerst-Lahti and Rita Mae Kelly. Ann Arbor: University of Michigan Press, 67–92.

Kohlberg, Lawrence. 1966. "A cognitive-developmental analysis of children's sex-role concepts and attitudes," in *The Development of Sex Differences*, ed. Eleanor E. Maccoby. Stanford, Calif.: Stanford University Press.

Krook, Mona Lena: 2009. *Quotas for Women in Politics: Gender and Candidate Selection Reform Worldwide*. New York: Oxford University Press.

Kymlicka, Will: 2002. *Contemporary Political Philosophy*. New York: Cambridge University Press.

Lake Research Partners: 2012. "Female State Legislators Project," dataset collected for Political Parity, a program of Hunt Alternatives, Cambridge, Mass. Datafile shared with author, based on survey with 176 female state legislators.

LatinasRepresent (a joint initiative of Hunt Alternatives and the National Hispanic Leadership Agenda): 2014. Interview with Congressman Juan Vargas on Social Justice. Available online at https://www.youtube.com/watch?v=ivPip6h_1XU (accessed February 14, 2016). More information on LatinasRepresent available at https://www.latinasrepresent.org/ (accessed February 14, 2016).

Lawless, Jennifer L.: 2004. "Politics of Presence? Congresswomen and Symbolic Representation," *Political Research Quarterly*, Vol. 57, No. 1. (March): 81–99.

Lawless, Jennifer L., and Fox, Richard L.: 2005. *It Takes a Candidate: Why Women Don't Run for Office*. New York: Cambridge University Press.

———: 2008. "Why Are Women Still Not Running for Public Office?," *Issues in Governance Studies*, Brookings Institution. Available online at: http://www.brookings.edu/papers/2008/05_women_lawless_fox.aspx (accessed January 5, 2010).

———: 2010. *It Still Takes a Candidate: Why Women Don't Run for Office*. New York: Cambridge University Press.

———: 2013. "Girls Just Wanna Not Run," report from the Women & Politics Institute, American University. Available online at https://www.american.edu/spa/wpi/upload/Girls-Just-Wanna-Not-Run_Policy-Report.pdf (accessed February 14, 2016).

Lawrence, Regina G., and Rose, Melody: 2010. *Hillary Clinton's Race for the White House*. Boulder, Colo.: Lynne Reinner Publishers.

Layman, Geoffrey C.; Carsey, Thomas M.; and Horowitz, Juliana M.: 2006. "Party Polarization in American Politics: Characteristics, Causes, and Consequences," *Annual Review of Political Science* 9: 83–110.

Leighley, Jan E.: 1995. "Attitudes, Opportunities and Incentives: A Field Essay on Political Participation," *Political Research Quarterly* 48(1), March: 181–209.

Leighley, Jan E., and Vedlitz, A.: 1999. "Race, Ethnicity, and Political Participation: Competing Models and Contrasting Explanations," *Journal of Politics* 61(4), November: 1092–14.

Lessig, Lawrence: 2015. *Republic, Lost: Version 2.0*. New York: Twelve/Hatchette.

Liberty Voice: 2014. "Harvard University Tops List of Colleges with Congress Member

Alumni," *Liberty Voice*. Available online at http://guardianlv.com/2014/02/harvard
-university-tops-list-of-colleges-with-congress-member-alumni/ (accessed March
30, 2014).

Little, Thomas; Dunn, Dana; and Deen, Rebecca: 2001. "A View from the Top: Gender
Differences in Legislative Priorities among Legislative Leaders," *Women and Politics*
22(4): 29–50.

Long, Robert: 2012. "Sen. Olympia Snowe Urges Return to Founding Fathers' Blueprint
in Farewell Speech," *Bangor Daily News*, December 13. Available online at http://
bangordailynews.com/2012/12/13/politics/sen-olympia-snowe-to-give-farewell-
speech-to-us-senate-on-thursday-afternoon/ (accessed February 14, 2016).

Lopez, Mark Hugo, et al.: 2006. "The 2006 Civic and Political Health of the Nation:
A Detailed Look at How Youth Participate in Politics and Communities," CIRCLE
(Center for Information and Research on Civic Learning and Engagement) Report.
Available online at http://civicyouth.org/the-2006-civic-and-political-health-of-the
-nation/ (accessed February 19, 2016).

Lublin, David: 1999. "Racial Redistricting and African-American Representation: A
Critique of 'Do Majority–Minority Districts Maximize Substantive Black Representation in Congress?'" *American Political Science Review* 93(1): 183–86.

MacFarquhar, Larissa: 2007. "The Conciliator: Where Is Barack Obama Coming
From?," *The New Yorker*, May 7.

MacKinnon, Catharine: 1991. "Reflections on Sex Equality Under Law," *Yale Law Journal* (March).

———: 1993. "Rape, Genocide, and Women's Human Rights," in *Mass Rape*, ed.
A. Stiglmeyer. Lincoln: University of Nebraska Press.

———: 2000. "Disputing Male Sovereignty," *Harvard Law Review* 114:. 135–78.

———: 2001. *Sex Equality*. New York: Foundation Press.

———: 2007. "Women's Status, Men's States," Lecture at the Radcliffe Institute, Harvard
University, April 19.

Maisel, L. Sandy, and Stone, Walter J.: 1997. "Determinants of Candidate Emergence
in U.S. House Elections: An Exploratory Study," *Legislative Studies Quarterly* 22(1):
79–96.

Maisel, L., Sandy; Stone, Walter J.; and Maestas, Cherie D., Principal Investigators:
2008. "The Candidate Emergence Study (CES)," description of multi-year study.
Available online at: http://ces.iga.ucdavis.edu/ (accessed January 9, 2010).

Mandel, Ruth: 1981. *In the Running: The New Woman Candidate*. New Haven, Conn.:
Ticknor and Fields.

Mansbridge, Jane: 1983. *Beyond Adversarial Democracy*. New York: Basic Books.

———: 1986. *Why We Lost the ERA*. Chicago: University of Chicago Press.

———: 1993. "Feminism and Democratic Community," in *Democratic Community:
NOMOS XXXV*, ed. John W. Chapman and Ian Shapiro. New York: New York
University Press, 342–77.

———: 1999a. "Should Blacks Represent Blacks and Women Represent Women? A
Contingent 'Yes,'" *Journal of Politics*, Vol. 61(3): 628–57.

———: 1999b. "'You're too independent!': How gender, race, and class make many plural feminisms," in *The Cultural Territories of Race: Black and White Boundaries*, ed. Michèle Lamont. Chicago: University of Chicago Press 291–317.

———: 2003. "Rethinking Representation," *American Political Science Review* 97(4): 515–28.

———: 2009. "Everyday Activists and Emergent Collective Action," unpublished manuscript, in submission process.

———: 2014. "What Is Political Science For?," *Perspectives on Politics* 12(1): 8–17.

Mansbridge, Jane, and Shames, Shauna: 2008. "Toward a Theory of Backlash: Dynamic Resistance and the Central Role of Power," *Politics and Gender* 4(4): 623–34.

Marschall, Melissa J.; Ruhil, Anirudh V.S.; and Shah, Paru R.: 2010. "The New Racial Calculus: Electoral Institutions and Black Representation in Local Legislatures," *American Journal of Political Science* 54(1): 107–24.

Massachusetts General Court (state legislature): 2010. Website of member biographies. Published by the Massachusetts General Court. Available online at https://malegis laturegov/People/House/ (accessed June 2, 2010).

Matson, Marsha, and Fine, Terri Susan: 2006. "Gender, Ethnicity, and Ballot Information: Ballot Cues in Low-Information Elections," *State Politics and Policy Quarterly* 6(1): 49–72.

McDonagh, Eileen: 2009. *The Motherless State: Women's Political Leadership and American Democracy*. Chicago: University of Chicago Press.

McGlen, Nancy E.; O'Connor, Karen; van Assendelft, Laura; and Gunther-Canada, Wendy: 2002. *Women, Politics, and American Society*. New York: Longman.

McGlennon, John, and Mahoney, Ian: 2012. "State Legislative Competition in 2012: Redistricting and Party Polarization Drive Decrease in Competition," report for The Thomas Jefferson Program in Public Policy at the College of William and Mary. Available online at http://www.wm.edu/as/publicpolicy/documents/st_leg _comp_2012_final.pdf (accessed March 30, 2014).

McIntosh, Peggy: 1989. "White Privilege: Unpacking the Invisible Knapsack," *Peace and Freedom Magazine* (July/August): 10–12. Available online at http://nation alseedproject.org/white-privilege-unpacking-the-invisible-knapsack (accessed February 20, 2016).

Mendelberg, Tali: 2001. *The Race Card: Campaign Strategy, Implicit Messages, and the Norm of Equality*. Princeton, N.J.: Princeton University Press.

Metcalfe, John: 2012. "The Skyrocketing Costs of Running for Mayor in a Major U.S. City," report in CityLab/The Atlantic. Available online at http://www.citylab.com /politics/2012/11/skyrocketing-costs-running-mayor-major-us-city/3814/ (accessed February 15, 2016).

Moncrief, Gary; Squire, Peverill; and Jewell, Malcolm E.: 2001. *Who Runs for the Legislature?* Upper Saddle River, N.J.: Prentice Hall.

Montoya, Lisa J.; Hardy-Fanta, Carol; and Garcia, Sonia: 2000. "Latina Politics: Gender, Participation, and Leadership," *PS: Political Science and Politics*, 33(3): 555–61.

Moran, Caitlin: 2012. *How to Be a Woman*. New York: Harper Perennial.

Morgan, Edmund: 2003. *American Freedom, American Slavery, 2nd edition*. New York: Norton.

Murray, Mark: 2014. "113th Congress Not the Least Productive in Modern History," *NBC News*, December 29. Available online at http://www.nbcnews.com/politics /first-read/113th-congress-not-least-productive-modern-history-n276216 (accessed February 14, 2016).

Mutz, Diana C.: 2007. "Effects of 'In-Your-Face' Television Discourse on Perceptions of a Legitimate Opposition," *American Political Science Review* 101(4): 621–35.

Mutz, Diana C., and Reeves, Byron: 2005. "The New Videomalaise: Effects of Televised Incivility on Political Trust," *American Political Science Review* 99(1), February: 1–15.

Myers, Dowell: 2008. *Immigrants and Boomers: Forging a New Social Contract for the Future of America*. New York: Russell Sage Foundation.

National Journal: 2015. "Wanted: Millennial Candidates for Congress," *National Journal*, May 6, 2015. Available online at http://article.wn.com/view/2015/05/06 /Wanted_Millennial_Candidates_for_Congress/ (accessed February 15, 2016).

National Post: 2013. "Posted Toronto Political Panel: Good grief, it costs a grotesque amount of money to become Mayor of Toronto," *National Post* (Toronto, Canada), February 4. Available online at http://news.nationalpost.com/toronto/posted -toronto-political-panel-rob-ford (accessed February 15, 2016).

NCRW (National Council for Research on Women), CAWP, and the Center for Responsive Politics: 2014. "Money in Politics with a Gender Lens," research report. Available online at http://www.regender.org/sites/ncrw.org/files/moneyinpolitic swithagenderlens_0.pdf (accessed April 1, 2014).

NCSL (National Conference of State Legislators): 2009. "State Legislators Data," NCSL. Available online at http://www.ncsl.org/Default.aspx?TabId=14766 (Latino) and http://www.ncsl.org/Default.aspx?TabId=14781 (Black) (accessed June 4, 2010).

———: 2014. "2010 State Legislator Compensation Data," NCSL. Available online at http://www.ncsl.org/research/about-state-legislatures/2010-legislator-compensation-data .aspx (accessed March 31, 2014).

———: 2016. "Overview of State Laws on Public Financing of Campaigns," NCSL. Available online at http://www.ncsl.org/research/elections-and-campaigns/public -financing-of-campaigns-overview.aspx (accessed February 15, 2016).

Niven, David: 2006. "Throwing Your Hat Out of the Ring: Negative Recruitment and the Gender Imbalance in State Legislative Candidacy," *Politics and Gender Journal* 2: 473–89.

Norris, Pippa: 2007. "Women Leaders Worldwide: A Splash of Color in the Photo Op," in *Women, Media, and Politics*, ed. Pippa Norris. New York: Oxford University Press, 149–65.

Norris, Pippa, ed.: 1997. *Passages to Power: Legislative Recruitment in Advanced Democracies*. New York: Cambridge University Press.

Norris, Pippa, and Lovenduski, Joni: 2010. "Puzzles in political recruitment," in *Women, Gender, and Politics: A Reader*, ed. Mona Lena Krook and Sarah Childs. New York: Oxford University Press, 2010.

———: 1995. *Political Recruitment: Gender, Race, and Class in the British Parliament.* New York: Cambridge University Press.

Nye, Joseph S.; Zelikow, Philip D.; and King, David C.: 1997. *Why Americans Don't Trust Government.* Cambridge, Mass.: Harvard University Press.

O'Connor, Karen: 2003. "Do Women in Local, State, and National Legislative Bodies Matter? A Definitive Yes Proves Three Decades of Research by Political Scientists," research overview report published in pre-conference "Briefing Book" for White House Project 2003 Conference, "Why Women Matter." Available online at http://scholar.harvard.edu/shaunashames/files/whp_wwm_briefing_book_post_conf.pdf (accessed March 31, 2014).

The Onion: 2008. "Black Man Given Nation's Worst Job," News-in-Brief, November 4. Available online at http://www.theonion.com/article/black-man-given-nations-worst-job-6439 (accessed February 15, 2016).

Open Secrets: 2014. "2012 Presidential Race," Open Secrets Report. Available online at http://www.opensecrets.org/pres12/ (accessed March 31, 2014).

Osborn, Tracy: 2012. *How Women Represent Women: Political Parties, Gender, and Representation in the State Legislatures.* New York: Oxford University Press.

Owens, Ernest: 2016. "The Ernest Opinion: Water Bottle Donations Aren't Going to Save Flint," *Metro U.S.*, January 29. Available online at http://www.metro.us/ernest-owens/the-ernest-opinion-water-bottle-donations-aren-t-going-to-save-flint/zsJpaC—dSPQpPVa8ciw/ (accessed February 22, 2016).

Paizis, Suzanne: 1977. *Getting Her Elected: A Political Woman's Handbook.* Sacramento, Calif.: Creative Editions.

Palmer, Barbara, and Simon, Dennis: 2006. *Breaking the Glass Ceiling: Women and Congressional Elections.* New York: Routledge.

Parlapiano, Alicia: 2015. "How Presidential Campaigns Became Two-Year Marathons," *The New York Times*, April 16. Available online at http://www.nytimes.com/2015/04/17/upshot/how-presidential-campaigns-became-two-year-marathons.html?_r=1 (accessed February 15, 2016).

Patterson, Thomas E.: 2000. "Doing Well and Doing Good: How Soft News and Critical Journalism Are Shrinking the News Audience and Weakening Democracy and What News Outlets Can Do About It," Faculty Research Working Paper, Shorenstein Center, Kennedy School of Government. Available online at http://ksgnotes1.harvard.edu/Research/wpaper.nsf/rwp/RWP01–001/$File/rwp01_001_patterson.pdf (accessed July 12, 2007).

———: 2003. *The Vanishing Voter: Public Involvement in an Age of Uncertainty.* New York: Vintage.

Paumgarten, Nick: 2007. "Field Studies: Girl Counter," *The New Yorker*, September 3 and 10.

Pearson, Kathryn, and Dancey, Logan: 2011. "Elevating Women's Voices in Congress: Speech Participation in the House of Representatives," *Political Research Quarterly* 64(4); 910–923.

Pew Research Center: 2009. "Income Distribution within Religious Groups," Pew Research Center Report. Available online at http://www.pewforum.org/2009/01/30/income-distribution-within-us-religious-groups/ (accessed March 25, 2014).

———: 2011. "Faith on the Hill," Pew Research Center Report. Available online at http://www.pewforum.org/2011/01/05/faith-on-the-hill-the-religious-composition-of-the-112th-congress/ (accessed March 25, 2014).

———: 2014a. "Millennials in Adulthood," Pew Research Center Report. Available online at http://www.pewsocialtrends.org/2014/03/07/millennials-in-adulthood/ (accessed February 16, 2016).

———: 2014b. "Political Polarization in the American Public," Pew Research Center Report. Available online at http://www.people-press.org/2014/06/12/political-polarization-in-the-american-public/ (accessed February 14, 2016).

Phillips, Anne: 1991. *Engendering Democracy*. University Park: Pennsylvania State University Press.

———: 1995. *The Politics of Presence*. New York: Oxford University Press.

Platt, Matthew: 2008. "Participation for What? A Policy-Motivated Approach to Political Activism," *Political Behavior* 30: 391–413.

Plutzer, Eric, and Zipp, John F.: 1996. "Identity Politics, Partisanship, and Voting for Women Candidates," *Public Opinion Quarterly*, Vol. 60: 30–57.

Political Parity (Hunt Alternatives): 2014. "Shifting Gears: How Women Navigate the Road to Higher Office," a report by Political Parity, a program of Hunt Alternatives. Available online at https://www.politicalparity.org/research/shifting-gears/ (accessed February 14, 2016).

Polity IV Project: 2016. "About Polity," Center for Systemic Peace Report/Project. Available online at http://www.systemicpeace.org/polityproject.html (accessed February 14, 2016).

Polsby, Nelson: 1983. *Consequences of Party Reform*. New York: Oxford University Press.

Powell, Robert: 1990. *Nuclear Deterrence Theory: The Search for Credibility*. New York: Cambridge University Press.

Prior, Markus: 2005. "News v. Entertainment: How Increasing Media Choice Widens Gaps in Political Knowledge and Turnout," *American Journal of Political Science* 49(2), July: 577–592.

Public Policy Polling: 2013. "Congress Somewhere Below Cockroaches, Traffic Jams, and Nickleback in Americans' Esteem," Public Policy Polling Report. Available online at http://www.publicpolicypolling.com/main/2013/01/congress-somewhere-below-cockroaches-traffic-jams-and-nickleback-in-americans-esteem.html (accessed February 14, 2016).

Redstockings: 2016. "Consciousness-Raising & Pro-Woman Line Papers, 1968–72," Available online at http://www.redstockings.org/index.php?option=com_content&view=article&id=45&Itemid=59 (accessed February 18, 2016).

Reingold, Beth: 2006. "Women as Office Holders: Linking Descriptive and Substantive Representation," paper prepared for presentation at the "Political Women and

American Democracy" Conference at the University of Notre Dame, May 25–27. Available online at http://rooneycenter.nd.edu/assets/11302/reingold_conference .pdf (accessed March 31, 2014).

Reingold, Beth, and Harrell, Jessica: 2010. "The Impact of Descriptive Representation on Women's Political Engagement: Does Party Matter?" *Political Research Quarterly* 63(2): 280–94.

Riker, William H., and Ordeshook, Peter C.: 1968. "A Theory of the Calculus of Voting." *American Political Science Review* 62(1): 25–42.

Rosenfeld, Diane: 2008. "Correlative Rights and the Boundaries of Freedom: Protecting the Civil Rights of Endangered Women," *Harvard Civil Rights–Civil Liberties Law Review* 43: 257–66.

Rosenstone, Steven J., and Hansen, John Mark: 1993. *Mobilization, Participation, and Democracy in America*. New York: Macmillan.

Rosenthal, Cindy Simon: 1998a. "Getting Things Done: Women Committee Chairpersons in State Legislatures," in *Women and Elective Office: Past, Present, and Future*, ed. Sue Thomas and Clyde Wilcox. New York: Oxford University Press.

———: 1998b. *When Women Lead*. New York: Oxford University Press.

Rosenthal, Cindy Simon, ed.: 2002. *Women Transforming Congress*. Norman: University of Oklahoma Press.

Rosenstiel, Tom, et al.: 2007. *We Interrupt This Newscast: How to Improve Local News and Win Ratings, Too!* New York: Cambridge University Press, 134–35.

Sanbonmatsu, Kira: 2003. "Gender-Related Political Knowledge and the Descriptive Representation of Women," *Political Behavior* 25(4): 367–88.

———: 2006. *Where Women Run: Gender and Party in the American States*. Ann Arbor: University of Michigan Press.

Sapiro, Virginia: 1983. *The Political Integration of Women: Roles, Socialization, and Politics*. Urbana: University of Illinois Press.

Sarkees, Meredith Reid, and McGlen, Nancy E.: 1999. "Misdirected Backlash: The Evolving Nature of Academia and the Status of Women in Political Science," *PS: Political Science and Politics*, Vol. 32, No. 1 (March): 100–8.

Schattschneider, E. E.: 1942. *Party Government*. New York: Holt, Rinehart and Winston.

Schlesinger, Joseph: 1966. *Ambition and Politics*. Chicago: Rand McNally.

Schlozman, Kay Lehman: 1990. "Representing Women in Washington: Sisterhood and Pressure Politics," in *Women, Politics and Change*, ed. Louise A. Tilly and Patricia Gurin. New York: Russell Sage Foundation.

Schlozman, Kay Lehman; Verba, Sidney; Brady, Henry; and Shames, Shauna: 2012. "What Shall Be Done?," in *The Unheavenly Chorus: Unequal Political Voice and the Broken Promise of American Democracy*, ed. Kay Schlozman, Sidney Verba, and Henry Brady. Cambridge, Mass.: Harvard University Press.

Schneider, Monica; Holman, Mirya; Diekman, Amanda; and McAndrew, Thomas: 2015. "Power, Conflict, and Community: How Gendered Views of Political Power Influence Women's Political Ambition," *Political Psychology* 36(3).

Schneir, Miriam, ed.: 1995. *Feminism in Our Time: The Essential Writings, WWII–Present*. New York: Vintage.

Schumpeter, Joseph: 1976 [1942]. *Capitalism, Socialism, and Democracy*. London: Allen and Unwin.

Schroeder, Patricia: 1998. *24 Years of Housework . . . and the Place Is Still a Mess: My Life in Politics*. Riverside, N.J: Andrews McMeel Publishing.

Shames, Shauna: 2001. "The Un-Candidates: Gender and Outsider Signals in Women's Political Advertising, 1969–98." Unpublished senior thesis in the Departments of Social Studies and Women's Studies, Harvard College.

———: 2003. "The Un-Candidates: Gender and Outsider Signals in Women's Political Advertising," *Women and Politics Journal* 25 (1/2): 115–47.

———: 2014. "Report on Female Gubernatorial Candidate Races," report to the Barbara Lee Family Foundation, Cambridge, Mass.

Shah, Paru, and Marschall, Melissa: 2011. "The Supply Side of Minority Representation: When and Where Do Minority Candidates Run?" Paper prepared for presentation at the annual meeting of the American Political Science Association (APSA). Available online at http://democracyobserver.org/papers/Shah%20Marschall%20Davis%20MPSA%202012.pdf (accessed March 31, 2014).

Shea, Daniel M., and Sproveri, Alex: 2012. "The Rise and Fall of Nasty Politics in America," *PS: Political Science* 45(3): 416–21.

Shelby, Tommie: 2005. *We Who Are Dark*. Cambridge, Mass.: Belknap Press of Harvard University Press.

Smith, David, and Roberts, Dan: 2016. "State of the Union: Obama Regrets Era of 'Rancor' and Ponders Divided America," *The Guardian* (UK), January 13. Available online at http://www.theguardian.com/us-news/2016/jan/12/obama-state-of-the-union-address-2016-partisan-poison-congress (accessed February 18, 2016).

Smith, Jacquelyn: 2013. "The Law Schools Whose Graduates Earn the Biggest Paychecks," *Forbes.com*. Available online at http://www.forbes.com/sites/jacquelynsmith/2013/03/14/the-law-schools-whose-grads-earn-the-biggest-paychecks/(accessed March 31, 2014).

Spencer, Steven J.; Steele, Claude M.; and Quinn, Diane M.: 1999. "Stereotype Threat and Women's Math Performance," *Journal of Experimental Social Psychology* 35: 4–28.

Squire, Peverill: 2000. "Uncontested Seats in State Legislative Elections," *Legislative Studies Quarterly* 25(1): 131–46.

Steele, Claude M., and Aronson, Joshua: 1995. "Stereotype threat and the intellectual test performance of African Americans," *Journal of Personality and Social Psychology* 69(5): 797–811.

Stevenson, Randolph T., and Vavreck, Lynn: 2000. "Does Campaign Length Matter? Testing for Cross-National Effects," *British Journal of Political Science* 30(20): 217–35.

Stokes, Atiya Kai: 2003. "Latino Group Consciousness and Political Participation," *American Politics Research*, Vol. 31, No. 4: 361–78.

Stout, Christopher, and Tate, Katherine: 2013. "The 2008 Presidential Election, Political Efficacy, and Group Empowerment," *Politics, Groups, and Identities* 1(2): 143–63.

Strachan, Cherie: 2002. *High-Tech Grass Roots: The Professionalization of Local Elections (Campaigning American Style)*. Washington: Rowman and Littlefield.

Strauss, Julie Etta: 1998. *Women in Congress: The Difference They Make*. Unpublished dissertation, Northwestern University.

Sturm, Susan: 2001. "Second Generation Employment Discrimination: A Structural Approach," *Columbia Law Review*(101)3: 458–568.

Swers, Michele: 2002. *The Difference Women Make: The Policy Impact of Women in Congress*. Chicago: University of Chicago Press.

———: 2013. *Women in the Club: Gender and Policy Making in the Senate*. Chicago: University of Chicago Press.

Tate, Katherine: 2003. *Black Faces in the Mirror: African Americans and Their Representatives in Congress*. Princeton, N.J.: Princeton University Press.

Tatum, Beverly: 2003. *"Why are all the Black kids sitting together in the cafeteria?" and Other Conversations About Race*. New York: Basic Books.

Thomas, Sue: 1994. *How Women Legislate*. New York: Oxford University Press.

———: 1997. "Why Gender Matters: The Perceptions of Women Officeholders," *Women and Politics Journal*, Volume 17.

———: 2002. "The Personal Is the Political: Antecedents of Gendered Choices of Elected Representatives," *Sex Roles* 47(7/8): 343–53.

Thomas, Sue, and Wilcox, Clyde: 1998. *Women and Elective Office*. New York: Oxford University Press.

———: 2005. *Women and Elective Office: Past, Present, and Future*. New York: Oxford University Press.

Thomsen, Danielle: 2014. "Ideological Moderates Won't Run: How Party Fit Matters for Partisan Polarization in Congress," *Journal of Politics* 76(3): 786–97.

Tilly, Louise A., and Gurin, Patricia, eds.: 1990. *Women, Politics, and Change*. New York: Russell Sage Foundation.

Time Magazine: 2014. "The Incredible Rise in Campaign Spending," *Time*, October 23. Available online at http://time.com/3534117/the-incredible-rise-in-campaign -spending/ (accessed February 15, 2016).

Tolleson-Rinehart, Sue: 1994. "The California Senate Races: A Case Study in the Gendered Paradoxes of Politics," in *The Year of the Woman; Myths and Realities*, ed. Elizabeth Adell Cook, Sue Thomas, and Clyde Wilcox. Boulder, Colo.: Westview Press.

———: 2013. *Gender Consciousness and Politics*. New York: Routledge.

Tolleson-Rinehart, Sue, and Stanley, Jeanie R.: 1994. *Claytie and the Lady: Ann Richards, Gender, and Politics in Texas*. Austin: University of Texas Press.

Trost, Christine, and Grossman, Matt, eds.: 2005 *Win the Right Way: How to Run Effective Local Campaigns in California*. Berkeley, Calif.: Berkeley Public Policy Press.

Uhlaner, Carole Jean, and Schlozman, Kay Lehman: 1986. "Candidate Gender and Congressional Campaign Receipts," in *Journal of Politics* Vol. 48: 30–50.

Uhlaner, Carole J.; Cain, Bruce E.; and Kiewiet, D. Roderick: 1989. "Political Participation of Ethnic Minorities in the 1980s," *Political Behavior* Vol. 11(3), September: 195–231.

U.S. Census Bureau: 2012. "Table 1: Enrollment Status of the Population in College/ Graduate School: All Races, by Sex," Population Division, U.S. Census Bureau. Available online at https://www.census.gov/hhes/school/data/cps/2012/tables.html (accessed March 30, 2014).

———: 2014. "Table 3: Annual Estimates of the Resident Population by Sex, Race, and Hispanic Origin for the United States: April 1, 2000 to July 1, 2008 (NC-EST2008–03)," Population Division, U.S. Census Bureau. Available online at http://www.census .gov/popest/national/asrh/NC-EST2008-srh.html (accessed June 4, 2010).

U.S. Department of Justice: 2014. "Attorneys General of the United States 1789–Present," available online at http://www.justice.gov/ag/aghistlist. php?sortby=last (accessed March 30, 2014).

U.S. House of Representatives Clerk: 2014. "Office of the Clerk of the U.S. House of Representatives," available online at http://clerk.house.gov/ (accessed March 30, 2014).

U.S. *News and World Reports*: 2010. "Law School Rankings," *U.S. News and World Reports*. Available online at http://grad-schools.usnews.rankingsandreviews.com /best-graduate-schools/top-law-schools (accessed March 30, 2014).

*UVA Today*: 2007. "Surveys of British and American Employees Conclude Women Must Work Harder," *UVA Today*, Nov. 27. Available online at http://www.virginia .edu/uvatoday/newsRelease.php?id=3370 (accessed January 13, 2009).

Valian, Virginia: 1999. *Why So Slow?* Cambridge, Mass.: MIT Press.

Vargas, Juan: 2014. Interview with staff of Political Parity, a program of the Hunt Alternatives Fund. Washington. Video recording of interview shared with author.

Verba, Sidney; Schlozman, Kay; and Brady, Henry: 1995. *Voice and Equality*. Cambridge, Mass.: Harvard University Press.

Waldfogel, Jane: 1994. *The Family Gap for Young Women in the U.S. and U.K.: Can Maternity Leave Make a Difference?* Cambridge, Mass.: Wiener Center, John F. Kennedy School of Government, Harvard University.

Wattenberg, Martin P.: 1991. *The Rise of Candidate-Centered Politics: Presidential Elections of the 1980s*. Cambridge, Mass.: Harvard University Press.

———: 1996. *The Decline of American Political Parties, 1952–1994*. Cambridge, Mass.: Harvard University Press.

White House Project, The (TWHP): 1998. *Framing Gender on the Campaign Trail*. TWHP Report. New York: TWHP.

———: 2000. *Style Over Substance: Spotlight on Elizabeth Dole*. TWHP Report. New York: TWHP.

———: 2005. *Who's Talking? An Analysis of Guests on Sunday Morning Talk Shows*. TWHP Report. TWHP.

White, Ismail K.: 2007. "When Race Matters and When It Doesn't: Racial Group Differences in Response to Racial Cues," *American Political Science Review* 101(2): 339–54.

Wilkins, David, and and Gulati, G. Mitu: 1996. "Why are there so few black lawyers in corporate law firms? An institutional analysis," *California Law Review* 84: 493–625.

Williams, Joan: 2000. *Unbending Gender: Why Work and Family Conflict and What to Do About It*. New York: Oxford University Press.

Witt, Linda; Paget, Karen; and Matthews, Glenna: 1994. *Running as a Woman*. New York: Free Press.

Wright, Richard: 2005. *The Ethics of Living Jim Crow*. Los Angeles: BukAmerica Inc.

Wrighton, J. Mark, and Squire, Peverill: 1997. "Uncontested Seats and Electoral Competition for the U.S. House of Representatives Over Time," *Journal of Politics* 59(2): 452–68.

Young, Iris Marion: 1990. *Justice and the Politics of Difference*. Princeton, N.J.: Princeton University Press.

———: 1994. "Gender as Seriality: Thinking about Women as a Social Collective," *Signs* 19(3): 713–38.

Zaller, John: 1992. *Nature and Origins of Mass Opinion*. New York: Cambridge University Press.

# INDEX

# ABOUT THE AUTHOR

Shauna L. Shames, Assistant Professor of Political Science at Rutgers University–Camden, received her PhD from Harvard University. Previously, she worked in nonprofit and feminist organizations in Washington, D.C., and New York, including the National Organization for Women (NOW) and the White House Project.